THE CALL OF
SPIRITUAL EMERGENCY

THE CALL OF
SPIRITUAL EMERGENCY

From Personal Crisis to
Personal Transformation

Emma Bragdon, Ph.D.

1817

Harper & Row, Publishers, San Francisco

New York, Grand Rapids, Philadelphia, St. Louis
London, Singapore, Sydney, Tokyo, Toronto

Credits appear on page 244.

For information about spiritual emergence processes beyond the scope of this book, or for referrals to professional help in any part of the world, contact the Spiritual Emergence Network, c/o Institute of Transpersonal Psychology, 250 Oak Grove Avenue, Menlo Park, California, 94025, USA.

FIRST EDITION

Library of Congress Cataloging-in-Publication Data

Bragdon, Emma
    The call of spiritual emergency : from personal crisis to personal
transformation / Emma Bragdon—1st ed.
      p.   cm.
    Includes bibliographical references.
    ISBN 0-06-250104-6
    1. Spiritual life. 2. Psychology, Religious. 3. Psychiatric
emergencies. I. Title.
    BL624.B635   1990
    291.4—dc20   89-29710
                                      CIP

---

90 91 92 93 94 VICKS 10 9 8 7 6 5 4 3 2 1

This edition is printed on acid-free paper that meets the American National Standards Institute Z39.48 Standard.

For those who dedicate themselves
to bring to light the Love
that underlies all that is happening at this time.

Contents

Chapter 5
Spiritual Practice 77

Chapter 6
Physical Stress 103

Chapter 7
Emotional Distress 119

Chapter 8
Sexual Experiences and Spiritual Emergency 139

Acknowledgments

This book has been given life by many people. Christina Grof has kindly encouraged me to contribute my voice to the field of spiritual emergency, which she initiated with her husband, Stanislav. I appreciate the Grofs' dedication to circulating information about spiritual emergency and their making way for new voices to enrich the song.

Tom Grady at Harper & Row helped with the first outline for this book after Shoshana Tembeck Alexander proposed that I further develop the ideas from *A Sourcebook for Helping People in Spiritual Emergency*. I am indebted to their initial encouragement and timely inspiration. Continuing as my editor, Shoshana gave of her big mind and kind heart—helping me bring these ideas down to earth. I am grateful for her wisdom and generosity. Mark Salzwedel at Harper & Row was a considerate and gentle companion as he taught me about the intricate steps of the publishing world.

The territory I cover in this book comes from a broad spectrum of life experience, and I needed consultation with colleagues in reviewing areas of the text. John White, Ph.D., contributed his eye for detail with kindness and tact. Arthur Hastings, Ph.D., helped me to see with new perspectives. The maturity of his knowledge was a refreshing and inspiring influence. Mary Culberson, Ph.D., has been a consistent, supportive presence with whom I could discuss the clinical issues of helping people in spiritual emergency. Aminah Raheem, Ph.D., masterfully encouraged me to be true to my own experience in her insistent, enlightened way. Laura Sosnowski's personal realization of the transpersonal realms was a constant mirror to me of the power and healing represented in the worlds beyond ego.

Finally, I need to express my profound appreciation to my friends and clients who offered their stories so that others might hear and learn from them. Interviewing people on the subject of their spiritual crisis points was an intimate and always fascinating process for me. I hope that the love and openness I was given is transmitted through the text to the readers. These stories and the unique individuals they represent are true gifts to this world as it struggles to become spiritually awake.

Most of the people interviewed for this book requested that I disguise their identities. I have made every attempt to honor that wish without sacrificing pertinent information: age level, sex, career orientation. The territory of spiritual experience is extremely personal in nature, exploring to the very roots of what makes life meaningful. Stories and information are shared here in the spirit of reaching out to others needing guidance on the path which is our birthright—spiritual emergence.

from *Shamanism: Archaic Techniques of Ecstasy* by Mircea Eliade:

Medieval legends tell of a "bridge under water" and of a "sword-bridge" which the hero (Lancelot) must cross barefoot and bare-handed; it is "sharper than a scythe" and it is crossed "with great pain and agony." The initiatory character of crossing the sword-bridge is also confirmed by another fact: before he starts over it, Lancelot sees two lions on the further bank, but when he is there he sees only a lizard; successfully undergoing the initiatory ordeal in itself makes the "danger" disappear.

1

The Sword-Bridge

Spiritual emergence is a natural process of human development in which an individual goes beyond normal personal feelings and desires—ego—into the *transpersonal*, increasing relatedness to Higher Power, or God. There are usually critical points in that process when a person feels disoriented and for a time is unable to function as usual in ordinary life, relationships, work, chores, etc., while he becomes acclimated to more subtle levels of consciousness. The end result is positive transformation, observable in increased compassion, creativity, and a desire to be of service to all of life. Like crossing a sword-bridge, this transition time demands more focused inner attention and special care, so as to see things as they really are. The stress of the situation may make things appear more threatening than they actually are. As the story of Lancelot suggests, it may seem that one is walking toward two hostile lions when actually there is only a small, shy lizard on the other side of the sword-bridge.

When spiritual emergence is punctuated by profound emotions, visions, psychosomatic illness, and compelling desires to behave in unusual ways, including suicidal thoughts, the spiritual emergence becomes a crisis, a *spiritual emergency*. Although the course of growth toward higher levels of functioning and perceiving life follows a predictable progression; spiritual emergency is generally unpredictable, erupting chaotically and spewing forth contents of the psyche that demand attention.

Spiritual emergencies happen in a number of ways. Both spiritual study and inner psychological exploration can precipitate intense spiritual experiences. Resuscitation technology and many types of drugs, including anesthetics, can trigger intense spiritual phenomena. Other catalysts to spiritual emergency are emotional or physical distress, time of life, and extraordinary sexual experiences. How and when spiritual emergency happens is discussed in depth in subsequent chapters. A synopsis of techniques for helping someone in spiritual emergency is in the concluding chapter. The intention of this book is to build a bridge for positive communication between those people going through the experience and the people who care for them—both personal friends and professionals.

In order to address a broad spectrum of people, I have attempted to find simple terms and relatively simple instructions for managing a spiritual awakening. The path into transpersonal levels of consciousness is tricky, and tests us at every turn. People must seek the help they need relevant to their level of understanding of spiritual emergence.

Historical Perspective on Spiritual Emergency

The term *spiritual emergency* was coined by Christina and Stanislav Grof, M.D. The concept of spiritual emergency grew out of Dr. Grof's research in nonordinary states of consciousness in a clinical context as well as Christina's personal experiences and work with other people.

Together the Grofs have been exploring the mysteries of spiritual growth, articulating the patterns in which it unfolds, and developing psychotherapeutic modalities to encourage spiritual opening. They found themselves paying particular attention to the needs of people who had spontaneous, unexpected spiritual openings in social contexts which were unsympathetic and unsupportive. Many of these people had no guidance, no encouragement, no companionship, no conceptual framework to help them find their way in integrating these experiences in a healthful manner. Christina Grof founded the Spiritual Emergency Network at Esalen Institute in Big Sur, California, in 1980 as a referral service to assist such people in finding supportive counselors and friends who were prepared to help them integrate spiritual awakening phenomena. At its inception a few work-scholars came each month to train with the Grofs. Together they collected referral names and addresses, produced educational materials, started a library, and published a newsletter.

In 1985, the Spiritual Emergency Network was moved to the Institute of Transpersonal Psychology in Menlo Park, California. Shortly after the move, the name was changed to the Spiritual Emergence Network (SEN) in order to emphasize support of the whole process of spiritual emergence and not only the crises of dramatic transition points. Since 1985, the Spiritual Emergence Network has branched out, and now offers educational workshops, lectures, and conferences to the public, and sponsors the publication of a newsletter, journal and educational materials, as well as continuing to expand its networking.

There are now over forty regional centers throughout the world, providing educational materials and referrals to people who seek this specialized support service. The Grofs travel worldwide, educating people about spiritual awakening phenomena and the Spiritual Emergence Network, as well as continuing their writing and conducting a training program for certification in helping people in spiritual emergency.

My own role at the Spiritual Emergence Network is in writing educational materials, including editing the *Spiritual Emergence Network Journal*. I also teach workshops about the field of spiritual emergence/emergency based on my first book, *A Sourcebook for Helping People in Spiritual Emergency*. The *Sourcebook* synthesizes the seminal work of the Grofs and other leaders in the field of transpersonal psychology with my own perspective. I have been involved with Eastern yogas, shamanism, and transpersonal psychology for twenty-five years. During this time, I have lived within several spiritual communities and worked as a Neo-Reichian therapist. My intimate involvement with the intricacies of spiritual development in myself and others has made me particularly aware of the dovetailing of spiritual and psychological growth.

What does this close relationship between spiritual and psychological growth mean in terms of spiritual emergence? It means that we cannot move forward spiritually unless we are also willing to deal completely with our personal psychology, especially developmental issues from early childhood that pattern the way we perceive and react to the present. In the first half of this century, Wilhelm Reich, M.D., in his study of body psychology, and Carl Jung, M.D., in focusing on wholeness and the quest for meaning, each supported this theory. Various ancient esoteric traditions throughout the world have been built on this premise. More recently, Stanislav Grof, M.D., Ken Wilber, and other theoreticians have tied this idea to the psychology of transformation and the thrust of human evolution.

This book brings these theories close to home, helping to demystify an area of experience often seen as alien or academic. Stories volunteered from my clients and members of spiritual communities, all ordinary people, expand our understanding of the stresses in our world that pull increasing numbers of individuals toward spiritual emergence. Transpersonal experiences can happen to anyone—a child, an adolescent, an adult, young or old. These experiences can happen spontaneously or with intention. They can happen anywhere: on a mountainside, in a therapy office, in church, in bed. They can catalyze feelings of deep peace or ecstasy. Perhaps some of us have these experiences quite often; but unless we have a name for them, they often pass us by unrecognized.

Ultimately, it is the responsibility of our institutions, especially our religious and medical establishments, to accommodate the needs of the public. Social service institutions are currently in a period of transformation, making changes in structure to respond to new needs. Special facilities in hospitals set aside for hospice care and natural childbirth are two examples of recent changes. It is now time for us to make organizational changes to more gracefully support spiritual emergence during the critical processes that carry us beyond the conventional norms of human development. Suggestions for this are included in this book. Realizing these institutional changes is the current goal for many of us involved with helping people in spiritual emergency.

The Transpersonal Levels

Transpersonal levels of experience go beyond personality and personal concerns. How do we know we are reaching these levels? What does it look like and feel like to have a transpersonal experience?

Ken Wilber, in *The Atman Project,*[1] has described three levels of transpersonal experience—*Subtle*, *Causal*, and *Atman* (in ascending order). At these levels people have access to a fluid creativity from a higher order of inspiration than the personality. This kind of intelligence is native to geniuses such as Mozart. The transpersonal levels also offer the possibility of communing with entities of higher intelligence who personify wisdom, love, and compassion. For example, true psychic channels move to the Subtle level when they bring forth guidance from higher levels of consciousness. In the transpersonal realms, there is often a feeling of boundlessness, of being beyond the limits of time and space. Unusual things may appear as visionary inner experiences, or as actual externalized apparitions. Mental telepathy, healing abilities, psychic phenomena, are native to these realms, as is, ultimately, complete absorption in Higher Power, or God. Following is a more definitive description of each level.

The Subtle Level

The Subtle level is a level of conscious awareness that includes extrasensory perceptions indigenous to the body, as well as experiences apparently divorced from the body, such as *out-of-body experiences* (OOBE) and *psychokinetic* phenomena (objects moving without a physical catalyst). The Subtle level can be experienced in many and diverse ways that are directly related to a system of energy centers in the body, called *chakras* in Sanskrit, that are of a higher order than physiological organ systems. The chakras activate a higher order of perception than our five senses. Following are examples of Subtle level transpersonal experiences. The majority of Americans have experienced at least one of these.

A woman is sitting in a church/synagogue/temple where prayers are being invoked for someone who is ill. The woman has an inner feeling that she knows the person who is ill, or she senses his experience, even though she has never met him.

A new mother wakes in the middle of the night, keenly in tune with her baby, who sleeps in his room. She goes to him and finds that he has an unexpected high fever and needs her immediate care. She was using, albeit unconsciously, her "sixth sense," or ESP.

A woman is watching a sunset in the mountains. The beauty of the changing light overwhelms her. She becomes rapt in bliss, feeling a deep love and gratefulness for being alive.

A young man sits in meditation at the bedside of a sick friend and senses the presence of a higher energy, what we might call an *angel*, full of love and divine compassion, attending the ailing friend.

A man goes to a counselor for a *past-life regression* and has a deep emotional experience of himself as living five hundred years ago in another space/time orientation. Through the experience, he finds understanding and healing of several of his current relationships.

A child has a winged pixie as her playmate for several years. Together, they explore the natural world, play with leaves and acorns, dance on the grass.

The Subtle level is a dimension of conscious awareness—consciousness beyond but including material reality. In this dimension, life is sensed as having mythic proportions. People are brought into more direct and conscious relationship to their own life force, or *prana* in Sanskrit. It is not unusual to sense vibrations and streaming energy in the body, or even to see these manifestations of life energy in other people or natural elements. People more aware of the energy of their own humanness have a sense of belonging to the human race with a potent inner meaning never accessible before. This renewed awareness of dimensions beyond physical, objectified reality are often the basis of inspiration in the arts. Dante expressed his direct experience of Subtle realms this way:

> Fixing my gaze upon the Eternal Light
> I saw within its depths,

Bound up with love together in one volume,
The scattered leaves of all the Universe . . .
Within the luminous profound subsistence
Of that Exalted Light saw I three circles
Of three colors yet on one dimension
And by the second seemed the first reflected
As rainbow is by rainbow, and the third
Seemed fire that equally from both is breathed.

The Causal Level

Few people experience Causal level consciousness for an extended period of time. They may experience it in deep meditation as a result of spiritual discipline or for a short period as a result of deep relaxation, being inspired by music, or nature, or a loving relationship. We have called these short periods "peak experiences." Some mind-altering substances can bring about Causal level experiences. It is a state of perfect ecstasy, bliss, untainted by any distracting thoughts, desires, or moods. The Causal level includes the awareness of Subtle and material dimensions, but also goes beyond them to the full realization of union with God. It is a state of being at one with Higher Power, or God, "love-in-oneness." At the Causal level there is no sense of time, only of eternity.

Michael, thirty-three, is an executive in an advertising agency in Los Angeles. He was committed to his spiritual growth, and researched ways in which he could accelerate his development. He wanted to realize God-consciousness within himself, and was willing to work hard to accomplish that. He attended a meditation retreat in 1987, with these results:

After three days of meditation and focus from 6:00 A.M. to 10:00 P.M. each day, I had opened up tremendously. I began sensing myself as just light. I would close my eyes and feel that my body was just full of light. For almost twenty-four hours I no longer assumed the roles and expectations I usually identify with. I even had to watch someone else at lunch to remember what a fork was for. The world was totally fresh and new! It made no difference who I was, who anyone was. Personal differences had very little importance. Most important was fully experiencing that we are all part of one thing. I knew beyond a shadow of a doubt that we are all one body. Never before have I felt so totally fulfilled, so completely ecstatic.

Michael's wife was extremely disturbed when she saw Michael after his retreat, because he could not be personal with her for twenty-four hours. He was completely absorbed in the Causal level.

Most religious traditions consider a teacher to be very important at this transitional point of spiritual growth. As Michael's experience illustrates, students moving more fully into transpersonal realms need reassurance and direction in letting go of life as they have seen it, letting go of the boundaries of time and space, letting go of themselves as the ones who witness life. Students need reassurance that dissolving these boundaries will not result in death or craziness, but rather in an opening to fuller life. They need guidance in integrating Causal level experiences into the rest of their lives so that relationships to partners, children, and jobs still proceed and grow in a natural course.

While we are in meditation, the world may disappear. Yet out of meditation we still need to be grounded in the world—to drive safely, to know how to teach moral values to our children, to get to work "on time," to be respectful of the values and mores of our culture.

The Atman Level

The Atman level is beyond the Causal but includes all dimensions below it—the material, Subtle, and Causal. Atman is a dimension of consciousness so completely immersed in the Highest Power that nothing else exists in awareness. Thus, this state brings perfect ecstasy—yet it is mysteriously beyond any emotion. Indications of the Atman level exist in mystical religious texts, but they are always referred to as being beyond description. It is the ultimate *unity experience*, where the witness to life and that which is witnessed are one and the same. Wilber writes, "[T]he entire World Process then arises, moment to moment, as one's own Being, outside of which, and prior to which, nothing exists."[2] The eternal Now is all that exists.

Having an experience of any of the higher realms does not necessarily mean that people will be in a crisis. However, even when they have openness, trust, and flexibility, it is still a challenge to let go of their habitual ideas of the world and enter a world of psychic phenomena, timelessness, boundlessness, limitless energy, and inspiration. Approaching these realms, even though they offer ecstasy and love, is often disorienting and can cause profound fear.

The way we ordinarily deal with short visits to higher realms of consciousness is to say to ourselves, "Something magic happened to me. I feel so lucky; what a miracle it was." We don't usually view these miracles as signposts guiding us to a whole new territory of our lives where we are capable of sustaining clairvoyance, clairsentience, communion with archetypes and angels, ecstatic bliss, and union with God. But that is indeed what can happen and what, I believe, is our true course in natural development.

Who Needs Help?

Increasing numbers of people are reporting their experiences of transpersonal levels due to spiritual practices, global changes, and resuscitation technology. Such people often feel isolated and confused. They need a conceptual understanding of their experiences and a sense of connection to others who are more familiar with this dimension of life and can offer some guidance and orientation.

I have been unusually fortunate in my ongoing process of spiritual emergence. From the time of my introduction to meditation through the last twenty-five years, I have had highly developed teachers in meditation, shamanism, intuition training, body therapies, and analytic psychology. I have also had the benefit of a community of "spiritual friends," people with whom I share mutual interest and sympathy in the ups and downs of spiritual awakening. This has meant that both my own process of spiritual emergence and my learning to be a *helper* to others have been supported in an enlightened way. I have had excellent role models as my counselors, medical help attuned to spiritual values of reverence for life, an academic background strengthening my conceptual understanding of human development, and a home community centered around spiritual growth.

I am very concerned for the people who have not been as lucky as myself. I have known of people who have killed themselves as a result of being isolated and overwhelmed with spiritual experiences. This happened to my mother. I have had clients who were intent on exploring their inner life whose families perceived them as crazy and wanted to put them on psychiatric medications to stop the spiritual experiences. These are stories that illustrate spiritual emergence processes of a critical nature, stories in which individuals are taken by storm with no one to guide them, no friends or family to support or encourage them, no community to contain them. Most of these individuals do not have the benefit of a conceptual framework to understand what they are experiencing. In the worst case, they have a framework that classifies their experiences only as evidence of mental disease. Their fears, their disorientation, are amplified to the degree that they become incapacitated, so flooded with the contents of their unconscious that they have no capacity to cope with these things. Often these people are hospitalized. These are stories of spiritual emergency. Some of these stories are told throughout this book.

I, and others who work at the Spiritual Emergence Network, have heard hundreds of stories from people who have been hospitalized inappropriately. I continually see people in my practice who keep asking, "Am I crazy to be experiencing these things? Where do they fit into my life?"

Questions about where transpersonal experiences fit into personal development can be answered reassuringly for those in spiritual emergency: "There are times when regressive behavior and severe disorientation are part of spiritual growth. Get the help you need, and go with the process." The friends, family, and helpers of people who are in spiritual emergency can also find relevant information, reassurance, and resources for locating professional help.

Hopefully, all people will benefit by further familiarity with the vocabulary that covers spiritual experiences and transcends religious differences. The English language has not given us terms to conceptualize many of the refined aspects of spiritual emergence phenomena. Many of the words I introduce are taken from Sanskrit, the classical language of India, which is rich in terms describing states of consciousness. This vocabulary in itself could be standardized and thus contribute to improved communication between health care professionals, clergy, hospital administration, teachers, and the general public. A glossary of terms is included at the back of the book for easy reference.

The following chapters may be helpful if you are looking for guidance and reassurance in understanding your spiritual experiences; if you are trying to understand a friend or family member who is undergoing strong spiritual experiences, if you are involved in a crisis of spiritual emergency, and need to find a helper who can support you in an appropriate way; or if you are looking for ways to make changes in a social service organization so as to accommodate spiritual emergence phenomena.

The metaphor of the sword-bridge dramatically illustrates the difficulty of spiritual emergence: the confrontation with oneself and one's belief system, the letting go of known territory which is safe, the vulnerability and sense of aloneness, the acute need for spiritual allies, the uneasiness of facing the other side which is imagined as overwhelming. How this metaphor that described Lancelot's journey is realized in modern life will be explored throughout this book. In the following chapter, I tell the beginnings of my own story.

2

Spiritual Emergence Is Not Crazy!

One day when I was seven years old, I was swimming with my cousin Anna underneath a dock in a lake. We were playing between the boards that supported the metal drums on which the floor of the dock was built. One of us would hide from the other—swimming down, and then coming up unexpectedly in a new place, spouting water. At one point, I dived down deep, so Anna had no chance of seeing me. I looked up for a place to emerge. This time I saw a crisscross of boards; the floor of the dock seemed woven with the boards of the supporting structure. I saw no place to surface. Seconds passed. Out of air, I panicked . . . blacked out. Close to death, my consciousness dived deep within me—to a place where there was no more fear, to a place of absolute peace and acceptance. There, the feeling of fear was just a vague memory. In this way, I discovered the kingdom of Higher Power, a deep experience of sacred energy that I would never be able to forget, that I would always know as "home." I had begun to relax into it completely when I burst to the surface of the lake, right between two boards with barely enough space for my head to pass.

Everything changed for me from the moment of that experience. Instead of fearing death, I now knew that death would be a passageway into the ultimate peace that I had felt when I nearly drowned. From that day onward, I distinctly led life in two dimensions—one life as a physical being who loves ice cream and close contact with others, and wants to survive to have the pleasures of this life; the other life as a spiritual being who is a part of that sacred energy that is complete peace and unconditional love that will live after my physical being dies.

Ever since infancy, I had had intense experiences I now would call "spiritual." Looking at rays of sunlight coming through a window into my crib would take me into ecstasy. My favorite friends were nature spirits in the forest near my home. But ever since that moment of nearly drowning, I have always been in touch with what I recognize as the deep, steady stream of Higher Power within me; my ordinary mind is like a bubbling brook animating only the surface of my consciousness. These experiences continued as I grew. Psychic phenomena, mental telepathy, ESP, clairvoyance, clairsentience, became a normal part of my life. I used to think that this was unusual—in fact, I used to think that people would treat me like a crazy person if I revealed the kinds of things that I was experiencing. Now, I know that most people have had at least one of these kinds of experiences. Still, we struggle to find words to describe them, and most of us have some fear of talking about them.

However, it was not until I completed my research for my doctoral dissertation in psychology that I realized the extent to which spiritual experiences are "normal." As I interviewed person after person in my study for writing *A Sourcebook for Helping People in Spiritual Emergency* (Lightening Up Press, 1988), I saw that these experiences not only are common but also have a place in natural human development. In my work as a psychotherapist, I became convinced of the value of spiritual experiences in enhancing mental health. I continually saw these experiences serve as stepping-stones to higher levels of functioning in the form of higher creativity, a sense of equanimity and peace, a desire to serve others, and the development of psychic abilities—even the capacity to do hands-on healing work.

People in our culture are afraid of speaking openly about their spiritual experiences, because psychic phenomena—such as experiencing past-life sequences, receiving clairvoyant, clairsentient, or clairaudient impressions, or speaking with disembodied spirits—have been considered symptomatic of psychosis. Most psychiatrists, psychologists, and even clergy have believed that most spiritual experiences are indicative of either retarded development or emotional disease. This opinion has diffused into our texts on mental health, and thus also informed other health care workers—nurses, counselors, hospital administrators, etc.

One client of mine, a research biochemist, had had an intense spiritual experience during the birth of her first child. She was in labor on a gurney in the hallway of the hospital, waiting to be wheeled into the birthing room. She was not under any medication. Her husband and a nurse were attending her. Suddenly, her body began to shake all over. She felt streams of light throughout her system. This continued for over an hour. No one in the hospital understood what was happening to her. They gave her medication to suppress the symptoms, and treated her as if there were something wrong about her. Believing them, she maintained that sense of herself for years, dreading another "occurrence," not realizing that the brilliant light and powerful energy rushes vibrating through her body had been a legitimate spiritual experience having to do with the awakening of *kundalini*—a form of spiritual awakening described below. In the course of our work together she came to realize her experience as one of union with Higher Power.

Are We Becoming a Nation of Mystics?

Despite the discounting and repression of experiences such as the one my client had in childbirth, people are in fact beginning to acknowledge their spiritual experiences publicly. Andrew Greeley and pollsters at the University of Chicago reported the results of their most recent findings in 1987.[1] In the United States, 42 percent of the adult population revealed that they had "had contact with the dead"; 67 percent of widows have had "contact with the dead"; 73 percent believed in life after death; 74 percent believe that after death they will be "reunited with dead loved ones." In terms of psychic phenomena, 67 percent reported that they had experienced extrasensory perception; 67 percent had experienced *déjà vu*; 31 percent had experienced clairvoyance.

These figures have been echoed in national surveys by the Gallup Organization.[2] From 1980 to 1985 their surveys indicated that 15 percent of Americans have had a near-death experience; 43 percent have had an unusual spiritual experience; 71 percent believe in life after death; 95 percent believe in a universal spirit or God. In 1986, 67 percent of teenagers reported that they believed in angels. Studies in the 1970s by Greeley and his associates showed 15 percent to 30 percent less activity in terms of spiritual experiences—with only 27 percent of adults reporting contact with the dead; 59 percent reporting *déjà vu*; 58 percent reporting ESP; and 24 percent reporting clairvoyance.

Either the numbers of people having spiritual experiences are increasing, or people are more courageous about admitting that they are having these kinds of experiences. Is this an indication that more of us are crazy? Are we a nation of psychotics? Or are we a nation of people now opening to share with each other a level of spiritual life we have not yet spoken about?

The Positive Results of Spiritual Experience

I believe the numbers indicate that it is natural to have spiritual experiences as part of human development. Clearly, a byproduct of these experiences is that they enhance creativity and compassion, the ability to relax and be at peace with oneself, and the desire to be of service to others. These qualities are all useful in maintaining and improving the quality of individual and collective life on this planet. Thus, the development of these qualities may be indicative of our evolutionary pattern.

Evidence of these positive results is described in research on people who have for a time been clinically dead and then come back to life—a *near-death experience*, people who have awakened spiritual energetic forces, kundalini, in their own body, cross-cultural studies of shamans, and highly creative individuals.[3] Dr. Kenneth Ring recognized a pattern of change in behavior in the majority of people who had had near-death experiences. These resembled the results people also achieved from intense kundalini awakenings brought on spontaneously or by spiritual practices like meditation. He found that people usually have no increased fear of death, believe in the existence of higher force(s) that are unconditionally loving and compassionate, perceive the universality of all religions, become more spiritual and less identified with any specific religion, often acquire the ability to heal and other psychic abilities, and out of increased compassion seek to improve the quality of life of other people.

The creativity born of spiritual experiences is documented in the biographies of our inventors, musicians, writers, and artists. Puccini described the inspiration for his *Madama Butterfly* in the following way:

> The music of this opera was dictated to me by God; I was merely instrumental in putting it on paper and communicating it to the public.[4]

Brahms described it this way:

> When I feel the urge I begin by appealing directly to my Maker. . . . I immediately feel vibrations which thrill my whole being. . . . In this exalted state I see clearly what is obscure in my ordinary moods; then I feel capable of drawing inspiration from above as Beethoven did. . . . Those vibrations assume the form of distinct mental images.[5]

George Sand speaks of her writing thus:

The Wind plays my old harp as it lists. . . . It is the other who sings as he likes, well or ill, and when I try to think about it, I am afraid and tell myself that I am nothing, nothing at all.[6]

Inventors often speak of getting their inspiration from dreams or the *hypnagogic* state, a state of consciousness between dreaming and waking. Thus, the source of their inspiration comes from the resources of the higher unconscious. Albert Einstein received valuable information through a waking vision. When he was resting on top of a hill one day he imagined himself traveling to the sun and returning. The experience "felt" to him as if he had traveled in a curved line. This insight led to his developing his famous equation, "Energy is equal to mass times the speed of light squared." Sir Frederick Grant Banting found his laboratory procedure for the mass production of insulin in a dream state.

How is it, then, that we have for such a long time thought spiritual experiences to be indicators of madness, and messages from the unconscious to be primarily workings of repressed emotion? How could our psychologists and doctors have been so misinformed? The issue is not misinformation, but rather, whether individuals have *the capacity to integrate the experiences* into their daily lives. If an individual does not have the wherewithal within himself or the guidance he needs to accommodate intense spiritual experiences, such an experience may accelerate a disintegration of his mental health, just as any intense physical or emotional experience might likewise overwhelm him. This is the madness society fears. But if an individual has the capacity to integrate the spiritual experience into her ordinary day-to-day life, it enhances her life, giving her access to higher levels of human development beyond ego. This is called spiritual emergence.

Spiritual Emergency Versus Psychosis

Spiritual emergency is a term that describes critical points in the process of spiritual emergence. Spiritual emergency marks a period of spiritual experiences that is overwhelming, when a person is struggling to integrate the feelings, thoughts, perceptions, and energy associated with the episode. It can happen that the crisis may be incapacitating for a time, making it impossible to carry on normal activities of work or childrearing. In this case, the person needs the care of someone who perceives his inner experiences as meaningful. This helper would be a support person who follows him through the full cycle of his crisis and helps him find a conceptual framework to make sense of the experience.

Intense spiritual experiences and inspired states of mind may often look similar to psychosis. In a purely spiritual experience persons may be preoccupied with an inner experience to the extent that they may not care to communicate with others. Instead, their communication is taking place with inner guides or higher forces. If given the proper context and guidance, persons undergoing these experiences can reach higher levels of functioning and bring spiritual gifts to their human community. On the other hand, visual and auditory hallucinations, delusions, and inability to communicate are symptoms of psychotic behavior that may indicate a person is falling from a normal level of functioning into a diseased state. Psychotic states that are pathological, rather than gateways to higher functioning, are very real, and need to be treated by health professionals.

Spiritual Emergence: My Story

I never confused my own spiritual awakening with mental disease, because of the excellent guidance I received. My process of integrating my spiritual experiences illustrates many types of transpersonal experiences. It depicts a spiritual emergence process that has not included a severely debilitating spiritual emergency. I never had a crisis that incapacitated me for a period of more than a few moments. Still, after each of my intense awakenings I felt disoriented, alone, and often fearful as I tried to integrate the experiences.

When I was still very young, at eighteen, I met Graf von Durkheim, who modeled for me how to hold ordinary reality simultaneously with the extraordinary spiritual dimension, and thus to integrate the two. He was a psychoanalyst, an intuitive, a meditator, a man of God, and an author (*Hara: The Vital Center in Man*). People who were lost or wanted assistance in their personal development came to him. He had them meditate, and he gave them therapy. He helped them integrate their spiritual experiences into their lives.

Within two years, I met several other teachers of this type. In fact, at twenty, I transformed my life: I went from being an art student to being a Zen Buddhist nun, just so I would have more access to teachers who would help me learn how to dovetail my ordinary consciousness with my expanding awareness of spiritual dimensions. I was intent on learning this.

While following a monastic lifestyle, for the first time I felt at home in this world. For the first time I felt I could live out my private life and my innermost longings. Tassajara Zen Mountain Monastery, nestled in the mountains behind Big Sur in California, was also the first place I met a group of people my age like myself. I could sense the longing they had, which matched my own: We all wanted to return to who we were in essence, to liberate ourselves from the attitudes and concepts of the collective society around us. We were all trying to get away from the deep pain we had seen in our parents and other relatives, and experienced through their stories of World War II or their personal lives of depression and alcoholism. We were all dedicated to finding a way to live on this planet that would not generate war and depression.

We rose at 4:30 A.M. for morning meditation. We went down to the meditation hall, an all-stone building with no heat. It was below freezing most mornings. We sat on our meditation cushions in long rows, facing the wall. We sat for forty minutes, trying to remain totally still to improve our concentration, to align with our will to stop all suffering. Several times during the day we repeated this vow:

> Sentient beings are countless —
> I vow to save them all.
> Tormenting passions are innumerable —
> I vow to uproot them all.
> The gates of the Dharma* are manifold —
> I vow to pass through them all.
> The Buddha's way is peerless —
> I vow to realize it.

We were practicing an Eastern form of meditation based upon the teachings of the Buddha. Although most of us at Tassajara had grown up in Christian or Jewish families, none of us had found satisfactory ways in our churches or synagogues that offered direct access to the experience of Truth.

After forty minutes, we had a walking meditation for five minutes, then sat again for forty. This was followed by a study period in the dining hall, then a return to the meditation hall for twenty minutes of chanting and breakfast in silence. The day proceeded ritually, with work, meditation before lunch, chanting, lunch as a meditation in a ritual form, a short break, work, bath, chanting before dinner, dinner in ritual form, a break, then either a lecture or meditation. This was the measure of our days. I was twenty-one years old at the time.

In order to have the privilege of joining this life, I was asked to show my commitment in the traditional way. I was to sit continuously for five days, rising from my meditation only for chanting and meals, a bathroom break, or to sleep at the scheduled time at night. During these five days, through the chill of the morning and the 90° heat of the afternoon, the flies crawling over my lips, the devastating aching in my knees, I reached the depths of despair and the heights of ecstasy.

---

*Levels of truth.

My feelings covered all the territory: anger, rage, sadness, helplessness, power, joy, hysteria, peace, love, gratitude, longing, satisfaction, fear, courage, willfulness, surrender, excitement, boredom, endurance, ease. I would never be able to blame another person for giving me these feelings—they were all within me, just waiting to burst out in some unpredictable rhythm.

Accompanying this roller coaster of feeling were body sensations that were wholly new to me. As I relaxed deeper into my experience of my true self, the tensions that had held me captive as I tried to fit the mold of who I should be to fit into the collective world began to release. Suddenly my body would begin to shake, as if my spine were a whip in the hand of some invisible force. I would bounce and shake as if I were astride a wild bull. Afterward I would feel a calm, a sense of being more whole and closer to my essence. Somehow my body knew how to shake me in order to return me to who I was, to unbind me from the rigid conditioning that had confined my body as well as my thoughts and my feelings.

So the five-day meditation was one of the greatest gifts I had ever received. It taught me that my own body was a guide to my essential self. It taught me that I am not only a sensitive receiver, responding to the stimulation of others, but an organism looking for ways to express itself. The meditation helped me to study the action of my inner life, which seemed to move from high drama to undisturbed quiet, notwithstanding that no "thing" was happening to me; I was just sitting there.

One of the other gifts I received during my time at Tassajara was the opportunity to make the acquaintance of a wise old man. When Lama Govinda arrived for a visit, I had no doubt that he personified wisdom and compassion; he had the regal quality of someone who had attained those human virtues and carried them gracefully. When he stepped out of the car, he put on his maroon mitred Lama's hat. He wore a matching long maroon robe. His white beard gently fell to the top of his chest. His face was lined with the deep marks of age. His eyes bestowed a depth I had never seen in a human being. In them were the worlds I longed for and identified with. In them were his travels to Tibet, his training as a Lama, his research as a scholar, his isolated hours as a writer. I was lucky enough to be chosen to attend him and his wife during their stay.

Through Lama Govinda, Suzuki Roshi, and the other teachers who came to stay at Tassajara, I realized that wisdom and compassion could be manifest in the world today, in this technological wasteland where people hardly meet, much less commune with each other. I no longer tried to think of questions to ask my teachers to show I was not crazy or to demonstrate how smart I was. I knew that my task now was to sit, to focus, and to do my work, and I could trust my own inner process to enlighten me.

Again, I was fortunate. I was in contact with a community of people who gave me their friendship and their support. Our mutual companionship shielded us from the devastating loneliness that is often part of the path toward wholeness. The Buddhist texts we were reading gave us a conceptual framework within which to place our experiences. The simple tasks—keeping warm, cooking, gardening, and building in a natural environment—helped keep us grounded in the physical world.

Still, it was not always easy to gracefully interweave the ordinary and extraordinary worlds.

Some of the phenomena that monastic life utilized to teach me about the nature of existence were astonishing. One early morning, during study period, one of the more verbal monks stood up to talk to the group. I looked up at him, and suddenly saw right through him. Literally—as if his cells had dispersed into thin air. I could see the table and chair and the wall behind him. No vestige of him remained. Then, within a few seconds, he again appeared in my field of vision. I could no longer see behind him. This made me realize the power of the mind to create a consensual reality and move beyond it! Plato was correct. We live in darkness in our ordinary consciousness. If we are fortunate enough to find some true light at all, we can see, only briefly, a reflection of the real truth.

Sometimes my experiences were frightening. One night after evening meditation, I was walking alone up the valley a short way from my cabin. Suddenly, I sensed what I can only call the roar of the universe. I heard it not with my normal hearing, but inside my head, to the point where I felt deafened in every cell of my body. Dimensions of sound that I had never heard before pressed in on me as if my whole body were an eardrum. I was terrified. I felt very alone and small. Words cannot describe this experience. There was no place to turn to for protection except the comfort of a friend's touch. Yet I knew human companionship was no real match for the overwhelming experience pressing in on me. I knew I would have to face this monster by myself. At that time I could not imagine what I would have to become to conquer it, but I knew I would need help to strengthen myself.

Intent on coming to terms with the Pandora's box of my inner world, I also sought explosive techniques of expanding my consciousness. After nine months of being at the monastery, when I was living in San Francisco within the Zen Center community, I asked Allan, my dear friend, to initiate me into the world of LSD. As the trip began, I became wondrously ecstatic. I was immersed in the inner worlds that felt like home to me. I reconnected with the source of inner wisdom that I'd had at birth. I was an American Indian shaman giggling at the effort of men and women to find the truth. The truth was so obvious! What did they need—a sledgehammer to hit them on the head to awaken them? Coming back down into ordinary consciousness was traumatic. I felt the mantle of fear, the self-doubt, the everyday concerns of what I had to do to survive. It seemed the inner wisdom again had to be covered, stay underground, so I could function as a wage-earner, shopper, student, etc. I turned to Allan for comfort, to hold me, to acknowledge the reality of all that I had seen and to acknowledge my ambivalence in coming back into the ordinary world, to acknowledge the difficulty of balancing these two worlds.

I was reading Carlos Castaneda's books. They speak about two worlds, the *nagual* and the *tonal*. The ordinary and the extraordinary. The world of time and space, and the world beyond time and space. The rational, logical world and the world beyond reason, the dimensions of unity and wholeness. My own inner experiences, relevant literature, my continued spiritual practice, Suzuki's lectures, the visiting Buddhist priests, the community of friends at the Zen Center—this whole environment supported my becoming more familiar with maintaining the balance between these two worlds.

My life was changing radically. I was seeing the worlds, but I was struggling to know how to integrate them in my own life. It seemed to me I was a visitor to one world or the other. But where did I really belong? Was I a wife, a nun, a waitress, an East Coast girl, a hippie, a disciple of Suzuki? Could I be invisible? What was I made of? What was my body telling me as it shook uncontrollably during meditation? Was that just a letting go? Was it kundalini awakening? What had I got myself into?

I decided to go to a psychotherapist who could work with both my physical shaking and my mental sorting-out process. I chose a Neo-Reichian therapist. In our first session she asked me to breathe fully up into my chest, and she did some massage on my tense areas. I sobbed without end. The amount of emotion I vented surprised me. My emotions had not caught up with my spiritual experiences. Many of my emotions were still tied to my very human desire for closeness, continuity, predictability. There was a deep grief at having lost contact with my blood family and letting go of the life that I had lived. There was enormous fear of giving myself over to this new way of life with all its unknowns. There was a deep need to feel loved and to love, and apprehensions about my ability both to give and to receive. I felt a deep insecurity in who I was in this world. How could I maintain my vow to save all sentient beings if I was so locked in my own suffering?

I continued therapy while I pursued a life devoted to meditation. Both helped me to understand myself and be myself, and to begin to answer the questions I had about my life purpose. I began to see that on both a physical and an emotional level I needed intimacy, give and take, deep sharing. Intellectually, I needed as much information as I could get about how to live my life so that I could move comfortably between the two worlds. Spiritually, I needed to keep expanding, opening to the extraordinary truth I held in my own psyche and surrendering to be of service to help other people get out of their own suffering.

> Sentient beings are countless—
> I vow to save them all.
> Tormenting passions are innumerable—
> I vow to uproot them all.
> The gates of the Dharma are manifold—
> I vow to pass through them all.
> The Buddha's way is peerless—
> I vow to realize it.

I was introduced to Harry Roberts at this time. He was a white man in his early sixties who had been adopted by a Yurok Indian shaman in northern California when he was four years old and trained by him to be the spiritual leader of the Yurok. Harry was a man of many worlds: a white man, a red man, a shaman. He taught horticulture at a local college. He had taught survival skills in World War II for the U.S. Army. He was a celebrated prizewinner in boxing and in ballroom dancing.

Until his death twelve years later, Harry was a powerful physical force in my life, teaching me how to make this world my own; how to survive in the woods, by the ocean, in the sacred power spots; how to reckon with beings of other dimensions; how to plant and harvest a garden; how to respect the transition from the ordinary to the extraordinary. He was my teacher and my friend. I could come to him with my experiences with animals, ghosts, and gods. I could cry on his chest like a baby when my heart hurt or I was sick of this world.

When I was twenty-three years old I decided to marry Tim, another Zen student. Harry placed his sacred stone in Tim's and my hands and married us in a private ceremony of the soul. That same day Tim and I were married in a public Buddhist ceremony. The wedding took place on a bluff overlooking the entryway of the Russian River into the Pacific Ocean. The reception was down the hill in the garden of a potter. Tassajara breads and the San Francisco Zen Center's finest catering were laid out on the pottery tables. A bluegrass band played. Chickens, ducks, cats, and dogs roamed among us as we danced. My family was there. My Zen Center community was there. Harry smoked fresh salmon on racks above the alder chips he had gathered for the occasion. It was a mixture of Brueghel, Appalachia, Zen monastery, blue-blood East Coast family, and northern California. It was a happy time. All of my worlds were together on that day.

Two months later, Tim and I conceived our son, Jesse. A new life began. We lived in San Francisco in an unobtrusive apartment in Noe Valley. He worked as a carpenter. I worked as a bookkeeper at Alaya Stitchery, which sold meditation cushions. We continued to meditate and follow Suzuki's teachings. We visited Harry Roberts often. I practiced hatha-yoga and exercised to prepare for natural childbirth. These months were my last months of childhood innocence and ease.

When I was seven months pregnant, I received word that my mother had killed herself. Less than two months later, I gave birth to a beautiful boy. Within the next twelve months, I experienced the deaths of Suzuki Roshi (leukemia), my employer (suicide), and my sister-in-law and her husband (killed by a drunk driver). Then I had a miscarriage, my father's companion died (overdose of drugs for heart disease), and then my father died (complications of alcoholism). My husband and I could not weather the stresses of this time together, so we separated. Our divorce came shortly thereafter.

I think the only things that enabled me to live through this emotional war zone were my connection to my son, Jesse, my desire to nurture and protect him, and my connection to Harry Roberts and my therapist at that time. These very human connections made me want to keep my body healthy and use these heavy emotional experiences to grow spiritually. Without the comfort of Harry's and my therapist's companionship, their witnessing, their wisdom, and their strength, I don't know if I could have kept myself together. The money I inherited at my parents' deaths also helped in a literal way to keep my body and soul together. This inheritance relieved me of the worldly stress of having to work, so I could afford to have quiet time for myself, be with my baby, and receive psychotherapy.

Paradoxically, I was experiencing so much death at the very time I was giving birth and becoming a mother. It was a clash of opposites, and the golden key to my opening new doors of understanding. The grief was too big to feel. There was too much disaster to come to terms with. My baby's needs were immediate and present. I went from numb withdrawal to feeling exquisite joy for each moment I had, because I felt that at any moment someone else whom I loved would be taken away. I was being forced to live in the present moment because the past held no promises and the future was unpredictable at best. Life and Death, the archetypical opposites, had made love on my doorstep. Now, change was the only constant—except for the predictable diapers and nursing. Those tasks kept me grounded.

In the midst of this year, little miracles awakened me to the knowledge that there was a plan for my life, and it was good. One summer day I went for a bike ride with my son. We were both dressed in shorts and light T-shirts. He was strapped in the childseat on the back. As we cruised along at a moderate speed, a dog ran in front of the bike, causing it to fall and Jesse to be catapulted out of his seat. He fell onto the pavement and rolled along the asphalt. Before he hit, in that split second, I prayed my hardest that he be protected. My prayer was an arrow to the center of God, unwavering and without doubt. I then fell (getting heavily scraped on hands and legs), got up, and with dread walked over to my child, who was not stirring or making a sound. He looked up at me with a smile, as if he had just been floating on a cloud. He never cried. He didn't have a scratch on him. I never found a bruise.

My prayers were also answered speedily when I decided to buy a house in Sebastopol, California. One morning I meditated on exactly what I wanted—a red house on a hill with a view, a rental cottage in back, two-plus acres a short distance from Sonoma State College, where I was to finish my B.A. degree. I contacted an agent. That afternoon the very house I had imagined came up for sale at the price I could pay. Nothing like it had been for sale for months. It was a dream come true.

From these beginnings, twenty years ago, I have gone on to train myself in spiritual work and psychological work so that I too can help people to integrate their spiritual experiences with their ordinary reality, to reach levels of development beyond ego. I have tools to develop myself in my own ongoing spiritual emergence. Even better, I belong to a community of friends and colleagues who want to support each other and be supported in the continued awakening process of ourselves and our clients.

Numbers of people are going through passages of human development into transpersonal dimensions. My story is just one illustration of this course. The next chapter delineates a general map that is applicable to all people. It charts the territory more distinctly as forms of spiritual emergence and the composition of psychological issues in that landscape. Metaphorically, we are entering into a wilderness experience—meeting the naked elements of life, trusting we have what we need to sustain and protect ourselves. Just as it is safer to have companionship in the wilderness, it is also advisable to have a spiritual friend with whom to share the journey into transpersonal realms. This becomes crucial in spiritual emergency.

3

The Forms of Spiritual Emergency

Louise is a psychiatric social worker. Her husband, Wes, is a psychiatric nurse. They have been married over twenty years and have three children.

Louise's dramatic initiation into transpersonal realms was sudden but not surprising. Louise was ready to open to new dimensions of herself. She had been studying archetypal psychology. She had been deeply engaged with her spiritual development, mainly through her Christian faith. She was unusually self-aware.

At one point Louise wanted to experiment with MDMA, a psychoactive drug, when it was still legally available. Prior to this experiment, Louise and Wes were personally unfamiliar with recreational drugs. Since many of her patients had abused drugs, Louise wanted to try a drug "trip" once, because she felt it would help her understand her patients in more depth. She and Wes prepared themselves carefully for this initial experience. They felt sure the drug they obtained was pure. Both of them were in good health and chose the sanctuary of their home as an appropriately safe setting. It was a powerful and positive experience for her:

> I experienced heat in my heart—as if someone had lit a fire. The energy of love was pouring out of me. I felt so connected to other people! I could even channel love to people who were hundreds of miles from me; it seemed they really received it.
>
> I no longer felt as if I was so much in need of receiving love, to fill a hole in my life. That shifted. Now, I just wanted to give love because my heart was so full!

Following the trip, Louise felt fine, although a little tired, which is a typical response to drugs. However, three days later, when Louise was watching a television program that included pictures of the atom bomb exploding, the contents of her unconscious mind also exploded, flooding her mind uncontrollably. This continued for two weeks.

> I felt like a small child. I didn't want my husband to leave me alone. We spent hours in bed together, with him just holding me. He was like my anchor. This bond we made kept me in my body—otherwise I would fly into my head, completely absorbed in my inner life . . . as if I was participating in an age-old myth. I was deeply immersed in right-brain, symbolic, metaphorical thinking—the magical thinking of a small child.
>
> I talked to Wes about all the things I was experiencing. I was particularly aware of the forces of evil and the forces of good. I felt I could see them. I felt obsessed with wanting to protect my children from the forces of evil, and even tried to make things they could wear to ward off these forces.
>
> I felt I had to allow an inner atom bomb to go off inside my mind, and that others needed to be willing to have it go off inside their minds if we are to avert an outer atom bomb going off and destroying us all.

Louise was filled with energy, and needed only a few hours of sleep a night. She was especially aware of energy coursing through her left side, next to her spine. She would often stretch to try to accommodate this flow of energy more easily. Her senses were especially acute, and everything took on a special meaningfulness. Louise's family and friends were able to be both supportive and understanding.

> My husband was wonderful. He understood that this was a kind of purification I was going through that would enhance my life. He knew that if I was taken to the hospital, they would give me antipsychotic medication to stop the process, so he decided to be with me at home, to support me in every way he could.
>
> He told our three teenagers what we were doing. They were quite able to accept it, and carried on their lives at home as normally as possible.
>
> We also had some very understanding friends. They brought in food and did errands for us. We really needed their help. We also needed them to leave us alone and not socialize during this critical time, which they were willing to do.

After two weeks, Louise slowly began returning to work, seeing only a few clients the first week. Within a month, she had returned to her regular workload. Over time, a dramatic shift took place in the nature of her practice. In addition to the couples having relationship difficulties and individuals with emotional problems, people began coming into her caseload who wanted to make contact with relatives who had passed away. This was new for Louise. She found she could help out by sitting quietly with her client, allowing the connection to be felt, helping the client work through unfinished business and discover the meaning of death in her life.

In all aspects of her life, Louise has found a new depth.

> I perceive myself as a handmaiden to Divine Mother, the feminine aspect of God. I want to channel divine love to others to help them become whole. I do what I am called to do. I feel very happy and, at the same time, peaceful. My clients are benefiting from my increased ability to love and to feel compassion for them. My practice is very full.
>
> My home life is wonderful too. I have a good relationship with my children. The experience has deepened the bond between my husband and me.
>
> In retrospect I know that this intense episode was a renewal, giving me inspiration about my own capacities as a healer and helping me release old patterns of fear and mistrust that impeded my development.

This episode of spiritual emergency illustrates many aspects of the phenomena of spiritual growth. First, Louise's experience took place in the course of normal development. Prior to this episode she had no severe emotional problem, and she was functioning very smoothly in her social world and at work. She was married, maintained a network of friends, and held a professional job. Louise's conceptual framework about her life process included spiritual growth—although her beliefs were not fixed to any particular religious creed.

In her crisis, she became absorbed in her subjective reality, opening new doors to insight. She had profound direct experience of universal themes of good versus evil, tension and surrender, male and female. She experienced being emotionally out-of-control, overwhelmed at times by new ways of perceiving her world. She was highly intuitive and loving during and after the crisis, becoming more and more involved in directing this capacity into helping others toward wholeness.

Breakdown or Breakthrough?

The Western world has not always considered the kind of experience Louise had after her drug experience as a positive part of human development, a *breakthrough*. Instead, barring organic problems, we would more likely call it a *breakdown*. Since we conventionally define maturity in a rigid way based on a person's maintaining emotional stability and an ability to perform consistently, any radical change we perceive in this pattern is generally seen as a breakdown. Of course, stability and dependability are essential for a culture that values efficiency, productivity, industry, and materialism. But perhaps there is more to life beyond this definition of maturity.

In traditions around the world that honor wisdom above efficiency, personal development didn't stop with physical age, emotional stability, or material well-being. Development was considered in a broader framework, which included reaching higher levels of compassion, fearlessness, sensitivity, and wisdom.[1] This is reflected in Wilber's developmental levels beyond ego—Subtle, Causal, and Atman—which I reviewed in chapter 1. When we use this model, which shows the possibility of growth beyond this fixation with material welfare, we open the possibility of episodes such as Louise's being breakthroughs into higher levels of functioning. The disintegration of old patterns may well be a burning away of obsolete ways of perceiving the world to make way for more clarity, a deeper self-assuredness, a greater wisdom, and a larger capacity for creative expression. Louise certainly functioned in a more expanded way after her episode.

We all have the potential of growing past conventional maturity into higher levels of functioning. It is the natural course of human development. In fact, most of us will access these higher realms, through experiences of closeness with God, divine inspiration, rushes of love, and sensing the transcendent.

Forms of Spiritual Emergency

In an episode of intense transpersonal experiences, the inner life will follow any of several patterns. Initially, six patterns were defined by psychiatrist Dr. Stanislav Grof and his wife, Christina Grof.[2] Any of these forms may appear alone, in conjunction with other patterns simultaneously, or serially. Louise experienced elements of three of the patterns simultaneously in the intensity of her episode. She was involved in the chaos of both Subtle level experiences and regressed states happening together. The final resolution was a stronger alignment with her life purpose. Her story and others are used below to illustrate all of the classic six patterns.

Opening to Life Myth

Louise was preoccupied with the archetypal mythic realms for a period of two weeks in her spiritual emergency. Immersing herself in this level expanded her insight and catalyzed an opening up to new dimensions that enhanced her family life and professional development. She experienced a renewed energy to be of service to humanity.

These are typical results of *opening to life myth*. What are these mythic realms? What is an *archetype*? What is a life myth?

Archetypal realms are the dimension of life related to universal human instincts (like the urge for power, meaning, survival, reproduction) perceived by the senses and/or manifested in fantasies and dreams.[3] They often reveal their presence only through symbolic images. Thus, a dream about a king almost always concerns the archetype of central power. It may indicate that the dreamer is concerned with issues of personal power, with taking authority. When you are opening to life myth, you are perceiving almost everything as a symbol of the larger archetypal realm. A tree is not just a tree, it is the Tree of Life. A picture of a nuclear bomb is not just a picture, it is a manifestation of evil. Thus, one's personal interaction with the archetypal realm becomes foremost. The material realm is important only as it is acted upon by the archetypes. Thus, Louise was obsessed with the conflict of good and evil and wanted to protect her children against the evil. She was not capable of making sandwiches, housecleaning, driving a car—the mundane, material things that often occupy a mother.

The inner world of a person opening to life myth is replete with dramatic archetypal images that portray profoundly significant themes to the person. It is as if they are reworking in their mind the creation of the world itself and social culture in that world. Images of kings and queens are prevalent, as are ceremonies and ancient rituals, cataclysms and disasters. Performing rituals, actually participating in the myths, is usually essential to a person opening to life myth. Louise was very involved with the myth of Psyche, who was on a journey to find Amor, the god of love:

> I would ask that candles be lighted at particular times, to mark stages along my journey. When I felt I was going into Hades, the underworld, to perform the last task, I had Wes get me some barley-rice cakes. I held these in my hand, as Psyche had on her journey. I did not give them to anyone, just as Psyche was told to do on her journey. When I recognized it was the "right" time, I ate them.
>
> Wes allowed me to perform these rituals. He felt if I did them, then I would be able to complete my journey and come out of the altered state I was in. He sensed that if I did not complete these ritual acts, I would remain caught in an altered state.

During her spiritual crisis, Louise received new understanding of world history, from its origins to the present, as well as her own beginnings to the present. The archetypal realm covered both personal and collective experiences simultaneously.

The person immersed in this opening may be unpredictable, highly emotional, and uninterested in, or unable to carry on, any normal routine of sleeping, washing, eating, and dressing. He or she may want to wander outdoors at all hours to commune with nature, dramatizing a "sacred" mission in his or her life myth, or be curled in bed for days in a fetal position, terrified to move. The desire to interact with the archetypal realms is that compelling!

However, the human body cannot withstand this kind of intensity indefinitely. Louise lost twenty-five pounds within the three weeks of her intense episode. In the case of opening to life myth, the episode usually lasts no longer than forty days. Interestingly enough, it often lasts exactly forty days. (Perhaps Christ's forty days in the desert were a part of his opening to life myth.) Then there is a period of integrating the new insights into one's daily life, and understanding the episode in retrospect. This period may last several years, with people continuing to reflect back and bring new understanding to their experience for the rest of their lives.

As we have seen, opening to life myth led Louise to a greater sense of service. Louise enriched her therapeutic skills and family life. She became more self-aware, and more sensitively tuned to others and the world around her. These are typical results of opening to life myth.

Differentiating this pattern of spiritual emergency from a psychotic episode that comes from an organic illness, or mental breakdown, can sometimes be very difficult. Special care needs to be taken in consulting a professional who can do a thorough diagnosis if there is any question about identifying spiritual emergency.

Shamanic Journey

Similar to opening to life myth, *shamanic journey* also carries a person into the depths of the archetypal realms. Either pattern can happen after a psychologically stressful situation. Shamanic journey may also be intentionally catalyzed through engaging in shamanic practices.

How is the shamanic journey different from opening to life myth? In shamanic journey the themes are more about birth, death, rebirth, and communion with natural elements (rocks, trees, birds, animals, the earth itself, etc.). There is typically a sense of traveling to "upper" realms of spirit or "lower" realms that are elemental or diabolical in nature. What marks the end of this journey is an inner experience of being birthed into one's real self, one's true essence in human form, interacting consciously with the world. The old self, the persona who would betray its essential self to pursue a worldly treasure, has symbolically died. Natural elements become *allies* (special spiritual friends) so that the lesson is not forgotten.

A shaman is a person, male or female, who is gifted with deep communion with natural elements and an ability to communicate with spirit realms—with spirits who have died, or disembodied entities who have never been in human form. Often shamans are healers and political authorities in their tribes. Shamanic practices are done to awaken or exercise the inner powers of the shaman.

This particular pattern of spiritual emergence is conventionally connected solely to ancient cultures from around the world. Our indigenous American-Indian cultures centered around important shamanic practices. All babies were named, and most young boys were initiated to manhood, through traditional shamanic practices. For example, on a *vision quest* a pubescent boy would go into the wilderness alone for several days and nights, naked, with a blanket and no food. Deprived of emotional contact and physical comfort, fasting from sleep and food, he was more likely to enter into an altered state of consciousness, connect to his life myth, and obtain a vision, an inner certainty, of his life direction. Other shamanic practices include healing rituals, purification ceremonies, drumming, and dances. All of these induce an altered state of consciousness in which people are more likely to contact their essential selves.

Since the rituals of ancient cultures have become more accessible to our modern culture, more Anglo-Americans are experiencing shamanic journeys. This may be the result of hearing music reminiscent of ancient cultures or personal contact with American-Indians, or through the stress of our times. Thus, a contemporary shamanic journey may be stimulated by deprivation of contact with loved ones and a sense of dying to one's past life. Visions from movies, light shows, television, or recreational drugs may take the place of visions from the ancient vision quest. Richard's story in chapter 9 illustrates this type of experience.

The shamans were often initially recognized by other members of their tribe because they would have a special dream or vision. This can also happen in our culture.

Jennifer, forty-nine years old, married, the mother of three grown children, working as an administrator in a large corporation, had a shamanic journey as a child. She had her vision and met her ally while playing alone one day.

> When I was about six years old and playing by myself in the basement of our home, I was somehow "taken to another world." In my mind's eye I saw a large eagle, full of love and compassion. It took me up into a place full of light where there were people who had already died physically. I was told there that I would be a healer to many people. This inner vision transformed my inner life. From that day, I knew what my life was about. But, I was not shown how it was that I would become a healer and teacher.

Preparation, prior to traditional vision questing, involves fasting and purification in a sweatlodge. Jennifer had many high fevers and dramatic undiagnosed illnesses as a small child. Many times she was on the threshold of death. These were her preparation, her fasting and purification. These "spiritual illnesses" often are also signs that a young person will have shamanic abilities as an adult. How these abilities become manifest is personal to each individual.

Jennifer met her ally in her vision. This was the eagle. From that day, any sign of an eagle, either physical or in a dream or fantasy, would be a signal to her that her spiritual friend was aware of her and helping her become strong within herself. Some family members gave her eagle feathers to remind her of her strength.

> Years passed. I went to high school. I was the prom queen. I was a cheerleader and very popular. I graduated from school and got married. Life went on in an ordinary way. I had my babies. I got involved in politics. I worked in Washington, D.C., for a congressman.
>
> When I was thirty-five, my vision reawakened. My teenage son, John, came home late one night. He suddenly collapsed, comatose from an overdose of recreational drugs. It was clear to me that he would die before an ambulance could get to our home, because his heartbeat was becoming progressively more faint and his breathing more uneven. I knew there was no choice but to bring him back to life through my knowledge of the other world [Subtle energies].
>
> I prayed to my ally, the eagle. I used my sacred eagle feathers in healing rituals as I prayed through the night. I prayed for him to be saved. I promised that I would fulfill my mission as a healer and teacher if he would be allowed to live. Early in the morning, John began to revive. My prayers were answered.

Jennifer's journey was a calling. For Jennifer, as for others who experience this pattern of spiritual emergence, it was a demand that she had to respond to. Life kept bringing her back to her calling until she embraced it fully. Jennifer now teaches nurses, doctors, and laypeople all over the United States about the use of Native American forms of healing. Through her healing ceremonies, some people experience remission from cancer and other forms of "incurable" illnesses. Her shamanic journey, at the age of six, made her aware of these very special gifts she had. Her willingness to respond to the calling has helped thousands of people toward increased well-being.

Kundalini Awakening

Kundalini is a Sanskrit word referring to a powerful energy that resides in the body. It is part of universal divine energy that purifies and strengthens the body. Most people are unconscious of it. It is said to be coiled like a sleeping snake at the base of the spine. As it awakens, it stimulates bizarre sensations in the body—flashes of heat and cold, muscle spasms, and streaming electrical pulsations are typical. Eventually, this contributes to discarding chronic tension in muscles and organs. The result is a more relaxed body, a consciousness awakened to transpersonal realms, a strong desire to be of service to others. Louise was responding to aspects of a kundalini awakening when she felt surges of energy in her spine. Our conventional definition of a spiritual experience—a sudden, overwhelming awareness of the presence of Higher Power, or God—is included in kundalini awakening.

Following is the story of Jill, a thirty-nine-year-old mother of four young children, who experienced an episode of kundalini awakening. It all started around the time that a close friend of hers, Kathy, died. Kathy's daughter and Jill had attended Kathy during the months prior to her death. The three of them became very close, and Jill was inspired by Kathy to focus on God as love.

> As Kathy became frail from the cancer, she also seemed to transform; a metamorphosis was taking place. If ever she saw that I was troubled, she used to repeat the phrase "Let go, let God." I was in awe of the love that flowed between Kathy and her daughter. Love filled their home. I was deeply affected by Kathy's transformation from a woman who was extremely independent and closed to her feelings to a very loving, happy, completely trusting woman whose spirit almost seemed to become love itself.

The intense focus of attention on something other than one's own personal needs often precedes a kundalini awakening. In Jill's case, shortly after Kathy died, she began to experience energy in a new way:

> I felt my heart was five feet wide. I had so much love in my heart, I didn't know what to do with it. I was really very uncomfortable. I wasn't sleeping well. I was anxious. I wasn't interested in eating. The worst of it was that I would get spaced out around my children. I didn't like the quality of my mothering. I wasn't really present with them.
>
> I tried to resolve these problems as I used to. I would pray, but be too anxious to listen for a response. I needed more help because I was only getting more anxious and spacy.

Jill started therapy. That helped her learn to accept her feelings and begin to understand them. Her body was trying to integrate the inrush of new energy and learn how to express it. However, her previous patterns of behavior, based more on fear than love, held her suspended in a state of anxiety. Something had to change. This tension is familiar to a person on the threshold of a kundalini awakening. After seven months of therapy, a very strange thing happened to her:

> I was saying good night to a friend when my legs started jerking and
> I collapsed to the floor, out of control, my legs and arms flailing. I had
> extreme nausea. There was an arc of pain from my heart to my solar
> plexus. I couldn't get up. I couldn't do anything. So, I surrendered to
> the jerking that would cycle through me every few seconds. This
> intensity lasted about two hours. By then I was exhausted, scared,
> and feeling bewildered. I had more tremors on and off all night. The
> next day I was filled with fear.

The intense physical release that Jill experienced is a good example of
what happens in a kundalini awakening. Often the body is out of
control for a period of time. Some people move spontaneously into
yoga postures, or *mudras*. Most people feel rushes of energy moving
up their spine. Around the time of the awakening there can be anxiety,
depression, anorexia, insomnia, even amnesia. Hypersensitivity to
stimuli is common, so there is a great desire for a quiet environment.
Psychosomatic symptoms, such as a change in visual perceptions, may
come and go. These energetic and physiological changes and mood
shifts can be consuming.

After that night and for weeks, Jill needed to be in a quiet,
nonstressful place, with the comfort of a close companion who would
let her be herself and take care of her. Her parents thought she might
be going crazy, that she might be having a nervous breakdown. Jill
knew intuitively that she was okay. She also knew that if she went to
the hospital or saw a regular physician, she would be given drugs to
stop her symptoms. Then she would be in real trouble and much more
confused—and, she thought, maybe I *would* go crazy! Deep inside her,
she knew what she needed—that her healing, or "coming together,"
would take time. She needed to avoid crowded areas, like big shop-
ping centers. The lights, confusion of sounds, and impersonal space—
all the stimuli—totally overwhelmed her. In those situations she
couldn't think anymore. She would get extremely anxious and disoriented.

Jill is blessed with a supportive husband who took over the care
of the children and almost all of the home care. He was very understanding when Jill wanted to stay at a friend's house where she could
be quiet. Her house was anything but quiet! Jill needed to rest. She
needed to let go of all the roles she had been playing as wife and
mother and just be herself for a while. Even the smallest decision was
often upsetting to her during this time.

> In this hypersensitive state I seemed to be more receptive to feel-
> ing the Spirit of my Heavenly Father, and thus receiving guidance
> from Him. I also became more telepathic, more sensitive to other
> people's feelings. If I was around someone with strong feelings, I
> would pick up these feelings with my own body. These feelings
> would be so intense that at times I got confused as to whether the

feelings were really mine or someone else's. Feeling the emotions of others increased my compassion and deepened my desire to help other people in a meaningful way.

She wasn't ready to fully resume her responsibilities at home for several months. She knew she did not want to continue to live as she had been living. She wanted to change her relationship with herself, her friends, and her family, and eventually figure out ways she could be of service to others. At some point, she wanted to work out the long-standing problems she had with her parents. She wanted to be a better mother and wife. She knew it would take time and patience to make such changes. She needed to have time available to be by herself, to exercise to improve her physical stamina, to be in nature, and to go to sacred places, where she received insight from Higher Power into her life.

Jill's awakening had a profound impact on the quality of her life. She became more self-aware. She has a fuller emotional and sexual expressiveness. She has a sense of being closer to Higher Power—and able to welcome the ways that it manifests through her. A year after the experience, Jill told me:

> The process of change I went through was both marvelous and terrifying for me. I didn't like being out of control, but I knew I was on the course that was right for me. Eventually, I learned to surrender to the process and be less self-critical and more patient. I often felt bad that I couldn't be more available to my family at times when they needed me.

Now, Jill is basically happy. She has some real peace in her life. She is not so controlled by her fears. Her husband said, "Before Jill fell apart, she used to be angry all the time, and now she is loving, accepting of others, and able to be present."

At times Jill lets external pressures overwhelm her, and she forgets to take time for her continuing internal growth process. She has a deep understanding of why so many prophets in the Scriptures went into the wilderness to seek the counsel of the Spirit and thus further their own growth. Perhaps for Jill the spiritual emergency was a forced retreat. It was a time of letting go of fears that were no longer serving her and learning more about who she is, learning to love herself—which then gave her the freedom to love others.

Just thirteen months after her "falling apart," Jill has been accepted by a school to take a monthlong advanced vision quest training course. She said she never would have done this two years ago, but it feels just right now.

Jill's story illustrates a profound transformation process that offered a new beginning in life. Jill is moving into the world, taking a new position vis-à-vis the church, her family, and her role in life. An excerpt from another woman's story illustrates the dramatic opening to intuition and direct knowing that is another aspect of kundalini awakening. Cynthia's story illustrates that the awakening can be very brief.

Cynthia is the mother of two children, and a student in graduate school. She has been deeply involved in the Christian religion all her life, and is a student of Jungian psychology. She was in the library by herself at the beginning of her experience. The intensity lasted only a few hours; however, the experience itself changed her profoundly.

> Suddenly, I began to have this sense of an enormous energy. My eyes would come to a word, and then rushes of energy would move up my spine. Then, it was as if a door opened up in my head, and I realized I could ask any question I wanted, and I would get an answer.
>
> I asked to see the relationship between good and evil. I saw them coming together in my mind's eye. I saw their dance, their real relationship. I still can't describe it in words, but I know it unquestionably. I saw that in essence all things are at one with each other. I saw that over and over.
>
> Once I gave way to the experience and let go of my fear, I felt ecstatic. Still, it was not easy to be with other people. I was shaking all over. It was difficult to walk. The experience really shook me on every level—physical, intellectual, and spiritual.
>
> As soon as I was able, I took a walk outside underneath the trees in a park. This helped me come back to myself so that I could function, driving a car, conversing with others, and continuing my day.

Kundalini awakening episodes may last minutes, hours, or weeks. Cynthia did not experience the length of disorientation that Jill had. For Cynthia, the experience lasted just hours instead of weeks. However, each of them speaks of her experiences as being transformative— opening her to a realization of the greater unity of all things and a profound sense of inner peace.

Emergence of a Karmic Pattern

Have you ever been to a new place and felt you have been there before, but you don't know when? Perhaps you have met people for the first time, yet felt as if you knew them already. The more intimately you feel you know the place, or the person, the more eerie the experience is. How could it be? You scan your memory for the time, but come up with nothing. This is similar to *déjà vu*, the sense of having witnessed a scene earlier even though it is just now unfolding before your eyes. Such events are unexplainable and disorienting.

When this type of experience is intensified to the point of being overwhelming or profoundly disorienting, it is a spiritual emergency.

It is infrequent for an opening to *karmic pattern* to be the only catalyst of a spiritual emergency. Like a powerful dream, the opening happens, is surprising, and stimulates reflection and new insight. It can help you see a certain pattern in your life that seems to run deep, as if it has been there for lifetimes.

Before Cynthia had the kundalini awakening just mentioned, she had an opening to a karmic pattern: She was with her husband, Jack, on summer vacation. Because she had been so deeply involved with the church, teaching Bible school since she was a teenager, she wanted to see a lot of churches in Europe. It was in Bingen, Germany, that she had an experience that struck awe into her.

> We were in a museum looking at some of the clothing that people had worn in the Middle Ages. I was enjoying myself, just relaxed and happy, when, suddenly, I looked casually at one picture of a nun, and a whole lifetime of experiences unfolded itself before my eyes. I recollected being a nun like the woman in the picture. I knew exactly how to put on a series of undergarments to wear my habit correctly. I remembered what my responsibilities were at the convent. I remembered how we spoke to each other, what we ate, how long we slept. I could sense what the place smelled like! That's how real it was to me.

This kind of inner recognition, unexpected, consistently involving all the senses simultaneously, as well as the emotions, is characteristic of an emergence of a karmic pattern. It does not always indicate past-life experiences that are historically identifiable. It may be attached to an inner knowingness—as if one's very cells had lived a life as part of another being. Then there is a definite sense of feeling someone or something other than yourself, for example, an Egyptian slave, a queen, a rock, or a bear. This kind of experience may give you insight into your way of taking authority. When emergence of a karmic pattern first happens, you often want to research whether it could be "true." Cynthia sought out books that could describe convent life in the Middle Ages. She found information that completely authenticated what she had "seen."

Although her Christian upbringing had not encouraged her to believe in reincarnation, Cynthia had no other way to explain her recollection. She had never been exposed to the information about this convent in a class or a book. The recollection explained her devoted involvement in the church in this lifetime. It was a repetition of some of the aspects of an earlier life, part of a pattern she was drawn to.

What is the meaning of a karmic pattern? *Karma* is a Sanskrit word relating to the law of cause and effect. Every action leaves an effect. Every effect has a cause. One's personal karma relates to the accumulated benefits one has earned through positive action or a pocket of ignorance one needs to enlighten. Cumulatively, one's karma may be envisioned as gold stars or black marks that determine what lessons must be addressed in life. Karma is accumulated through lifetimes, being carried like a scorecard from lifetime to lifetime. How did Cynthia relate to her experience as part of a karmic pattern?

> I believe my intention to find unity with God was incomplete in Bingen, and so I have my current lifetime to progress still further on my path. My good deeds in the past have earned me good karma where I now have wonderful friends and family, financial and emotional support for my spiritual journey. I feel my life would not be complete unless I shared this journey with my husband. I couldn't do that when I was in the convent.

Knowing yourself as having participated in many different lifetimes in many roles gives depth to your experience of yourself, your capacities, and your motivation. Cynthia used her experience to acknowledge her kinship with the religious life. Since her husband and family were basically supportive of this direction in her, her renewed commitment to spiritual direction was not a threat to them.

However, in a family that was alienated by the new information gained in an emergence of a karmic pattern, this kind of spiritual emergence could be very disruptive. Imagine a boy of seven, interested, like his peers, in baseball, bicycles, pizza, etc. His mother excitedly shares with him an insight she had gained in a past-life regression (a psychotherapy session designed to evoke emergence of a karmic pattern). The mother, in this case, had seen that she used to be the boy's lover in a past life, but he rejected her. She now sees that is why they have such a difficult time communicating at present. It would be a very unusual young child who could take this information and not feel confused by it. Children need to know that there are strong boundaries between the generations—that there is a dependable structure to the family. The boy is somehow being accused of incest— although the sexual relationship occurred in another lifetime. He might feel, Is it true? Will Dad be upset? Should I apologize to Mom? For what? A normal child in this culture does not need to be burdened with this kind of complication when he has no background with which to deal with it.

An emergence of a karmic pattern may come about in a special dream at night, in meditation; in a fantasy that spontaneously erupts during the daylight hours, especially when we are meeting new people or visiting new places; when we consult a psychic who clairvoyantly sees the past lives of her clients; in a deliberate past-life regression using hypnotherapy; through experiential therapies, like holotropic breathing; in the dentist's office with nitrous oxide; in surgery under the influence of a general anesthesia; in experimenting with recreational drugs; when we are reading a story or historical description. No matter how they occur, these experiences usually leave us with healing insight into our present-life dilemmas. Sometimes they lead to spontaneous physical and emotional healing.

Do you have to believe in reincarnation to experience the benefits of opening of a karmic pattern? Although many consider these experiences to be from past lives or even future lives, you do not have to believe in reincarnation to have the powerful healing effect this opening promotes. Treating the opening like a meaningful dream can lead to the same insights and healing.

Psychic Opening

This pattern is often connected to the emergence of a karmic pattern in that opening the doorway to past lives often opens the doorway to your deeper sensitivities, the "sixth sense," at the same time.

Psychic opening refers to experiencing an ability to see clairvoyantly, to feel clairsentiently, or hear clairaudiently. These abilities allow you to perceive, in pictures, or in bodily sensations, or in inner sounds, information about the environment and other people that is not objectively available. These abilities are particularly helpful for anyone in the healing arts needing to diagnose health problems. Attention needs to be paid to the confusion of psychic opening that is a true experience of Subtle levels and the occurrence of auditory, visual, or kinesthetic hallucinations indicative of psychological complexes or organic disease.

The opening of psychic abilities may happen suddenly or gradually. Some people are born with psychic abilities and never lose them. People who discover psychic abilities later in life often report that the abilities were there in early childhood but went underground for several years when the child was trying to fit into a culture that did not condone being "psychic."

The awakening to, or recollection of, psychic abilities will happen most easily in a social environment that accepts having these abilities as positive. This may happen in a stressful situation, where having the sixth sense may save a life. It could happen in a workshop in intuition training or sensitivity training, in consultation with a psychic, or in therapy.

Claudia, forty-seven years old, a psychiatric nurse, entered into therapy in order to know herself better. Claudia had never experienced bodywork before, and wanted to know what it was like. After several months, she was doing some deep breathing in a therapy session in order to relax into herself.

I suddenly began experiencing myself as an old wise person. I felt my eyes were deep pools to the universe. I was a healer who could love, who could really see, who could let go of anger as if letting a bird go in the wind. My hands were buzzing with energy.

During this time in my life I began exploring hands-on healing with people. Everyone I worked with told me that I seemed to know, without them telling me, exactly where they were hurting and how to touch them to take away the pain. This scared me at first. I didn't know how I knew! Then, since it helped people, I figured, "Well, why not use it?" So, I do use it more and more frequently. And I still don't know how it works.

Psychic abilities have also been useful in finding lost objects. For example, the police employ psychics to track down lost objects, lost children, or criminals. Military groups have explored using psychics for "seeing" the secrets of their enemies—where missile sites are located, etc.

On a lighter note, psychic abilities can manifest in a number of mundane ways. One person I know, who is not a newspaper reader or an educated shopper, can "sense" where to go for the best deal on a specific item of clothing at any particular time. Another person, uneducated in car mechanics, simply "knows" what is going wrong in a car by closing his eyes and asking his intuition. Many successful fishermen apply their sixth sense to going where the fish are and "knowing" what the fish will take for bait.

Harry Roberts, who I mentioned in chapter 2, grew up with the Yurok Indian tribe in northern California. As a youngster, he played by the Klamath River with his friends. As he grew older, he realized he had "fish medicine." He could stand on a hill looking down to the river and see with his inner eye where the fish were located. When he was at the river, he could reach his hand gently into the water and simply pull out a fish.

In Eastern psychologies (Hinduism in particular and especially Yoga psychology), the opening to psychic abilities is a sign of getting closer to opening to Higher Power, the most sacred and powerful energies in the universe. The psychic abilities, *siddhis* in Sanskrit, are thought to be connected to the fifth and sixth chakras, energy centers physically located around the throat and center of the brow. When these energetic centers are open, not only can you perceive information not objectively obvious, but you can communicate with beings who are not visible because they live in a dimension not usually perceptible to us.

The small group who started the Findhorn Community in the coastal sand dunes of northern Scotland exemplified the benefits of this ability to commune with other dimensions. Eileen and Peter

Caddy, along with their friend Dorothy Maclean, worked directly with the spirits of different vegetables and fruits in the planting and maintenance of their garden.

On July 28, 1964, Dorothy received this information from the angel of the landscape:

> In the tremendous growth in the garden, you have evidence in form of how power when recognized is made manifest. We of the deva world have been contacted, recognized by you, and thus given "hands and feet" which we would otherwise not have. As power within you is not awakened until it is recognized and called forth, so must you call forth our powers.[4]

As a result of the daily instruction Dorothy and Eileen received from the *devas*, or spirits, of each plant, they produced flowers and vegetables that were recordbreaking in quality and size. "In the worst possible soil for roses, ours bloomed to perfection. . . . Foxgloves, which normally grow to three and four feet in rich soil, grew to eight and nine feet in our sandy garden."

Their success in the garden became an inspiration to horticulturists as well as spiritual seekers. The Findhorn community has now grown to become a sanctuary for people who have psychic abilities and/or want to develop a closer communication with the positive dimensions of the natural world. As the community has grown over the past twenty-five years, it has become an internationally renowned educational center that fosters the spiritual emergence process beyond, but still including, horticulture. Through the psychic opening of a few people, the spiritual emergence process of many have been served.

Possession

> What is light is always balanced with what is dark. What is good is always balanced with what is bad, what is love is balanced with what is hate. What is purity is balanced with what is evil. And so, in the creation of the light beings, there was also creation of the dark ones, for that [duality] is the nature and the formation of this plane. . . . When there is separation from the desire to return to wholeness, the dark forces enter. So a being who says for a moment, "I give up, I do not see how I will find my wholeness again," this one opens a doorway, and the dark shadow enters in.
>
> —LYNN BREEDLOVE, channeling on the
> nature of possession. February 1989.

Usually, we think of "possession" as a person being taken over, controlled, by an evil entity or by a soul whose body has died. We believe the victim, if not delusional, needs exorcism by a priest, priestess, or someone familiar with magic. This victimization, helplessness, and opening to predatory spirits is certainly the most frightening definition of possession. It is easy to see that this experience may catalyze a spiritual emergency.

In addition to possession as an event involving the Subtle realm, there are other forms of possession that are more psychologically based. Think of a young boy, the child of quiet, unexpressive parents, who develops an avid interest in violent and aggressive sports. He, too, is "possessed" by his interest. He may also be "possessed" by the *shadow* of his parents—that is, compelled to live out the shadow of his parents. The shadow represents those parts of us that we feel uncomfortable claiming as our own. Children often act out the shadow of their parents. It is nature's way of creating wholeness. If the parents became more whole, accepting their own shadow side, the boy would not be compelled to act out their shadow. He would then be freer to find his own wholeness.

In my opinion, most people who are possessed are under the influence of a shadow—their own or someone else's. These dark forces must be identified and worked with psychologically in order to stop what is experienced as "invasion" or "victimization." The most well-developed cases of possession by a shadow are people with *multiple personality disorder*. They have completely cut themselves off from their shadow to the extent that their shadow takes on an independent personality structure. In less extreme cases there is simply the *dissociation*—a refusal to claim an aspect of the self—that I mentioned above. Although dissociation seems less difficult than multiple personality disorder, it may be potentiated by religious dogma and lead to devastating results. Think of a rigidly devout Fundamentalist who sees anger in his child and believes him to be "possessed by the Devil." He beats the child physically as an exorcism. Some children die from this treatment. If the parent had claimed the shadow of his own anger, the child would not have fallen victim to the parent's projection.

The third definition of possession is related to enhanced contact with beings of higher intelligence. This is called *channeling*. In this instance, a person willingly allows his or her own body to be used by a higher intelligence to allow increased communication of wisdom to those not in contact with that source.

Understanding what possession is, where entities come from, how to protect against negative possession and find a place for channeling, and how to claim your own shadow can be a time-consuming and anxiety-producing experience in itself. Where does one go for help? What kind of exorcism really works? What kind of psychological therapy is appropriate? Whom do you trust?

Lynn Breedlove is a gifted psychic in Santa Cruz, California. For twenty years, Lynn has had many Subtle level experiences. For over seven years, she has been in direct communication with all kinds of disembodied entities, both negative and positive. In dealing with a person who has been taken over by an evil entity, Lynn speaks to the entities that have invaded a person in a prayerful manner. She asks what message they bring and prays that they be healed and blessed and united with their wholeness. As a channel, Lynn also receives positive uplifting information from disembodied entities to assist in healing people.

When people think they might be possessed, Lynn helps them integrate the energy of the shadow elements, disidentify with the disempowering aspects of being a victim, and claim the empowering aspects of being sensitive to themselves.

> Trust the validity of your experience. Do not deny that what you see, feel, or hear may be true. Talk to someone you trust about your experience, someone who can accept the validity of possession. As you speak to him, you may find within yourself what help you need to be rid of the invading energy. Perhaps your trusted friend will have an idea that seems to feel right to you. It doesn't necessarily have to be reasonable or logical, and you don't have to believe in it. Almost anything can work. The most important thing is to believe that it *may* work. It could be an exorcism by a Catholic priest, or a bath in salt-water, a prayer to Mother Earth, and/or psychotherapy and centering exercises like meditation or martial arts.

Anyone who can truly validate the possessed person's experience, help him go into it directly and not escape from it, will also simultaneously be helping him evoke information needed for the appropriate remedy. "The remedy is hidden inside the experience itself." However, the helper must have confidence and skill in what the process involves, which includes skill in recognizing symptoms of mental and organic illness. The romance of being "possessed" may be a cover for a person not finding an effective route to cope with dissociated aspects of himself.

If you are possessed by a disembodied entity or a shadow, you may lose all consciousness of yourself. Your voice and gestures change. This happened to a sixteen-year-old girl, Galen, who came to me for help. She had been sitting with a few friends after school and had gone into a reverie, losing consciousness. This was not caused by a drug trip or any organic problem. Something happened about which she has no memory. Fifteen minutes passed. When Galen "awoke," extremely groggy, her friends were yelling at her to wake up and shaking her all over. The girls were all terrified. They told Galen she had been speaking with a man's voice, her face had taken on a demonic look, her eyes had even seemed to change color. They made her leave the room with them and do calisthenics outdoors. They also prayed with her that the demonic force would leave her alone. This helped her. She has not been "possessed" in the same way again, but she has become more aware of herself in new ways.

Galen has learned that she has psychic abilities, healing abilities, and a familiarity with spiritual realms. Her confronting her possession—going through the fear that she was crazy, seeking support from counselors, questioning her own ideas about the nature of this world, and finding ways to manage her sensitivity—has given her a greater sense of self-worth. She is more connected to her compassion. This has brought a new dimension to the way she expresses affection to friends and family. She also knows that she does not want to be "possessed" by these sensitivities. She wants to educate herself about them, maybe take a few classes about psychism, and wait to cultivate her abilities when she is older. She wants to lead the life of a regular high school student now. Thus, she is more self-aware, and more in charge of her way to manage her interest in transpersonal realms. Confronting possession, and resolving the issues it presents, is a process of gaining a stronger sense of self.

It is not necessary to experience possession by losing consciousness as Galen did. Lynn is able to maintain awareness of what is being spoken through her at the same time she has given herself over as a channel. She is also able to choose which entity is to come through her and what questions she wants to have addressed. She says that her intentions to connect to the most holy energies are essential to her work in these realms, as is her asking for protection if negative energies present themselves.

This kind of method has been developed over years of entering into the Subtle realm and bringing knowledge of that realm into normal life. Lynn is far from being helplessly victimized by disembodied entities. Although she, like Galen, was also frightened of her abilities and her bizarre experiences when she first began to open up psychically, Lynn has integrated channeling into her life. Now, she can talk to an angel, then gracefully excuse herself to attend to making her husband's lunch or maintaining their lovely home. She is as much a part of this world as any person. The only difference is in her unusual skill in moving flexibly between the Subtle astral realm where the disembodied entities exist and the physical realm. Also, as a psychic counselor, she helps people achieve insight into life problems, resolve disturbances, and improve both physical and spiritual well-being.

People who are most susceptible to being possessed are people with weak boundaries, like Galen and other young people. They do not yet have a strong sense of who they are. People who are so sensitive to others that they lose touch with themselves while feeling someone else's feelings also have weak boundaries. A lack of self-esteem generally accompanies this condition. When self-acceptance and self-confidence build, there is less likelihood of being victim to negative forms of possession—psychological and/or psychic. So being possessed may be a call to gain that strength in oneself.

Synthesis of the Forms

In review, individuals usually experience the forms of spiritual emergence simultaneously and serially. The very beginning of my story from chapter 2 is an example. As a child, I experienced my soul, beyond time and space, when I almost drowned. This was a shamanic journey of sorts—a death of my old sense of self and a new birth into a renewed sense of self based on my identification with my soul. In the process of being underwater desperately trying to find my way to the surface, I was experiencing the archetypal realms—dark versus light, life versus death. I had imagined a monster living in the lake, the bogey man my brother warned me about to tease me. This was a shadow figure that I was afraid would possess me. I was opening to my life myth—the roots of my lifelong interest in transpersonal realms and the shadow. Shortly after coming to the surface and catching my breath, I realized I could now see the world in a new way. For instance, I could see with my inner eye that my cousin was not yet engaged consciously with her soul. I had become more psychically open. Soon afterward, I began having dreams about Indians coming to get me at my home. This was precognition of my future involvement with shamanism and a cue to my opening to karmic patterns. As an adult doing past-life regression work with a psychotherapist, I experienced the knowledge of shamanism as if I had been a shaman in a previous life.

All of the above forms and the synthesis of the forms of spiritual emergence belong to the mythic realm where we are all potential heroes and heroines, on this earth to manifest our essential selves fully in a way that adds to the quality of life . . . whether we are healers or simply never-before-seen blossoms in the garden of humanity. The patterns of spiritual emergence fuel and accelerate this natural process of growth. It is a process of becoming more ourselves, more whole, and, simultaneously, closer to our connections with spiritual realms. It is a process that is beneficial—helping us be more perceptive, more capable of being of service, more creative, and more trusting of dimensions beyond our ordinary perceptions.

NOTE: Stanislav and Christina Grof reworked the initial six patterns to number ten patterns in their book *Spiritual Emergency: When Personal Transformation Becomes a Crisis*. This means that some of the above forms were divided into three separate patterns to more specifically describe the pattern and its catalyst. What was formerly *possession* became *possession states, communication with spirit guides and channeling,* and *experiences with close encounters with UFOs.* What was formerly *kundalini awakening* was split into *awakening of kundalini, episodes of unitive consciousness or peak experiences,* and *near-death experiences.* I have remained with the six original patterns in this text because I find it simpler to convey and grasp the material when the catalysts of spiritual emergence are not combined with the patterns of experience that they precipitate.

Entering the Transpersonal: A Zigzag Course

If the promise of these realms is so positive, why not just jump in? Where's the start? Well, once you are aware of having experiences from higher realms of consciousness, once you see where it is you want to go, it is not a straight line of development from conventional maturity to the transpersonal realms. Development to transpersonal levels does not follow a straight course. It is more like a zigzag line. From the moment we are conceived, we occupy one level, but may jump from that level to another, participating for short periods of time in other stages, higher or lower, before moving on to occupy the next-higher step of development. A child may not yet have reached maturity but be having Subtle level experiences when she plays with her "imaginary friends." A businessman who has reached maturity may be having transformative intuitive flashes, again from the Subtle level, when he does his relaxation exercises to music.

Likewise, this same businessman may regress back to less emotionally mature levels, wanting, for instance, a relationship with a sexual partner that allows him to be taken care of like a child by its mother. In having this relationship, he is trying to complete a stage in his own growth that is still not finished.

In a period of intense spiritual experiences, this same zigzag pattern is often sped up in such a way that a person with a strong sense of self may be opening to Subtle or Causal level experiences and the next minute be working with very regressed states of consciousness. Within this intensity, there is an impulse of the psyche to work through, to release the hold of the earlier stages, to liberate more energy to stabilize at a higher level of development. Psychological material that has not been metabolized from earlier times must be dealt with before the individual is free to move on more completely to higher levels. This is the reason why spiritual crises are like purification rites—they help to burn out those pockets in the psyche that still hold vestiges of "complexes," constellations of fixated energy resulting from incomplete developmental tasks from the past.

Louise's spiritual emergency helped her to move more closely to the Subtle realm, where she could work in harmony with the archetypal energies of sacred energy in its feminine form. In the process, she needed to go back into her own past and reexperience fears that she had as a small child: the fear of confronting the unknown; the desire to be held and be reflected in another's presence; the desire for the complete safety of being embraced only by what is known. This was a return to the psychological territory of a young baby with its mother. Once Louise lived out her intense desire for that kind of care (which she probably had not received enough of as a child) through the help of her husband who supported her so magnificently, then she could more independently integrate the deeply moving archetypal experiences she was having.

Another way of looking at this is that the archetypal experiences created a heat in her that flushed out old psychological material that needed to heal in order for her to grow. Both the content of the transpersonal experiences and the psychological material from the childish level were thus important at the same time in understanding her process. Her experience of the Subtle level needed to be validated. Louise needed to be reassured that it was okay to enter into that level of experience. And she needed a way to heal the complex from earlier in her life.

Crucial Support Issues

People in spiritual emergency need a particular kind of support. They need the freedom to regress to earlier levels, to work out unresolved problems from early life in a safe and supportive environment. They also need support to surrender to higher transpersonal levels. Support by someone who respects the process of spiritual emergency as a positive, life-enhancing development, not a disease or infirmity, is crucial.

Louise was fortunate to have in her husband, a resident psychiatric nurse, a person to care for her responsibilities, and a loving helper to attend her during her spiritual crisis. He could make decisions on her behalf. He could protect her safety. He knew how to make her more comfortable. He had the knowledge to differentiate her positive disintegration from a debilitating psychotic episode. He trusted that her experience was basically positive. He took time to help her process her issues from early life and actively encouraged her to explore the Subtle realms as well. Not everyone is so lucky.

In a more typical situation, family members are not schooled in transpersonal psychology and become terribly frightened by the bizarre behavior of someone in spiritual emergency. They band together, excluding the person in crisis, sure that this person has a disease, contributing to his sense of isolation. Often they decided that the person is probably having a psychotic episode and needs medication. They try, sometimes with deceit and desperation, to make him go to the hospital.

If Louise had been hospitalized during her episodes, she most likely would have been given medication to stop the symptoms: the inner visions, the intense emotionality, the increased sensitivity. Most physicians, including psychiatrists, categorically see all Subtle level experiences and deeply regressed states as symptoms of psychosis. The treatment is usually medication, to return to "normalcy." Antipsychotic medication would have prevented Louise from having Subtle level experiences. It would have cut her off from access to the regressed states that summoned her healing. Thus, it could have short-circuited her growth. It could have taught her that going into Subtle level experience was not good, and was in fact a symptom of pathology and not to be trusted. It might also have made her afraid of trusting her body's own wisdom—that she needed to regress for a time to take care of old business before she could move ahead.

Jill, whom I described under kundalini awakening, knew that medication was not the appropriate treatment for her. As her therapist, I supported her in that choice. I knew that she was going through a spiritual crisis. I checked for signs of deeper pathology on a regular basis and was convinced there was no need to hospitalize her. I talked to her husband and parents about ways to support the process Jill was in. Eventually, this network of trust and support between all of us provided the stability Jill needed to proceed through all the phenomena of the spiritual emergency.

Differentiating between spiritual emergency and pathological states is crucial to determining appropriate care. This must be done by a professional who is skilled in differential diagnosis—a psychotherapist, psychologist, or psychiatrist who is competent in the area of transpersonal psychology. *A Sourcebook for Helping People in Spiritual Emergency* gives guidelines for diagnosis and provides useful information for professionals and paraprofessionals about caring for someone in spiritual emergency.

After it is clear that someone is in a spiritual crisis, it is ideal for the person to be cared for in a homelike setting. See chapter 11 for some ideas on how to work with and support someone in spiritual crisis.

This chapter has defined the forms of spiritual emergencies and their relationship to psychological health. Spiritual crises are stimulated by a variety of circumstances, including lack of support and knowledge of spiritual emergence phenomena. Both spiritual study and inner work are typical catalysts to intense spiritual experiences. Many types of drugs, including anesthetics, can trigger intense spiritual phenomena. Other catalysts to spiritual emergency are emotional or physical distress, time of life, and extraordinary sexual experiences. All of these catalysts are discussed in depth in subsequent chapters. How a particular time of life may precipitate a spiritual emergence process is the subject of the next chapter.

4
Time of Life

One day I was preparing to drive into town with my four-year-old son, Jesse. I was sitting in the driver's seat when Jesse, standing behind me, leaned over and spoke close to my ear:

> I wish I could be an angel
> So I could catch a bird
> Then I'd be me again.
>
> But angels aren't true.
> The world says so.
>
> The world is an invisible mouth,
> And we are inside that mouth.
> Air comes out of the mouth.

I was amazed! I had never said anything to him like this. Neither had his father. I immediately told him how beautiful it was for him to see that and tell me about it. Then I quickly took out a pen and paper to jot it down.

To me, this poetic statement revealed Jesse's awareness of the spiritual nature of life and the hesitation of the adult world in accepting that reality. The angel represented Jesse's aspiration to be one with the embodiment of love and the freedom to fly. Jesse also recognized that the world—consensual reality—is more involved in consuming and talking—being a mouth—rather than being with the higher forces.

From early childhood through death, humans are on a constant seesaw between the pull of consensual reality and the longing for unity with a higher reality. This is a pulsation between the desire to control destiny in order to create personal happiness and the longing to surrender into the deepest truth, the nature of mind that is beyond desires, the background of all phenomena, Atman. You can see this pulsation dramatically in babies. Without conscious control, they can be consumed by a desire to be fed or held, yet as soon as their physical need is satisfied, they can drift into a state of mind that seems angelic, close to Higher Power. Once a *mature ego*, a stable sense of self based on separateness, has been established, then the pulsation from consensual reality to higher states of consciousness becomes less fluid and more controlled. From this vantage point of choice, we often face deep questions about what is meaningful.

Adolescence and *middlescence*, middle age, are times especially highlighted by a crisis of choice making. Is it most important to secure a lucrative job or a meaningful career? Or, am I designed for something wholly different, something riskier, having to do with my deepest self, my soul's purpose? What is my soul, anyway? How can I find it if it is there? This is the "Dark Night of the Ego." The goals that reflect ego desires are called into question, and there is a recognition of an emptiness that ego desires and old patterns of perceiving things cannot fill.

Facing death, either in seniority or as a result of illness, is also a time when people face a crisis of meaning. What is beyond physical death? Is there anything? Will I meet the souls of people I have known? Will I be judged? Who will judge me? Will I be born again back into this world? What do I have to do here and now in this world before I go on?

In this chapter, we will explore how specific times in life can be catalysts for spiritual emergence or emergency, why that is so, and how best to respond when it happens to ourselves or those close to us.

Childhood

One night when I was five years old, I woke up needing to go to the bathroom. It was summertime, and I was sleeping on the porch of our beach house. My mom and dad were inside in their bedrooms, asleep. So were my two brothers. There was no one else in the house. When I opened my eyes, I saw a man sitting in one of our chairs, looking out to the ocean. He was kind of old. I didn't sense he meant any harm at all. But I was breathlessly afraid. Then I watched him go out the door. He stepped into the air. Then he disappeared.

I didn't tell anyone about what I saw. I kept it to myself until I was nineteen. I was afraid it was not okay to see things like this. I was afraid people would be upset with me if I told them. No one in my family ever talked about stuff like this.

—JULIA, thirty years old, a counselor.

Young children, especially before the age of seven, are close to dimensions of reality in which they feel the unity of all things. They love fully, and they get angry without hesitation. Unless punished or suppressed, they are spontaneously expressive. They are not bound by linear patterns of thinking, by having to be rational. Time and space are fluid. Creative expression is not bound by self-consciousness. As a result, the whole world is magical, and they can enjoy it simply as that. They love magic shows. Their world is full of fantastic phenomena. The child's mind is absorbing new information at a fantastic rate.[1] Many children are effortlessly clairvoyant. They have not yet defined their personal limitations.

According to Erik Erikson's ideas on natural development, the child before seven is facing the following issues: Am I going to trust the world as a safe place or not? Do I have to feel ashamed of myself, or can I feel glad to be seen for who I am? Is it okay to take initiative and go in the directions I want to, or must I feel guilty about my interests?[2] During this phase, the child's primary attention is on his own biology—exploring his own body, getting physical needs met, understanding this world through exploring it physically. After seven, approximately, the child enters the stage of "latency" until puberty. At this point there is a stronger interest in acting on the external world. What can I do? What can I make? What recognition can I earn for my skills? The ego is beginning to take shape vis-à-vis the world.

The spiritual life of children may include Subtle level experiences, but children, not yet having a mature ego are not equipped to live at the Subtle level. The experiences of "unity" the child has are *prepersonal*, they are recollections of being at one with the mother, in her womb. They are not *transpersonal*, Causal or Atman, which involves transcending the ego.

What kind of spiritual experiences do children have? Adults regressed to early life through therapeutic techniques articulate in words what babies cannot say. These adults report:

> In the womb I felt completely at peace. I was in bliss. There was nothing I needed to do. I had everything I needed. I was completely happy. I could remember why I was born. I remembered my purpose in being born. I was excited to be here.

This recollection of the soul's purpose by the child is a "direct knowing" that comes with clairvoyance, clairsentience, and clairaudience. Especially before age seven, children may be very psychic. They may have past-life memories, be able to read minds, and perceive energy that is invisible to adults. It is easy for many children to become absorbed in an unbounded state of oneness with another person or an animal. This direct cognition stays with some children through early childhood. Eleanor told this story about her three-year-old son:

> He was in the backseat of my car in a parking lot waiting for me to unload the groceries. As I got in the car, he pointed at the woman in the next car and squealed delightedly, "Look, Mom, that lady just got married!" I asked him, "How do you know that?" He answered, "Because of the light around her face!"
>
> I got out of the car and introduced myself to the woman. She was dressed very plainly. I said, "Excuse me, my son seems to think that you have just gotten married. Is that so?" The stranger replied, surprised, "Yes, how did he know?"

This immediate cognition of the truth begins to fade when children become more entranced with critical thinking. This shift happens naturally around the age of six or seven. The world of concepts, especially the conventional reality valued in school, on television, and by the advertising industry become more dominant. Spiritual experiences are then apt to bring up fear for children, because they do not coincide with conventional reality. Most children who have had "imaginary companions" and/or seen entities invisible to adults begin to drop their contact with this realm.

Children, like Julia, who saw the man drift into the night, become swept up in the conventions of our consumer society. They become absorbed in finding their identity in the classroom and family hierarchy, making sure that they "fit in." Spontaneous cognition and intuition go underground while the ego structure and personality is thus being stabilized.

Spiritual Emergency in Children

Spiritual emergency cannot be diagnosed in a child as readily as it can be in an adult for many reasons. A child's communication skills are limited, and it is harder to measure what kind of experiences the child may be having. A child does not have a firm ego structure or a rigid conceptual framework about life that would be threatened by what an adult might perceive as bizarre experiences. The flexibility and openness of children allow them to accommodate spiritual experiences with much less difficulty than an adult. So spiritual emergency as a crisis of integrating intense spiritual experiences is not usually a problem. Julia was shocked by seeing the entity on the porch. She was also able to put the experience aside relatively easily, and distract herself with the more mundane aspects of life.

Spiritual experiences are problematic for children only when they are retreating into Subtle realms chronically as a defense from the pressures of their ordinary world. If there is no sign of mental illness, it could be that this preoccupation is caused by a physical illness or inappropriate care by a parent.

Among the women I have had as clients, each one who was physically or sexually abused as a child developed unusual psychic ability. Here, the emergency is actually their physical and emotional abuse. The spiritual experiences and psychic development come as a by-product of these crises. Some of these clients of mine are facile at out-of-the-body experiences. It was so difficult for each of these children to remain in her body, feeling the physical pain and conflicting emotions during the abuse, that she literally found a way to propel her consciousness onto the ceiling. (The relationship of physical abuse and Subtle experience is discussed in more depth in chapter 6.)

Living in continual fear of abuse, a child will develop a habit of constantly scanning the environment for any sign of potential danger—even a shift in vibration or feeling in the air. In this way, children teach themselves to read subtle vibrations and cultivate their psychic potential. The psychic powers are used as a defense mechanism to manage anxiety and pain—first around the abuse and then generally in other difficult situations. The psychic life of such a child can undermine his learning how to handle social difficulties in life because the child habitually "leaves," or is preoccupied with his own world and is thus less capable of handling external stress. This eventually develops into an emotional problem that incapacitates development. It needs to be addressed in psychotherapy or in therapeutic relationships to enable the child to learn alternative ways of coping with stress. Ideally, the child's spiritual experiences would be affirmed while new coping skills are being taught.

The spiritual life of a child is in crisis when the reality of the child's inner experiences is denied. For example: A child sees a red aura around an angry man and tells his mother about it. "Look at that man—there is red all around the outside of his shirt." The mother says, "No, you don't see that. That is impossible." Or: A child has a daydream in which she feels the presence of her grandmother, who is dead, and they talk together. The child tells her parent how happy she was to be with her grandmother. The parent replies, "That's a fantasy. You know your grandmother is dead. Don't be making up things."

In both of these two situations, the children are being taught to discount Subtle perceptions and the possibility that the Subtle realm exists. The children are also learning not to trust their own perceptions. Particularly for the most sensitive children, these admonitions from parents can make them feel alienated from their very ground of being. In contrast, having these perceptions affirmed can be the basis of children having deep trust in themselves and in their universe.

Encouraging Spiritual Emergence in Children

Adults who have maintained contact with the sense of unity and the Subtle level experiences they had as children have a touchstone, an anchor point, to guide them on the spiritual journey toward higher levels of consciousness. Children who maintain this connection with their spiritual life are less likely to have a spiritual emergency later in life. Helping children stay in contact with their unity experience and their psychic perceptions can have a beneficial effect on their development throughout life.

How can you encourage spiritual emergence in children? First, listen and watch. Second, affirm them.

Children who tell parents and teachers about their experiences of this nature are asking if it is okay to have these perceptions, or is there something "wrong" with or "weird" about them? Is it all right to have this? How does it fit into life? Am I wrong to perceive these things? Of course, the young child will not ask directly for this kind of reassurance, but the question will be there in a glance, a touch, a catch of the breath.

It is important to affirm the children's perceptions. Help them to talk about their experiences. Let them know that other people have these experiences. Let them know these experiences are an important part of life. Most important, help them to integrate their experiences in this realm into their everyday life.

When my son told me, "Angels aren't real, the world says so," I told him that angels *are* real. I showed him pictures of angels. Together we colored angel pictures. I also told him that people don't often talk about angels, and that many people *don't* believe in them. I reassured him that there is a place for angels in life, that even if they are invisible, they are really there to guide and protect us. Shortly after I told him this, Jesse's attention naturally moved to other things, like tying shoelaces and playing on his tricycle. After all, these too have a place, and normal children act out their knowledge that things of the ordinary world must be attended to. They want to accomplish the developmental tasks appropriate to their age, which have more to do with cultivating skills and acquiring emotional acceptance. This helps them to maintain a feeling of being safe in this world.

Adolescence

The developmental tasks of adolescence do not leave behind the more primitive needs of the child, but they go further—into developing a real identity. Young people must integrate all of who they were as children with the "vicissitudes of the libido . . . and the opportunities offered in social roles."[3] Ideally, adolescents congeal their sexual identity and settle on career directions. If there is real confusion about sexual identity in an adolescent, it is not uncommon for him to have psychotic episodes. Phenomena of spiritual emergence may be present in these episodes.

During adolescence (and again at mid-life), a conflict between ego identity and spiritual values surfaces. It is a time of urgent choices, choices that will affect the adolescent for many years to come. Should I go to college, or take a job that will give me direct experience? Should I get married, or stay open to other relationships? Should I travel, or save my money for ———? Should I stay in a job I don't enjoy but that gives me security, or go for what I really want to do? Should I have a child, or go to school? What is really most important in life? Then there is the pressure "to be grown up" to "have it all together," and, simultaneously, not to miss anything. Chaos.

Adolescents may well feel pulled to pieces inside by a variety of conflicting interests and loyalties. These pieces orbit around peer group pressure, personal desire, family, job, and/or church. What is more important: the school game, a family chore, contacting a girl-friend, getting to church, earning some money, or experimenting with a drug? Concurrently, developmental issues that have not been completed in childhood again come to the fore. For example, where basic trust in the world was not established in the phase where the infant bonded with its mother, the desire to trust and establish deep bonding may now become paramount. Indecision, flights into radically new directions, and/or adventuring into unconventional relationships are a sign of desperately trying to find completion, to free oneself to move in a more liberated direction away from obsolete patterns of behavior. Destiny calls each person to bring her ego and her soul into harmony.

Spiritual Emergency in Adolescents

The search for answers to these questions of meaning are what leads to the characteristic moodiness of adolescents. The young people who cannot find satisfactory ways to answer their questions directly often become chronically anxious and/or depressed. Many teenagers narcotize their pain and confusion through drugs and alcohol, which take them away still further from resolving the tasks of adolescence. In 1986, an estimated 4.6 million adolescents aged fourteen through seventeen—one in every three—experienced negative consequences of alcohol use, such as poor school performance, trouble with parents, or involvement with law enforcement personnel.[4] In the United States, one adolescent attempts suicide every ninety seconds. One is successful every ninety minutes.[5]

With or without the use of these narcotics and stimulants, some teenagers experience Subtle level experiences. These may add a new confusing element to the already unresolved fragments of life. Or the spiritual experiences may help the teenager find his or her role in life more quickly, and thus accelerate development.

Adolescents experience the whole spectrum of spiritual experiences. However, what is unique to this age is that with the rise of sexual energy, many teenagers also experience more pranic activity. This may manifest in unusual physical symptoms similar to kundalini awakening, e.g., tremors, energy streaming, flashes of heat or cold. Along with this physical activity, perceptual changes may occur: brightening of color vision, sharpness of visual perceptions, inner visions, inner sounds, increased sensitivity to touch. Psychokinetic phenomena happen most frequently in households where there is an adolescent.[6] It is as if the potent energy that has not yet found direction in the teenager catalyzes movement in the furniture and objects of her house. These phenomena may lead to spiritual emergency if the young person does not have help in understanding what is going on and make use of the excess energy in his life.

One sixteen-year-old young man told me that a close friend of his was curious about Satanism. Satanic forces are often of special interest to teenagers. Shortly after the two conversed about the rituals of Satanism, the friend saw a glass spontaneously lift off a table and smash against the wall. The event scared him so much he never considered exploring Satanism again. An adolescent who had taken up meditation for relaxation found that his presence began to have an affect on electrical equipment. When he walked into a room, the radio or television would suddenly have distorted reception. These episodes can be terribly frightening, especially if young people have never seen or heard of this phenomenon. They need to be told what it is. They also need to know that when they have a positive outlet for their creative energy, the phenomenon of psychokinesis will most likely vanish.[7]

Galen, the sixteen-year-old I referred to in chapter 3, was referred to me because her father was afraid she was showing signs of psychosis. Galen was performing well academically, she had a nice boyfriend, she played the piano, and she had good relationships with her parents and siblings. However, for the past four months she had been having experiences of a "dark cloud" descending around her. At first these came once a week; after four months she was having them sometimes two or three times a day. When Galen felt this presence, she would become afraid that one of her loved ones was in trouble. She would telephone her father, grandmother, or other relatives to check on them. Always they were okay. One day she was with some friends and "something else" took over her body. At one point, she seemed to wake up, but her friends later said, "It was not her. We were terrified." When she awoke, Galen still sensed a dark presence in the room that wanted to "get to her."

Galen is especially sensitive. She needed counseling about how to manage her sensitivities so she would not be likely to have these occurrences again. She also needed to identify the inner conflicts she was having and begin working to resolve them. She learned that drugs and alcohol would make it more likely she would continue having these bizarre experiences. She learned that her protection would come in aligning with Higher Power through prayer and being sure she got enough rest and proper nutrition. It was reassuring for her to talk to a few adults who were psychically open and functioning well in the world. Then Galen realized that her own psychic openness did not have to drive her crazy, as her father feared it would.

Possession is not particularly common in teenagers, but teenagers are especially susceptible to transpersonal experiences. Teenagers usually do not have a strong sense of themselves. They have more questions than answers. Their boundaries are weak. Their sense of boundaries becomes even weaker with drug or alcohol use. In contrast, their vital energy is very strong. This polarity is fertile ground for spiritual emergence phenomena. In addition, many teens want to explore beyond the area circumscribed by social conventions. Alcohol and drugs seem to provide a means of doing so. (The potential of drugs and alcohol to effect spiritual emergence is discussed in chapter 9 in depth). Sleep deprivation, physical training, arduous intellectual work, fasting from food or water, also can bring about altered states of consciousness. Any of these can catalyze forms of spiritual emergency.

Howard, at nineteen, went into a spiritual emergency after writing poetry for several days and nights without stopping. He was returning from a trip to Mexico by himself. He had had several days of a high fever, and was not in very good physical health. The general weakness mixed with his intense desire to "discover the elements of my inner nature and maybe something about the universal nature of life" brought him to have visions of his life in archetypal themes.[8] He was also compelled to follow his impulses to perform time-consuming ritual activities marking his "odyssey" into the true nature of his life. This was an opening to life myth, a classical spiritual emergency. Since Howard needed twenty-four hour care because he did not seem capable of taking care of himself, his father, a family physician, had Howard hospitalized in a psychiatric ward. He was cared for in the hospital for several months before he was released.

Caring for a Teenager in Spiritual Emergency

What do you do for a teenage son, daughter, or friend in such spiritual emergencies?

Galen's father first took her for consultation to a psychic counselor, then to psychotherapy. Galen was told by the psychic that the dark presence was a husband from a former life who was coming back to get her so that they could again be sorcerers together in another dimension. As her therapist, I taught her how to stay grounded so these "other energies" could not intrude on her to take her away. It was a great relief to Galen to objectify the energies that had seemed so amorphous and to realize that she was in control, that by grounding herself, she could make them go away, and thus be able to address her personal problems clearly. The skills to ground herself, to strengthen her boundaries through diet and exercise, were the most important tools she was given.

Galen was intrigued by the new information about past lifetimes, the possibility of having relationships that span lifetimes, the idea that she could be in direct contact with other entities. She realized in counseling that there were many parts of herself that were still "unconscious."

As her therapist, I helped Galen decide how much energy she wanted to devote to the transpersonal dimension of her life at this time. Again, Galen realized she had a choice. She could take control. She decided to attend some classes on spiritualism, but otherwise stay focused on her schoolwork, friends, and music practice. This experience helped Galen take possession of her own life choices.

Careful consideration is needed in assessing disturbances in troubled teenagers. Professional mental health care may be essential. For example, what appears as possession and could be handled through grounding techniques in some cases may in other cases be symptomatic of paranoid schizophrenia. A transpersonally oriented mental health worker is best qualified to make this distinction.

For the teenager in spiritual emergency, the following guidelines will be helpful. They are also useful in encouraging spiritual emergence. Adolescents need to learn how to get grounded in themselves and their power to make their own choices. They must find an outlet for their excess energy outside of compulsive habits that take them "out of themselves" (compulsive eating, watching TV, passively listening to music, sex, drugs, etc.). Positive outlets are creative movement, dancing, athletics, and physical work. These activities will help them be aware of and respect their own boundaries. Simultaneously, they need to establish a solid connection to Higher Power, some representation of the ultimate, universal, sacred energy.

Appropriate types of touch help teenagers feel their bodies and make them aware of their boundaries. Unfortunately, few teenagers feel comfortable getting hugged by their parents or friends. Their alternative is feeling "at loose ends," or being involved in sexual relationships for the sake of being held. If your teenager shies from being held or touched, you might talk with her about it, and ask her if it's okay if you give her a hug now and again. Ideally, adolescents can fulfill their natural needs for touch in affectionate, supportive relationships with people of all ages who care for them.

Another grounding technique, particularly useful in the face of psychokinetic phenomena, is guided meditation. I teach my younger clients to imagine that there is a cord that runs down the full length of their spine into the center of the earth, anchoring there. Then I have them envision a power that is all-compassionate and wise and embodies love. This might be Jesus, an angelic form, or some other figure they can imagine. I ask them to envision the aura of this powerful figure surrounding and protecting them.

Some teenagers are also open to repeating an affirmation, prayer, or mantra that further empowers this visualization. Swami Radha, a German woman now residing in Canada who teaches kundalini yoga, teaches the following affirmation, which appeals to people of all faiths and all ages. It is especially good for teenagers who may not feel comfortable with a particular personification of Higher power.

> I am created by Divine Light.
> I am sustained by Divine Light.
> I am protected by Divine Light.
> I am surrounded by Divine Light.
> I am ever growing into Divine Light.

Swami Radha recommends using this visualization at night before going to sleep, especially for those who feel fearful for any reason. Adolescents can also imagine their body and bed being surrounded by a spiral, like a cocoon, of Divine Light.

Adolescents who have experienced parapsychological phenomena often have many questions about the nature of life. Literature or films about the positive aspects of parapsychological phenomena can be especially grounding and reassuring. At the end of the book are references to appropriate books. The Spiritual Emergence Network may be contacted to find a teacher or therapist in your area who is familiar with giving guidance in the transpersonal realms to teenagers.

Mid-Life

The developmental tasks of adulthood are twofold. They begin with realizing the capacity to form and maintain intimate relationships (including business partnerships), and to maintain "the ethical strength to abide by such commitments, even though they may call for significant sacrifices and compromises."[9] The alternative is to be in a relationship that does not support intimacy, or to be isolated, self-absorbed, and/or lose ethical considerations. When a sex life that is physically satisfying, based on love, has been found and the quest for sexual identity has been completed, then adulthood has been reached. Of course, this can take many forms. It may involve partnership and a conventional nuclear family. It may involve periods of celibacy and consolidation of same-sex friendships. It may involve shared housing in unconventional communities. The second tasks of adulthood involve *generativity*. There is a deep investment in creating and guiding the following generations. The impulse to manifest creativity and productivity is especially strong during this stage.

"Mid-life Crisis" typically occurs in the mid-forties for both men and women. It is a time of personal assessment: Have I really achieved the intimacy I want? Have I really been all that I can be in my sexual expression? What do I really have to give following generations? Am I ready to let go of childrearing? Have I done what is most important for me to do in this life? If not, am I set up to do it now? If earlier developmental tasks have not been completed, they may rise up and become compelling: I have to learn how to trust someone! I have to feel all right about myself now, and to trust myself! I can't stand to feel guilty about who I really am anymore! I want to know who I am and express it! I know I have a unique gift to give! This critical time is similar to adolescence in three ways. There is a compelling appraisal of sexual adequacy and need, a desire for expansion into new areas, and a yearning to align with one's "true self," despite social convention or old habits.

A person in mid-life crisis often has the sense of having missed something, or a feeling of emptiness. The result is either a surge of energy to complete the uncompleted tasks or to individuate—to find one's own unique identity—or a downward spiral into despair: "It's impossible; I can't do it. I might as well not try. . . . I will stay in the marriage without intimacy. I will not try to form satisfying relationships; I am too old for that. I don't have anything to give. Other people have something special; I don't."

Spiritual Emergence and Spiritual Emergency in Adulthood

How do spiritual emergence phenomena interact with the developmental tasks of adulthood? In the adult who is in a personal relationship that is growing in a satisfying direction, where there is deepening intimacy, commitment to some mutually beneficial ethical standards, sexual satisfaction, and a positive expression of creativity (children, artistic and work-related achievement, etc.), spiritual awakening unfolds in every sphere. There may be spiritual highs in sex; surges of inspiration in artistic expression or at work; unexpected episodes of telepathy in close relationships; reveries of gratitude to Higher Power for the gift of life and the fruits of love. These individuals may notice that the presence of love truly is the source point of health. With body and mind in harmony, they move to transpersonal levels gradually and gently.

The adults who achieve this are few. Currently, the divorce rate is above 60 percent for both first and second marriages.[10] Over 25 percent of families with children are headed by single parents.[11] Adults are having to come to grips with isolation and solitude through divorce, separation, and single parenting. This breakdown in relationships is only one of the major stresses in our society.

More people are acknowledging the extent of dysfunctional behavior—our reliance on alcohol, drugs, codependent behavior, and child abuse/spousal abuse—to counter the frustrations of unhappy adult life. There is a rise of interest in Twelve-Step programs such as AA, Al-Anon, Narc-Anon, Co-Dependents Anonymous, Overeaters Anonymous, etc. There is a new desperate search for a way to carry on relationships that are life-enhancing. Ethical standards that were thrown out during the sexual revolution of the sixties are now being reconsidered in the face of the terrifying specter of AIDS and other sexually transmitted diseases. Feminism has demanded a reappraisal of what constitutes intimacy, gender-related roles in marriage, in church, in the workplace, and the value of childbearing vis-à-vis other forms of creativity. Women and men alike search for groups designed to help them find out and express their "real selves," to establish real trust.

In this volcanic ferment, there arises a desperate longing for meaning, for a sense of unity with what is beyond ego, for spontaneity, for direct knowing and unconditional loving. These are universal spiritual longings, often disguised as personal desires for "letting loose," merging with a partner in sex, having the thrill of new love. Often people in mid-life get involved in extramarital affairs, or numerous "one night stands," hoping to find something to answer this deep long-ing they feel, consciously or unconsciously.

Coeleen's story of her mid-life crisis illustrates many of the dy-namics of spiritual emergency characteristic of this time of life.

A Story of Mid-Life Crisis

Coeleen is an artist, an organizational consultant, and an art therapist. Now in her fifties, she shares her active life with a man who allows her plenty of solitude for her personal work.

> In 1968, I was thirty-five, married fourteen years, with four chil-dren between the ages of seven and thirteen. Then I discovered that my husband had been having an affair. My husband and I went to counseling first with our Methodist minister. But I was in such de-spair. It didn't really reach me.
>
> When my neighbor unexpectedly committed suicide around that time, I had a total "mental breakdown." I called the minister, know-ing I was in terrible trouble. I was thinking of killing myself. He referred me to an internist. I was put on tranquilizers and referred to a Freudian analyst who was head of the psychiatric unit at our hos-pital. I was not hospitalized. I stayed at home but got full household assistance. For a full year, I didn't want to go out socially; I preferred to be with the children. I was unable to work or be involved with anyone outside of my children. I also had a lot of back trouble. My analysis was helping me establish an ego structure, which I had never done before. I had spent my married life helping my husband be strong in who he was in the world and had missed finding out who I was.

A personal crisis which involves recognizing that you do not yet know who you are can be a starting point of spiritual awakening. Coeleen's world had been held together by an expectation that her life would be satisfactorily molded by the institution of marriage, and by the church. When her marriage broke apart and her minister could not handle Coeleen's personal problems, she had nothing to hang on to. Often this frailty of ego-structure goes hand in hand with a physical weakness.

The analysis and sanctuary at home (at one point restricted to a body cast for a month to help her back problems), led Coeleen to a profound spiritual experience.

> I was in the living room in the early afternoon. On intuition, I just knew I had to go sit in a specific chair in the dining room and face a particular direction. I saw no reason to do it, but I just did it any-way.

Shortly after I sat down, I became immersed in a feeling of light. It entered my body from the top of my head and flooded every part of me. My vision became very sharp. I became very sensitive to feelings. I had access to esoteric wisdom I had never understood before. I was really in a state of ecstasy—beyond all my problems. It was as if I found a place in myself where I was totally free to be fully me. Instantly, I had a profound understanding of who Jesus Christ really was, and what he stood for. It was all in this light.

Coeleen, like others in crisis at mid-life, gained access to this kind of experience after she had been working on building her sense of self. Now, contained by her own sense of self, she had the resources to hear the voice of her intuition and the belief in the importance of trusting her "gut" feelings. These had always been sacrificed previously, in order to accommodate the needs of her husband, her children, her social circle, before herself. Ultimately, in finding herself she was truly able to find God.

This epiphany lasted in its intensity for almost two weeks. During this time, I wanted to pay special attention to whom I was with and what I ate. If I ate simply, did not drink alcohol, and was only around people who were positive and loving, then I maintained ready access to the "special kind of knowing" which came with the awakening.

The core of the experience has never really left me. Only the high ecstasy and intensity moderated. Over twenty years have gone by, and I still have direct access to that place inside me of strength, freedom, and closeness to God's light. Sometimes I long for the intensity of the epiphany. But I know I don't really need it in my life. I got the message it brought!

Following the two-week episode, Coeleen reentered a full and active life, no longer obsessed by the trauma of her husband's unethical behavior. She became more involved with her children's lives outside of the home, at school and with friends. She became more socially active. She looked for ways to explore the territory that had become open to her, the territory of profound meaning. She started a women's group in her home with the goal of raising consciousness to support women in thinking "beyond diapers, recipes, home care, etc." She began studying group process at a training center, learning especially how to effect trust and empower people to be fully themselves.

Relationship to Religion

Coeleen tried to bring what she had experienced into the church, too. She told her minister about her epiphany. He said that it was very special, indeed a "religious experience." Coeleen then wanted to empower other people to have the same kind of experience she had had, but it didn't work out under the auspices of the church. Its formalities were too restrictive.

> I began to realize that my church, and most churches, do not really make room for people to be fully themselves. I knew *that* was essential to having spiritual experiences. Actually, I saw more spiritual experiences happening as a result of being in sensitivity training group processes than as a result of attending church services. I saw that people become so passive in church. They don't express themselves; they have little avenue for their own individuality, thoughts, feelings, creativity. I never saw anyone interrupt a minister giving a sermon if he or she disagreed with him. Part of the structure of the service is giving your power over to the minister as authority. I don't think it helps people who need to find themselves.

Many people who go through spiritual awakening at mid-life find a disillusionment with the church's rituals that had beforehand been important to them. These people discover a broadening of spirituality, a knowing that Higher Power is everywhere, not just in church; that Higher Power is in everyone, not just people of one particular faith. Coeleen dropped out of formal religion entirely. She went back to graduate school in psychology for a Master's degree. She counseled alcoholics in recovery. She also had a studio for her artwork. Her continued quest to be her full self and be of service to others in their similar journies set Coeleen up for another spiritual awakening ten years after the first one.

> This time I was at a retreat listening to a lecture on Jung. Suddenly, there was an explosion of energy in my heart and, again, the feeling of light pouring through me. Ten days later, still in the glow of the experience, I had an inspiration about creativity which became the basis of a book on creativity, workshops, and classes.
>   I am sure that people find themselves in their artistic expression—if they are allowed to do their work in an atmosphere of unconditional love, respect, and interest. What follows that definition of themselves as individuals will surely enhance their spiritual lives.

On the other hand, spiritual awakening does not always take people away from organized religion or other institutional settings. Many people intensify their involvement in their religious group after having spiritual experiences. Especially after a spiritual awakening, there is a strong desire to participate in some group that acknowledges spiritual development. The community itself helps to give structure and grounding to the unbounded feelings that are part of the transpersonal levels. Michael provided an illustration of a Causal level experience in chapter 1. He found himself needing to invest more energy in his relationship with his spiritual director and his spiritual discipline after having his opening. For the first time, daily meditation for an hour every morning became part of his life. Jill, quoted in chapter 3, rededicated herself to church activities with renewed interest following her kundalini awakening.

The Impact of Loss

Spiritual emergency in mid-life is often intimately linked with losses. For Coeleen, the loss of the loyalty of her husband and the loss of contact with her church catalyzed a Causal level experience that transformed her life. For other people, this opportunity for transformation comes through the death of a child or a parent, the loss of a job, loss of health, losing friends because of a job change or a divorce. (See chapter 7 for a further discussion of this.) These life situations are more prevalent in the middle years of life than in adolescence or childhood. Ironically, the loss of isolation—through getting married, moving into a community of friends, acquiring a satisfying work environment, bearing a child—can also catalyze a crisis. A client recently told me something I have heard from many others who are pulling out of negative patterns:

> I'm so used to feeling alone and being depressed. Now that I am happy with myself, know what I want to do, and am doing it, I hardly know myself. Sometimes I even look for something to bring me down. Then I catch myself, breathe a deep breath, and surrender to my good feelings again.

The loss of a loved one to death especially allows many people to penetrate the veil between this world and the next for the first time. In 1987, the Gallup poll found that 67 percent of widows report contact with the dead.[12] Forty-two percent of adults report having communication with the dead. Seventy-three percent of Americans believe in life after death. These are large numbers! They indicate that the majority of Americans are having transpersonal experiences. What are the results? Three of my clients report:

> It helped me not fear my own death. There is no death. No separation with souls. Physical death is only physical. The soul lives on.

> I felt relieved to know that my husband was happy in the next dimension. The car accident was so unexpected. We never had a chance to say good-bye. The telepathic communication with him after his death made me realize that I will never lose him completely. I know I will be with him again after my own death.

I didn't know why my mother had killed herself. In meditation I had a "direct knowing" that she was tired of the struggle in her life. She wanted to be with God. When it came to me, my body shuddered and became exquisitely peaceful. I knew beyond doubt she was happy to be released.

How are people integrating these experiences? Some remain quiet, not speaking about their experiences so as not to risk being thought crazy. Some easily accommodate their experiences, knowing they are not crazy, gradually changing their values or lifestyle to reflect what they have learned. Others suffer dramatically, not knowing how to adjust to the loss or the transpersonal experiences.

Dramatic losses or extraordinary gains destroy one's singular identification with previous roles. Suddenly, after a death, people no longer have the role of a wife, a husband, a son or a daughter. After a divorce, losing a lover, or a job, people feel as if they have lost part of themselves. Dramatic gains, such as having everything one has ever wanted, often break down old roles, too. From being ambitious, one has now "made it." One response to these changes is the dark night of the ego, where people reach beyond their old ego identifications—the roles—to a deeper identification beyond ego. This is a crisis of meaning, akin to the identity crises of adolescence. Again, it drives people to look outside of conventions to find the deeper meaning of life.

In the dark night of the ego, there is a desire to get rid of the old self, the old identification, which seems stifling. This destructiveness shows itself in thoughts of suicide, dreams about death, a preoccupation with dying and mortality. Coeleen's response to learning of her husband's infidelity was to want to kill herself. This wish was symbolic of wanting the death of the kind of relationship that had been holding her bound in a certain role. The wish was a statement: "Without the marriage, I am nothing." The wish was also tied to her own ultimate power to do with her life what she wanted. It was this creative power that became her guiding light.

Suicide

Teenage suicide is a growing problem in the United States, as described, and suicide is also an adult problem. In 1970, 23,500 people over the age of fifteen committed suicide. In 1986, 30,900 people in this age bracket killed themselves.[13] Taking into account the rise in population over sixteen years, that represents a 1.2 percent increase.

Although suicidal thoughts are a manifestation of emotional disturbance, at the very root of this state of mind is the longing for return to unity and a release from the conflicting demands of worldly concerns. The emotions become conceptualized as a physical death wish.

Very few people actually want to curtail their lives completely. Instead, most suicidal individuals have a passionate desire to become disentangled from a dominant theme in their life that is no longer vital to them in order to find something else more essential.

There is usually a desire in the suicidal individual to move beyond something or someone. This might be a desire to kill the voice of the "inner critic" that has always told them that they are not good enough; that they need to speak better, dress better; be kinder, more assertive, more together, more relaxed, tidier. It might be a desire to find the "higher position" of the witness—to be able to step outside of oneself, so to speak, and witness one's life, one's thinking, one's feelings from a more objective position, without being so caught up. The obsession might have at its heart the longing to find the center of inner wisdom and knowingness in oneself—the desire to get rid of all that stands between one's personal problems and that source of wisdom. Or it might be a longing to escape the confines of a relationship that is no longer workable without having to experience the emotions inherent in separation—guilt, abandonment, loneliness, anger, grief, and so forth.

No matter what the particular circumstances, the motivation in each case is a desire to move beyond the dominance of the ego and its emotions. Whether the quest is recognized or not, the individual often is seeking a more expansive realm of higher consciousness rather than total annihilation.

Obsessive thoughts of suicide also prevail in situations where individuals have consciously engaged themselves with spiritual emergence and desperately want to be released from ego attachments to end the life of duality, of seesawing back and forth. My mother was an example of this. She began to truly see the light at the end of the tunnel—the enlightened mind was dawning in her as a result of intensive years of meditation. This made her even more poignantly aware of her bondage in social conventions. She longed to resolve the conflict between responding to the needs of her family, community, and world and following her path to complete liberation. The bondage seemed too strong to overcome. Deluded by her passion to be liberated and feeling stuck in her inner conflicts, she killed herself.

Averting Suicide

How can we help potential suicides disengage from the emotional obsession and find the capacity for unity at the core of their dark night? In particular, how can adolescents and mid-lifers find release from the constriction they feel so acutely?

For the person contemplating suicide: Realize you are close to the very core of your life, a central place for making transformative change. Check for the possibility of physical disease as the cause of depression. Depressed thyroid condition or poor nutrition are two physical causes of mental depression. Barring physical illness, consider: What is it about my limited way of thinking or perceiving the world that I want to radically change? Or, Where is it I truly want to go? You may more effectively come to what lies at the root of your desire for death in the answers to these questions.

You will likely benefit from a trusted counselor or wise friend in this self-inquiry. This person may help in understanding the root of your issues and be able to point out your resources for making the changes you long for. Although professional help is not always necessary, it is advisable for anyone in a state of crisis to consult a physician or therapist for an assessment. In some cases, psychiatric medications may be essential to break the pattern of emotional cycling and obsessive thinking. Prolonged drug use may inhibit your ability to work through your inner search and find resolution. In extreme cases, twenty-four-hour sanctuary in a hospital setting with appropriate psychiatric drugs may be the most compassionate care for you.

For the family or friend of a person contemplating suicide: If there is *any* threat of suicide, take it seriously. You must assess the seriousness of the threat. Call a suicide prevention hot line to familiarize yourself with the signs of possible suicide and your community's resources for suicide prevention. Make sure that the depression and/or anxiety the person feels is not a direct cause of medication or illness.

Once physical causes have been ruled out, the person needs a companion with whom he or she can talk about his perceived problems candidly. Sharing thoughts and emotions can help define the problem and alleviate the utter loneliness that accompanies suicidal thinking. The relationship then can act as a container—offering more space to vent feelings and explore alternatives to suicide. Offering an explicit conceptual framework to help an individual think about her problem in a different light may be most helpful.

It will be the work of the companion/guide to introduce the idea of the developmental spectrum in chapter 1, to suggest the concept of the dark night of the ego, to begin talking about the longing for unity with Higher Power as a positive, human force within every human psyche. This is only appropriate for people who are not completely obsessed with suicide and have some attention available to reflect on their condition. It may be appropriate to tell stories of people who have been through suicidal thoughts as part of their spiritual emergence—and how these thoughts preceded major periods of expanded growth. The Greek myth of Amor and Psyche is especially good in such instances, as the protagonist, Psyche, contemplates suicide before completing each task set before her on her way to uniting with Amor (Love) and giving birth to their child, Pleasure.[14]

Other resources for positive and inspiring models for change are music and artistic expression, which evoke higher states of consciousness. Activities that can inspire change include rhythmic activity such as walking, jogging, dancing to melodic music, singing inspirational music—e.g., hymns or chants—yoga, martial arts.

Many people with whom I have worked have felt liberated by the concept that their suicidal thoughts are symbolic of a desire for them to make a profound change, a surrender to a larger process in their own psyche. Out of this concept ensues an adventure of discovery, a new way of perceiving life itself, sometimes a new, less conventional lifestyle. Psychotherapy, or spiritual practices such as solitary meditation, prayer alone or with a companion or in a gathering, can have a profound impact to catalyze the growth longed for at this time. It is a time for meaningful connection to be made with one's higher self and another person in the world who knows the landscape of such profound transitions and can act as a guide.

If your suicidal friend or relative is so immersed in his obsession that he cannot respond to any of the foregoing suggestions, you may have to take him to a hospital where trained medical personnel can assist him.

Helping A Mid-Lifer in Spiritual Emergency

> Swan, I'd like you to tell me your whole story!
> Where you first appeared, and what dark sand
> you are going toward,
> and where you sleep at night, and what you are
> looking for . . .
>
> It's morning, swan, wake up, climb in the air, follow me!
> I know of a country that spiritual flatness does not
> control, nor constant depression,
> and those alive are not afraid to die.
> There wildflowers come up through the leafy floor,
> and the fragrance of "I am he" floats on the wind.
> There the bee of the heart stays deep inside the
> flower,
> and cares for no other thing.[15]
>
> —ROBERT BLY, *The Kabir Book*

This poem lyrically suggests the guidelines for helping people in mid-life who are experiencing a spiritual emergency. Whether such individuals are contemplating suicide, searching for meaning, struggling to complete old developmental tasks, or are in one of the six forms of spiritual emergence—there are four elements which need to be attended to: grounding, education, catharsis, and sanctuary.

Grounding: Help them to feel a connection to the earth and a sense of community. A way to connect to the earth may be through exercise or being in nature. Rest and good nutrition are important grounding. A sense of community can be found in belonging to religious organizations, doing a spiritual practice with others, or joining a 12-Step program, consciousness-raising group, or therapy group. A sense of community may start with just one person, a trusted companion or counselor.

Education: Give them concepts to consider their crisis supplementary to a disease oriented framework. Start with the developmental spectrum which outlines moving from prepersonal to transpersonal levels. Allow them to map out where they are on this spectrum, define current issues. "Do you sense you are longing for transpersonal levels of consciousness? Do you feel you are battling with issues of identity? Are you trying to complete developmental tasks from earlier in life? How does this relate to your life story right now?" C. G. Jung, the noted Swiss psychoanalyst, regarded mid-life as the critical time for dealing with issues of entry to transpersonal levels.

Catharsis: Relating your life story to a trusted companion brings up a lot of feelings. Allow the individual in crisis to express the feelings. Encourage this catharsis. Pounding pillows on a bed, or ripping up the pages of an old phone book, are good releases for anger. Catharsis clears the way for some new energy and new insight. Letting go, surrendering to emotions, is a mini-death. It is essential to creating a space for new life to enter.

Sanctuary: Encourage people in crisis to make time for themselves to be quiet, to explore who they are outside of the demands the world places on them. This may be in a retreat setting that provides structure for self-inquiry. It could also be in a setting that is free of all structure. If there is no threat of people hurting themselves because of emotional obsessiveness, a day at the beach alone can be therapeutic. Generally, people in crisis know what they most need. They may, however, ask for some encouragement to follow through.

Late Adulthood and Preparation for Death

The majority of people experience at least one crisis of meaning in middlescence or adolescence. However, everyone faces a spiritual crisis preparing for the moment of death. If the questions about the meaning of life have not been faced before, they now rise fully, this time with a sense of urgency: What has my life been about? Have I got what I wanted? Have I done what I wanted? How much more time do I have to do the things I have missed doing?

Jack Kornfield, a Buddhist teacher and clinical psychologist, was called to assist a man in critical condition. He was a prominent San Francisco businessman who had never formed a meaningful connection with any spiritual tradition. In his late forties, married, with a few children, he suddenly found out that he had a brain tumor. Surgery was to take place in twenty-four hours. The likelihood of his surviving without severe brain damage was possible but not insured. His alternative to surgery was six more weeks of life while the cancer took him over.

The man was in a state of shock when Kornfield walked into his hospital room. Tears were streaming down his face. Fully lucid, the man gestured toward the pigeons on the window ledge in a kind of reverie. "I never noticed how exquisitely beautiful a pigeon is in flight. Each movement is so precious. Each moment is now so precious to me."

Kornfield sat with the man. Kornfield did not proselytize or try to convince the man to embrace religion at this desperate moment. Instead, he was there as a friend in an attitude of loving compassion and acceptance, appreciating the precious moments of life passing between them. This way of being, surrendering to the moment, helped the man come into his deepest self in a profound way.

The man had surgery the next day. The cancer was removed. He regained full use of his mental faculties. He then transformed his life. Living off his savings and no longer interested in making more money than he needed to live simply, he decided to have more time with his family and counsel people who are dying.

Transformation experiences and conversion experiences are not uncommon for people who have almost died and been allowed back to continue life. Of those who do return, many report a profound commitment to help others realize the spiritual nature of life, to find the source of unconditional love and true freedom. For people like the businessman just described, this means a radical shift in their own values and lifestyle.

If people have time to contemplate their life after they realize that death will soon be inevitable, their contemplation universally reveals that the value of life is measured in how much they have learned and how they have loved. A deep desire to mend difficult relationships, to forgive, to finally find love, arises. If time allows, the desire to have things in order, to be able to leave in peace, also comes up.

A Tibetan Buddhist scholar and teacher, Sogyal Rinpoche, has devoted himself to teaching Westerners about how to prepare for the moment of death so we do not experience a crisis but the flowering of our spiritual emergence. His teachings are applicable to people of any faith. The central idea is that the actual time of death tests our capacity for full surrender. The dying person needs to be able to surrender to Higher Power fully at the moment of death, and remain stable in that consciousness as she proceeds in the intermediary states immediately after death. Thus, the opportunity for full enlightenment, full realization of God, at the moment of death is available to all people, of all faiths.

What is the way to reach this enlightenment? Sogyal Rinpoche counsels us to live with the knowledge of death. Live in a way that you are prepared for death to take you at any time. Live without denying that death may take you at any time. This means to keep your physical things in order so you are not leaving a mess for someone else to clean up. It also means to practice detaching from all your ego desires and possessions, so that at the moment of death you can let them all go easily. Meditation and other spiritual practices are a means to this end. These exercises assist us in uncovering the true nature of mind, beyond feelings, concepts, perceptions.

The actual moment of death, when the physical energies are beginning to leave the body, is the time when ideally a spiritual friend would be present with the dying person to help guide him into total surrender to Higher Power or the highest consciousness. The prayers and positive thoughts of family and friends also affect the potential for the dying person's full surrender at death. Holding on to people who are dying may push them into a spiritual emergency if they are not feeling free to move with their spiritual emergence process of letting go of the physical plane.

The spiritual family, in the Buddhist tradition, is thought of as important as the truth itself. It is our spiritual friends who help us find our way when we get lost, or forget where we are going on our spiritual path. At no time is this more important than at death, when the dying person needs such friends to continuously send positive thoughts, recall the good memories, and pray for the liberation of their friend, and be willing to release him to Higher Power.

Helping the Dying Toward Spiritual Emergence

Again, the first order of business in helping a person in this time of spiritual emergency is to check out her physical well-being: "Are you in physical pain? Do you want to have pain-killing drugs? Does a doctor advise drug use?" Some drugs may make it possible for a person to stay awake to her spiritual focus without being overly preoccupied with pain in her body. Other drugs may dull sensitivities to the extent that individuals fall out of contact with themselves and others.

Second, help the person to finish her business with this world. This may be reaching out in forgiveness to a brother or sister who has been alienated for years. Or, it may be simply sitting quietly with friends or family. A dying person needs some time to say her good-byes and release her attachments to this world.

If there is no clergy called in by the dying person, a spiritual companion can assist the dying person at the moment of death to imagine the highest power she knows. This might be Jesus, Mary, Buddha, the universe, etc. Guide dying people into bringing their own energy into a point of focus and then sending it into the heart of that being of higher power. Have them then imagine becoming completely merged with that being of higher power. Help them to stay steady and undistracted in their focus, perhaps verbalizing that they let go of the body, let go of the past, let go of all that holds them to this world, reassuring them that everyone who is left is okay. "Go into the Light" is a simple phrase symbolizing this letting go that many relate to well, no matter what their beliefs are about the afterlife.

Then, after the person no longer shows vital signs, continue to imagine her merging into the heart of Higher Power. When you re-member her, recall the good things about her. Speak to others of the good memories. This also will assist the dying person in her transition.

Many times in life, from earliest memories in childhood to death, may bring spiritual experiences. Although we are more facile at as-similating these experiences after we have attained a stable ego, the transpersonal realms do not wait for the knock of the mature hand before the doors are open. It behooves us to support the value of transpersonal experiences in our young children and adolescents. This will give them an anchor point to return to when they have, or long to have, spiritual experiences later in life and need to find meaning in them. Mid-life and the time of preparation for death are opportune times to focus directly on spiritual dimensions of development. Many of the mundane tasks of life have been accomplished, and spiritual questions come to the fore.

When spiritual experiences erupt unexpectedly at various times of life, they often accompany the need for a reevaluation of one's spiri-tual focus. A spiritual experience will renew understanding of the goal of spiritual practices designed to catalyze spiritual development. The role of spiritual practices in spiritual emergence is the topic of the next chapter.

5

Spiritual Practice

Teresa loved socializing in the living room with her friends from town. She enjoyed the attention she always attracted. At fifteen years old, she was very beautiful, witty, and charming. Her father, finding her too undisciplined, too interested in boys, put Teresa under the care of forty Carmelite nuns. Teresa did not feel particularly close to God. She enjoyed pastries and nice clothes, like most normal teenagers.

In the convent, Teresa was willing to go along with the regulations. She said her prayers and attended chapel daily. She grew familiar with solitude, as she had a small cell to herself, but she looked forward to leaving the convent in two years and taking up a more worldly life again.

However, at seventeen Teresa came down with an illness that kept her in almost complete isolation for nearly four years. During that time, she often suffered immense pain throughout her body brought on by seizures that could not be diagnosed. She often lay completely paralyzed.

> They [the seizures] overcame her with the relentless fury of elemental events. No part of her body remained unaffected; no function stayed immune: no limb, no muscle, no nerve was safe from the blazing pain. And the agony of her "little deaths" resembled ever more the real agony of the great death.[1]

During her confinement, her relationship with God became her solitary point of focus. Twenty-one years old in 1536, Teresa of Avila committed herself entirely to the religious life. From the ordinary preoccupation with boys, food, and beautiful things, Teresa's life story evolved in an extraordinary way as she became a saint. Certainly her spiritual practice and her profound physical challenges were essential to her making this transformation.

Through the help of an uncle, who was a follower of Saint Francis, Teresa was exposed to an unspoken spiritual form of prayer, a direct communion with Higher Power, very unlike the verbal prayers that had become a formal routine in the convent. In her communion with God, Teresa gained access to a joy that was her only relief from physical pain. She depended on this communion to help her weather the subsequent attacks of her painful illness, which came unexpectedly throughout her early and mid-adulthood.

> The frightened nuns called her by her name. She remained motionless. They shook her, rubbed her, lifted her up. All their efforts were in vain. Her body remained cold and rigid as though she had died. As the attacks recurred, the illness extended its hold over Teresa's entire life. Some of her organs were never entirely free from pain. And from one attack to the next the respite granted her grew shorter and shorter.[2]

After twenty-five years, the attacks transformed in nature to ecstatic raptures. Teresa was then forty-three years old. People witnessed her in these states. Her pulse stopped beating, and her breath seemed suspended. Her whole body became rigid. Her hands and feet were so cold she was once assumed to be dead for four days. Yet Teresa came back from these states with renewed energy and deeper oneness with God. In the *Interior Castle*, she wrote:

> One feels that one has been wholly transported into another and a very different region from that in which we live, where a light so unearthly is shown that if during one's whole lifetime one would be trying to picture it and the wonders seen, one should not possibly be able to succeed. In an instant the mind learns so many things at once that if the imagination and the intellect spent years in striving to enumerate them, they could not recall a thousandth part of them.
> [In the raptures] an upward flight takes place in the interior of the soul and this with the swiftness of a bullet fired from a gun. . . . Sometimes, a feeling of the presence of God would come over me, unexpectedly, so that I could in no wise doubt either that He was within me, or that I was wholly absorbed by him.[3]

Clearly Teresa's communion with Higher Power and the purification process of her "disease" had opened the path for her to fully experience union with God. Solitude, renunciation, and communion with God were the life activities Teresa chose from the time her "illness" took hold of her until she was approximately fifty years old. The illness, which was never diagnosed, was likely a series of dramatic kundalini awakenings—purifying her body, mind, and soul. When the process of her spiritual awakening was complete, she no longer suffered the "seizures"—nor had she been crippled by them. Instead, she was full of energy and determination to make her contribution to her Carmelite order. She had harvested the fruits of her spiritual emergency.

The last years of her life were full of extraordinary accomplishments. In her late forties, Teresa began her own convent, based on a life of simplicity, solitude, and prayer—very different from the monastic life of her time, which was typically highly social and political. By the end of her life, eleven convents had been founded under her direction. The autobiography of her spiritual awakening, *The Interior Castle*, first written to justify the authenticity of her visions and spiritual experiences to the church fathers, had become a meaningful piece of religious literature. These were no small contributions for a woman in the sixteenth century under the domination of a tightfisted male-oriented society and the shadow of the Inquisition. On a more personal level, her spiritual emergence had taken her to the highest realms of consciousness by means of a strict religious practice. As a result, ecstatic bliss was familiar to her, as well as the ability to solve worldly problems creatively to serve her fellow humans. Her example served to revitalize the Church, drawing from the deepest depths of spiritual experience itself.

From the other side of the world, in a culture and a time very different from Teresa's, comes another example of a spiritual emergency fueled by disciplined spiritual practice. This story is of a common householder born in the beginning of the twentieth century who also endured depths of psychological and physical pain during his kundalini awakening.

Before his spiritual emergency, Gopi Krishna, an East Indian, enjoyed hours of meditation as part of his daily routine. Early in the morning and at night he would enjoy sitting quietly by himself, focusing on an image that symbolized his enlightenment. The rest of his time was spent at his job as an office worker, or with his wife and children.

The most dramatic aspect of his spiritual emergence happened when he was thirty-five years old, after he had been a practitioner of yoga and meditation for seventeen years. Unlike Teresa, Gopi Krishna had many years of spiritual discipline under his belt before the kundalini awakening that took him to the Causal level. One day that meditation bore fruit:

> Suddenly, with a roar like that of a waterfall, I felt a stream of liquid light entering my brain through the spinal cord. Entirely unprepared for such a development, I was completely taken by surprise; but regaining self-control instantaneously, I remained sitting in the same

posture, keeping my mind on the point of concentration. The illumination grew brighter and brighter, the roaring louder, I experienced a rocking sensation and then felt myself slipping out of my body, entirely enveloped in a halo of light. It is impossible to describe the experience accurately. I felt the point of consciousness that was myself growing wider, surrounded by waves of light. It grew wider and wider, spreading outward while the body, normally the immediate object of its perception, appeared to have receded into the distance until I became entirely unconscious of it. I was now all consciousness, without any outline, without any idea of a corporeal appendage, without any feeling or sensation coming from the senses, immersed in a sea of light simultaneously conscious and aware of every point, spread out, as it were, in all directions without any barrier or material obstruction. I was no longer myself, or to be more accurate, no longer as I knew myself to be, a small point of awareness confined in a body, but instead was a vast circle of consciousness in which the body was but a point, bathed in light and in a state of exaltation and happiness impossible to describe.

After some time, the duration of which I could not judge, the circle began to narrow down; I felt myself contracting, becoming smaller and smaller, until I again became dimly conscious of the outline of my body, then more clearly; and as I slipped back to my old condition, I became suddenly aware of the noises in the street, felt again my arms and legs and head, and once more became my narrow self in touch with body and surroundings.[4]

For the two years following his initial awakening, Gopi Krishna endured overwhelming psychological and physical problems that left him unable to function. For months at a time he was incapacitated by anorexia, incapable of assimilating any food, burning with an internal fire that affected all his organs. He felt fearful of the supernatural in any form. Like Teresa, he was wrapped in solitude, with no escape from the powerful energy that had taken hold of his life. His story is also another example of the dark night of the ego described in chapter 4.

... brief intervals of mental elation were followed by fits of depression much more prolonged and so acute that I had to muster all my strength and will-power to keep myself from succumbing completely to their influence. I sometimes gagged my mouth to keep from crying and fled from the solitude of my room to the crowded street to prevent myself from doing some desperate act. For weeks I had no respite.[5]

For those two years, the strain of supporting a husband so debilitated by spiritual illness was borne by Gopi Krishna's wife alone. This woman was dependent on a man who could barely care for himself on the most primitive level. Imagine yourself in her shoes—with a husband who could not work, could not do chores or child care, was physically ill and emotionally unbalanced and completely preoccupied with meditation and spiritual growth. It would be frightening. Gopi Krishna's family weathered poverty. There was no resource in the community to assist him in understanding his loss of health, or his emotional upsets. No physician, counselor, or spiritual teacher showed any capacity to diagnose and treat him. The family's only resource was their faith that the process of this awakening was positive and that the ill effects would eventually subside.

After months of aloneness in his struggle, Gopi Krishna was instructed by an inner voice of wisdom, a part of the enlightening energy transforming his body and opening him to psychic power, about a new way of meditating to bring balance. Still, it took several more years for him to become accustomed to his new energy level and the inner luminosity that grew to affect all of his sense perceptions, lighting his whole world:

> Wherever I went and whatever I did, I was conscious of myself in the new form, cognizant of the radiance within and the lustrous objectivity without. I was changing. The old self was yielding place to a new personality endowed with a brighter, more refined and artistic perceptive equipment, developed from the original one by a strange process of cellular and organic transformation.[6]

Toward the latter part of Gopi Krishna's life, the kundalini was no longer emotionally, physically, or spiritually overwhelming for him. Like Teresa, he was able to harvest the renewed energy, creativity, and desire to make a contribution to his world. Gopi Krishna wrote poetry in several languages and dedicated himself to teaching and research on kundalini, including founding an institute in India for that purpose. He authored fifteen books on kundalini, instructive for anyone in the process of that opening. Gopi Krishna died in 1984. On a personal level, he left a family that had been profoundly enriched by his spiritual awakening. On a larger global level, in his wake arose a wave of interest in the profound truth of kundalini and all the psycho-physiological manifestations of consciousness expansion. His autobiography, *Kundalini, the Evolutionary Energy in Man* (with commentaries by James Hillman, a noted Jungian psychologist), is a classic in the literature dedicated to understanding the role of spiritual experience and psychological transformation in human development.

In all the major religions of the world can be found examples of people engaged in spiritual practices who have been through intense and sometimes physically and emotionally debilitating periods of spiritual experiences and ultimately attained transpersonal levels of consciousness. The preliterate, although no less enlightened, ancient shamanic cultures also relate stories of individuals strengthened by cultural religious rituals, blessed with a special connection to spiritual forces. In all cultures, these people become the teachers and leaders, for they are living examples of the energy that draws us to spiritual practices and religious institutions in the first place. Through these people, we are reminded that it is possible to commune with the highest source of wisdom and love on a personal level. Through these people, we are reminded of the power behind spiritual practices.

We often think that such mystical experiences happened in the past to "special" people, but not today, in our time and in our culture. However, spiritual practices also awaken "normal" people as described by my own story in chapter 2 and other stories throughout this book. In addition, there are several spiritual teachers in our own century who have been through profound spiritual awakenings, attaining a level of transpersonal consciousness. They have told their stories to inspire and lend direction to others. Thomas Merton, a Trappist monk, relates his experiences in *The Seven Storey Mountain*. Bernadette Roberts, in *The Experience of No-Self*, tells the story of her spiritual odyssey, which involved being a Catholic nun for ten years and subsequently a mother of four children. Swami Radha, the German woman who followed a path of kundalini yoga and now heads a spiritual community in Canada, whom I referred to in Chapter 4, tells her story in *Radha: Diary of a Woman's Search*. Philip Kapleau, a newspaper reporter from New York, studied Zen Buddhism in Japan and came back to be a leader in the Buddhist movement in America. He tells his story in *The Three Pillars of Zen*. Flora Courtois began her dramatic spiritual journey without any spiritual practice and found her spiritual companionship later in Zen Buddhism. She tells this story in *An Experience of Enlightenment*. *Daughter of Fire* is the autobiography of Irena Tweedie, an English woman who attained her enlightenment through the spiritual practices related to Sufism.

The spiritual practices that each of these people maintained were all different. Some involved conventional, prescribed prayer; others didn't. Some involved complex rituals; others didn't. Some involved paying homage to certain deities or personifications of the Higher Power; others involved an absence of any Godhead. Some involved monastic life; others found no conventional religious institution to guide them.

However, each of the above individuals had an intense, authentic desire to realize the deepest truth about life and was willing to keep returning to that point of focus as essential. This profound, heartfelt yearning and intellectual-spiritual inquiry is the core of all spiritual practice. Holding the inquiry as highest priority in life is spiritual discipline. Psychological maturation, including letting go of past traumatic events and truly forgiving people who have hurt you, is inevitably part of the process of spiritual growth and becomes part of spiritual practice. Each individual's obstacles in this psychological maturation are often revealed in psychosomatic complaints and/or released through kundalini rising.

Now that we have seen how spiritual emergency happens as a result of spiritual practice, let us reflect on the role of religion in supporting spiritual growth and the role of psychological growth in spiritual development. At the conclusion of this chapter, we will look at an exemplary spiritual community that provides support for spiritual growth and allowance for psychological work within that context.

The Role of Religions in Spiritual Emergence

Spiritual practices and religious disciplines were created for people who want a technique to help them draw closer to that which is most sacred in life. Religions were founded to support people in their quest for spiritual union with Higher Power. Our ritual celebrations, prayers, hymns, chants, and sacrifices were also designed to lead us to authentic spiritual experiences, to know God. Our temples and cathedrals were built to remind us of the power and beauty of our heavenly origins, to provide us with a structure in which we can gather to perform religious rituals.

A distinction needs to be drawn here, however, between conventional religion and the path of spiritual emergence toward mystical union with Higher Power. Conventional religion is defined by prescribed ritual devotions that are performed routinely and passed down, generation to generation. These practices are designed to instruct parishioners on their moral and religious duties as well as affirm the concept that Higher Power and a community that believes in Higher Power are present. These practices are *external* authorities that influence our inner life. Spiritual emergence, on the other hand, is an *internal* process involving an individual's sense perceptions and emotional life first, then effecting change in thinking and external behavior. Although spiritual emergence may be catalyzed by religious practices, it may also erupt completely independent of conventional religious life, as is illustrated throughout this book. In fact, strict religious codes may even prohibit spiritual experiences from happening.

If we seek the highest truth, we must go beyond the conventional forms to the living experience of the most sacred universal energy. This can only be found in the living presence of a spiritual adept who has realized the Causal and Atman levels of consciousness or in one's own spiritual awakening to these dimensions.

Here we find a profound, albeit tragic, paradox. In truth, the very institutions designed to help us toward spiritual development, to know God, are often the very places that are most awkward in recognizing spiritual experiences or helping someone in spiritual emergency. Clergy and church or synagogue administrators often flounder under the challenge of differentiating true spiritual experiences from psychopathology, or deciding what kind of care is needed by a congregant distressed by results of spiritual practices. Our clergy are not generally chosen for their spiritual experiences and aptitudes so much as for their academic education, speaking, and administrative abilities. Because of this, many church and synagogue leaders have had few, if any, authentic spiritual experiences. Thus, they do not have the personal resources to counsel someone in spiritual emergency, yet may be afraid to admit it.

Few people find support in conventional religious institutions for their spiritual experiences. Special visions, contact with the dead or higher forces, telepathy, and other Subtle level phenomena are often considered delusional by priests, ministers, and rabbis. So, spiritually awakening people, who have these experiences, often seek companionship outside of formal religious institutions with others who share their experiences. In some cases these individuals lose the support of their religious community. In most cases the religious community loses the rich experience these individuals have to offer.

Julia grew up Episcopalian. In fact, she was the daughter of an Episcopal minister in Georgia. She is highly sensitive, empathic, and bright. When she was nineteen years old, in 1977, she had her first out-of-body experience.

> I was at home with a cold. During my meditation, I started rocking back and forth. Then, energy shot up my spine, and I went out the top of my head, through the roof of the house and out into space. I could feel wind in my sinuses. I was seeing planets. I could see my body back in the room meditating. While I was flying, my vibration was so intense I thought, "This is a faster rate of speed than humans can go." I was in bliss, but I also was remembering stories of people who couldn't get back into their bodies after an out-of-body experience. So, I attempted to get back.
>
> When I did get back, I felt scared. I knew I was out of control of the whole process. I was spacey for several days. I told my dad about it. He looked very scared and worried. He didn't offer me any advice or counsel. He didn't let me know about other people who had had this kind of experience. He didn't want to talk about it. This made me feel I was strange or wrong in his eyes to have had the experience.

Several years later, Julia moved to a community where she befriended people who were not estranged from the kinds of experiences she had had and continued to have. These people were involved in Subud, a spiritual community originating in Indonesia at the beginning of this century, which has high regard for Subtle level experiences and spiritual practice. In the comfort of her new community, Julia not only found assistance in exploring new dimensions of her consciousness, she also completed her education, graduating with a Master's degree in psychology and opening her private practice as a counselor. She is especially gifted in helping people in spiritual emergency.

The visions and direct communion with Higher Power that Teresa of Avila experienced were discredited time after time by her senior nuns, abbots, and bishops. It was often thought that she had become possessed by the Devil or some evil forces, and that the appropriate "treatment" would be exorcism. At one point, a small band of Jesuit priests were the only group who granted her spiritual experiences any validity. During this period, when she was still in the grip of the disease that racked her body with fevers and paralysis, she was in dire need of the love and support of her community. Yet it was not there. They provided her a solitary cell in which to live a "religious" life. They supported her ritual devotions. But when Teresa was in the process of profound transformation, her sisters and abbess were often at a loss as to what to do to support her.

The Psychological and Physiological Aspects of Spiritual Emergence

In the Bible, it is not made clear that spiritual awakening often involves profound psychological and physiological changes. Spiritual growth, increased knowledge of Higher Power, is the recognized goal of religious work for Christians and Jews. However, the landscape of the path is not well known. It is no wonder that Teresa of Avila's sisters at first interpreted her bizarre physical spasms as indicative of her negativity rather than identifying her illnesses as part of her spiritual emergence. It is no wonder that Thomas Merton was not given the consistent support that he needed in his times of depression but was instead discouraged from having the solitude, the sanctuary, he craved.

I don't mean to imply that Christianity or Catholicism do not have any means to recognize authentic spiritual experiences. Retreats are designed for prayer and spiritual practices, and spiritual directors assume that some people making a retreat will have strong visions and deeper cognition of the truth as represented in the Bible. However, in our Western religious traditions, the *psychological and physiological* aspects of profound spiritual growth are not widely known or accepted. Knowledge of these aspects is found in some spiritual directors and not others, depending on their own life experience and spiritual development and information about others' experiences.

In the texts of Yoga, Hinduism, and Buddhism, it is clearer that there is a psychophysiological result of spiritual practices. Yoga philosophy offers a direct route into working with this component of spiritual practice through the practice of hathayoga, a set of physical postures designed to prepare the body for union with God. Traditional Eastern meditation postures require sitting with a straight back to encourage the rise of kundalini energy up the spine. Gopi Krishna's books have made a generous contribution to the literature, and are relevant to people of all religions. His books and other texts (see References at the back of the book) recognize that the practices themselves, whether prayer, meditation, yoga, ritual, etc., should induce a kind of purification process that *literally* allows the refined energy of higher forces to enter the body, throwing off coarser energies. Thus, our religious rituals can catalyze spiritual emergence, but it can happen less painfully if we recognize the phenomena of this awakening. Both Teresa of Avila and Gopi Krishna might have had fewer problems in their kundalini awakening if they had seen a map of the landscape of spiritual emergency and been educated about the end result.

Spiritual emergence involves an emotional process, purifying out the "coarser energies" connected to worldly desires: lust, greed, anger, hatred, and fear. Often these are the results of past actions, karma, habits, or addictions. The Sanskrit name for these afflictions is *samskaras*. These samskaras always have a physiological component in chronic body tensions. For example, people who are motivated by lust and greed are often literally hard-hearted. They have chronic tension in the muscles surrounding the heart. It is more difficult for them to feel compassion or sympathy for others. People who are motivated by fear often are rigid in the back, shoulders, and neck.

When higher energies enter the body, the chronic body tensions begin to loosen their hold. In the process of this liberation from the samskaras, the body will go through physiological and/or psychological experiences. This may be dramatic at times, subtle or imperceptible at other times. It is not uncommon for a meditator to be sitting quietly and suddenly be wriggling all over, or having uncontrollable muscular spasms in some part of the body. Moods are also symptomatic of a release of samskaras. These may include irritability, sadness, joy, giggling, fearfulness, and anxiety. Moods also seem to be harder to control, which can be humiliating or frightening for someone used to being in control.

As the samskaras are released, there is increased energy and awareness. The natural biological energy can flow more freely through the body. And the energy of the universe, *prana* in Sanskrit, can also participate more fully in the physical body. This revitalizes the whole system. Especially with increased pranic activity comes a sharpening of all sense perceptions: Subtle perceptions of auras may become visible, vibrations of people may become palpable, direct contact with others who are at a distance, or dead, may become perceptible, etc. We begin to be in better contact with particular organs of our body. The organ of the heart can be felt in its subtle reactions to the world. Blood pressure can be regulated. Body temperature can be modified through focusing attention. It is also the increased pranic activity that makes it possible to have direct communion with higher forces, angels, and God.

Illness is often a time of burning away samskaras, of purification. The years that Teresa of Avila suffered with high fevers, pain, and paralysis may have been a bonfire of samskaras, enabling her simultaneously to open to higher energetic experiences and direct communion with Higher Power. Certainly, her intention supported this happening, because her thoughts were constantly directed toward God. Similarly, Gopi Krishna endured episodes of physical debilitation lasting for months.

Religious leaders need to know the landscape of this spiritual unfolding so they can truly work with the living process of spiritual emergence and not just the religious practices that are but vehicles to the living experience. Once we have learned the specifics of psychological and physiological opening in spiritual emergence, it is easier to recognize this theme in more conventional Christian texts.

Purification: The Dark Night of the Soul

While Eastern religions offer texts and practices that are more specifically relevant, there are two well-known themes in Christianity that deal with spiritual transformation through practices: the "Dark Night of the Soul" and Christ's temptation in the wilderness.

Jesus Christ was able to align himself with the refined energy of Higher Power after he had purified and strengthened himself through fasting, prayer, communion with God, and solitude. These spiritual practices thus helped him rise above personal ego desires and fears—the samskaras. When the Devil appealed to Jesus' desires and fears, Jesus did not yield to him, because he was occupying a higher level of consciousness than the ego. He was very close to the state of oneness with Higher Power, on the Subtle and/or Causal level.

> Then was Jesus led up of the Spirit into the wilderness to be tempted of the devil.
> And when he had fasted forty days and nights, he was afterward an hungered.
> And when the tempter came to him, he said, If thou be the Son of God, command that these stones be made bread.

But he answered and said, It is written, Man shall not live by bread
alone, but by every word that proceedeth out of the mouth of God.
Then the devil taketh him up into the holy city, and setteth him on
a pinnacle of the temple.
And saith unto him, If thou be the Son of God, cast thyself down; for
it is written, He shall give his angels charge concerning thee; and in
their hands they shall bear thee up, lest at any time thou dash thy foot
against a stone.
Jesus said unto him, It is written again, Thou shalt not tempt the Lord
thy God.
Again, the devil taketh him up into an exceeding high mountain, and
sheweth him all the kingdoms of the world, and the glory of them;
And saith unto him, All these things will I give thee, if thou wilt fall
down and worship me.
Then saith Jesus unto him, Get thee hence, Satan; for it is written,
Thou shalt worship the Lord thy God, and him only shalt thou serve.
Then the devil leaveth him, and, behold, angels came and ministered
unto him.[7]

Jesus Christ must have gone through psychological and physical
difficulties in the desert wilderness. Imagine being a young man,
barely thirty years old, out in the desert heat for forty days and nights
by yourself with no food. You want to commune with God. But certainly your days and nights are also punctuated by human needs: desires for food, for comfort, for human warmth. Perhaps Jesus felt these
too. Perhaps he also felt anger, even hatred, toward the Romans. Perhaps he went through a dark night of the ego, doubting if he could
accomplish what he wanted in his life. Perhaps he also feared for his
physical survival in the desert, or his survival in the community,
given that he did not want to accommodate the spiritual conventions
of his culture. In the midst of these physical and psychological difficulties that arose during his spiritual practices, perhaps Jesus, like
Teresa, also became feverish as he let go of samskaras.

In *The Dark Night*, Saint John of the Cross alludes to psychological
problems that beset those who are no longer beginners on the spiritual
road. In so doing, he recognizes that problems arise as people let go of
their impurities so completely that they become like light. Saint John's
treatise on this phenomenon offers some solace to any spiritual seeker
overwhelmed with depression. Saint John describes the depression as
an inevitable part of the path. He shows that people must go through
it—that it is *not* a senseless waste of time. He also describes emerging
out of it, purified.

The dark night of the soul is different from the dark night of the
ego described in chapter 4. In the dark night of the ego, the person has
been absorbed in her ego and is longing to come into direct relationship to her inmost soul and the higher self for the first time. The dark

night of the soul, on the other hand, is more advanced. It is a bridge to the perfect divine union of the soul with Atman, which is only available to those who are already proficient on the spiritual path, have already experienced the soul, and committed themselves to know Higher Power more completely. Thus, much of the pain of the dark night of the soul is in feeling rejected by the God one intimately knows already.

> This night . . . causes two kinds of darkness or purgation in the spiritual person according to the two parts of the soul, the sensory and the spiritual. Hence the one night of purgation will be sensory, by which the senses are purged and accommodated to the spirit; and the other night or purgation will be spiritual, by which the spirit is purged and denuded as well as accommodated and prepared for union with God through love.

> The soul, because of its impurity, suffers immensely at the time this divine light truly assails it. When this pure light strikes in order to expel all impurity, persons feel so unclean and wretched that it seems God is against them and they are against God. Because it seems that God has rejected them, these souls suffer . . . pain and grief.

> This, precisely, then, is what the divine ray of contemplation does. In striking the soul with its divine light, it surpasses the natural light and thereby darkens and deprives individuals of all the natural affections and apprehensions they perceive by means of their natural light. It leaves their spiritual and natural faculties not only in darkness but in emptiness too. Leaving the soul thus empty and dark, the ray purges and illumines it with divine spiritual light, while the soul thinks it has no light and that it is in darkness.[8]

The sensory and spiritual purgings Saint John speaks of are the physical and psychological purification related to samskaras. The purgation is a time of darkness, of turmoil, where perspective is lost. The commitment to become one with God's love has been made and the personality has been initially infused with Divine Light. Still, there is this painful time, truly a crisis in spiritual awakening, when we focus on elements of our personality that are not yet in the light and feel a "divine homesickness"[9] for the transpersonal states we have experienced.

The Role of Psychological Growth in Spiritual Emergence

The story of Christ in the wilderness and Saint John's interpretation of the dark night of the soul both point to the psychological difficulties of moving away from the pleasures of the senses and even the powers of the Subtle realm to stronger communion with Divine Light in the Causal and Atman levels. All spiritual growth includes Subtle level experiences, moodiness, unusual physical symptoms, and the necessity to work with psychological development and chronic physical tensions. Clergy, spiritual counselors, and spiritual practitioners exploring these areas will find important help in transpersonal psychology and bodywork, as well as from living spiritual adepts from any culture.

Neither the Bible nor *The Dark Night* identify the process of purification enough to educate religious people about the specific diagnosis and treatment of spiritual illnesses. For this we have to look at sources like *How to Know God: the Yoga Aphorisms of Patanjali*, derived from ancient Yogic texts, or Gopi Krishna's books. Both of these describe very precisely the rigors undergone in body and psyche. Or we have to look at modern Western psychology of the body that affirms that no characterological change is possible without corresponding physical change, and that the body is actually a direct contact point for bringing about psychospiritual change. Wilhelm Reich, M.D., was the originator of this thesis, and the neo-Reichian therapists that followed him have developed his ideas. John Pierrakos, M.D., Gay Hendricks, Ph.D., Graham Farrant, M.D., A. H. Almaas, Stephen Johnson, and Stanislav Grof, M.D., have all reflected on the value of intensive experiential bodywork as part of spiritual growth. (At the back of this book there are references to their books.)

The following story clearly illustrates the value of using psychological therapeutic techniques as preparatory to deepening spiritual work. Alicia, at twenty, was a dedicated student of Zen Buddhism. Every morning she would sit in meditation for forty-five minutes, the same at night. Her discipline and concentration helped her focus a tremendous amount of energy. After a few months of this practice her body began to shake uncontrollably halfway through each sitting. She went to her teacher to ask what she should do. He said, "Just keep sitting. The shaking is *makyo*."

She returned to her meditation cushion, unsatisfied with the answer. *Makyo* means illusion, or distraction, she thought. Is it wrong to have shaking? Does it mean I am trying to distract myself? I sense my body is trying to tell me something. I don't know what it is, but I sense it is worthwhile. Alicia went to a bodyworker. As she worked to release the chronic body tensions, her body became looser and more flexible. Often she would cry in her sessions as she got in touch with emotions of grief she had been keeping from consciousness all her life. As a result of this personal clearing work, Alicia discovered that her body did not shake so much in meditation, her concentration improved. This worked to speed and support the meditation. She felt more in tune with herself and more confirmed on her path to transpersonal levels of consciousness.

True awakening is enhanced by clearing away the psychological blocks and debris of old trauma. Maybe therapy is even a necessary element to spiritual development, because, in therapy, you can clear away samskaras, both psychological and physical, to prepare yourself to receive the more refined energy of transpersonal realms. As we become more self-aware and self-accepting of all our emotions, feel strong in our sense of self, and are no longer playing victim to the fears that lead to repression, we begin to receive spiritual experiences that add profound new dimensions to life. When Gopi Krishna gained confidence in himself, knew himself in his depths, trusted himself, then he became stable and could manage the kundalini energy that was awakening in him.

This is a very different understanding of the interface of psychiatry and spiritual development. In standard clinical psychiatry, spiritual experiences were considered to be mental or emotional aberrations — the result of regression to infantile states. Psychiatry seeks to terminate the regressive behavior, and thereby heal the patient. Catharsis is not always considered necessary; in fact, it is often inhibited through psychiatric medication. However, this orientation may also be inhibiting the seed of spiritual experiences from growing.

The convergence of personal development and spiritual development has never been clearly made by conventional religion or psychiatry. Only since the 1970s and the birth of transpersonal psychology have we had a discipline to order our thinking about the interconnectedness of personal growth and spiritual growth. Now, as we enter the 1990s, there is a highly charged discussion among transpersonal psychologists who are familiar with Eastern spiritual practices and spiritual teachers concerning the necessity of developing a strong ego structure before being able to support transpersonal levels of consciousness.[10] This does not mean that people cannot have authentic spiritual experiences before they have a stable ego structure. It does mean that a person has to have a strong sense of self, a sense of center and personal boundaries, before he or she can truly live on a level of consciousness that includes consistent experiences of communion with higher forces, the ability to do healing work, and other aspects of the Subtle and Causal levels. Before this level of ego is reached, individuals are still bound up in the conditioned responses of their childhood, seeing all of life as extensions of their family dynamics, with no freedom to move to a new level of consciousness.

Jenette, fifty-eight, came to me for therapy when she was moving out of the convent for the first time since joining as a teenager. She did not want to permanently leave the religious life but only to live on her own for a period. "I want to get to know myself," she said.

When she entered the convent, she had been taught to let go of her personal feelings and her personal history and not to develop any close friendships that might distract her from her relationship to Christ. Jenette was obedient and meek. When she heard by phone that her favorite sibling had died unexpectedly, the abbess told her not to cry and not to go to the funeral or meet with her family. Jenette obeyed.

Jenette did her best to repress feelings of wanting to go dancing with teenage friends, of wanting to have a close friend, of being affectionate with her own family. Others made her decisions for her about where she would live. Her options for choosing some form of work in the world were restricted.

With these limitations, it was very difficult for Jenette to form any sense of herself outside of her role as a nun. We usually define ourselves through our close relationships, our sense of history shared with our family, and our choices for work. Without these avenues for building a "self," Jenette never developed a sense of who she was.

By the time I met her as an older woman, she suffered from low self-esteem and depression. She had realized that her relationship with her Heavenly Father really followed the same form as the one she had with her natural father, who was remote, critical, not a loving person, unavailable to her. Being "married to God" brought her little satisfaction. Her personal relationships were few, and gave her little social connection. Her life often seemed meaningless to her. The vitalizing seeds of new spiritual experiences had little ground in which to take root to enhance her spiritual growth.

Jenette's therapy involved her becoming aware of how she had been given no "personal" attention all her life. The fourth of eight children, she had had no special place in her family. Again, in the convent, she did not feel she was significant as an individual. She felt she was useful only because she did not get in the way and could clean well. In the convent, as in her family of origin, everyone else seemed more important. When she was not so depressed that she couldn't feel her feelings, she was sad and lonely.

As she began to identify her real feelings, she realized how lonely she had been for personal contact all her life, how the life of her heart had suffered because she had been living in her head, following rules, but cut off from her own personal feelings, her dreams, and her yearning to be more connected with others. Acknowledging her longing with my encouragement, she began to reach out to others. She visited an Al-Anon group. She began learning how to communicate more directly with others, develop friendships not prescribed by rules of the convent, and take responsibility for her own life. She traveled to Hawaii and, for the first time, let herself relax and have fun. In doing bodywork therapy, she began to be more in touch with the life of her heart. This helped her gain confidence in herself and develop a *living* palpable experience of Higher Power as a sense of unity.

As Jenette gained confidence in herself and connected with a wider community of friends, her depression lifted. Her concept of God, her experience of God's love, now extended past the limited sense of a father who was remote and unloving.

Like Jenette, Joseph had been part of a Roman Catholic order for a number of years before he lapsed into a dark depression. His sleep was disturbed, he was beset with moodiness night and day, his body ached as if he had the flu. He went to the abbot of his monastery for advice. This man sent him to a psychiatrist, who did not happen to be a religious man or to have a transpersonal orientation. The psychiatrist did not know of the dark night of the soul. His medical texts on diagnosis did not include spiritual illnesses or the importance of letting go of samskaras. The doctor concluded that Joseph suffered from depression and prescribed medication to be taken for the rest of his life. Joseph returned to the monastery. As a side effect of his medication, he was now unable to remember his dreams and less able to feel his passion for the religious life or the deep connection with Christ. The drug dulled all his senses, taking him away from both his personal and transpersonal development.

Joseph continued this way for several years until he met a transpersonal psychologist. With his help, Joseph reappraised his situation and decided to discontinue medication. Subsequently, he saw the psychologist on a weekly basis to work through psychological problems dating back to his childhood. As he liberated himself from dysfunctional patterns of relating, opening to new ways of giving and receiving love, his energy for the religious life returned renewed.

Both Jenette and Joseph needed to do psychological work before they could move ahead with their spiritual development. Gopi Krishna and Teresa of Avila needed to plumb their own depths before they could work with the spiritual energies available to them. Alicia did her inner work with the help of a bodyworker. The need for such physical and psychological integration as part of spiritual development is not new. As Gopi Krishna tells us:

> The ancient teachers of Kundalini Yoga, taught by an experience extending for thousands of years, insisted on an exceptionally robust and hardy constitution, mastery over appetites and desires, voluntarily acquired control over vital functions and organs, and, above all, the possession of an inflexible will as the essentially needed qualification in those offering themselves for the supreme undertaking of rousing the Shakti [kundalini awakening]. An excellent condition of both body and mind, difficult to achieve in the unfavourable environment of modern civilization, is absolutely necessary in an enter-

prise of this nature to prevent the brain from giving way completely under the unbearable strain.

When accidentally the center begins to function prematurely, before the nerve connections and links have been fully established and the delicate brain cells habituated to the flow of the powerful current, the result is likely to be disastrous. The delicate tissues of the body in that case are likely to be damaged irreparably, causing strange maladies, insanity, or death.[11]

Consider again Gopi Krishna's story. He was in excellent health. He had cultivated his willpower and his ability to concentrate consciousness for twenty years before his dramatic kundalini awakening. He was brought up in a strictly religious home by dedicated parents. His personality was grounded in his intention to realize enlightenment. Even with this inner stability and dedicated family support, he was severely shaken by the increased pranic activity initiated through the kundalini rising. He had to face the torment of depression, self-doubt, anorexia, and debilitating physical weakness as part of his path to higher transpersonal levels. But he, like Teresa of Avila, did not have the advantage of a bodyworker or therapist to help.

Certainly, the experience of opening through the kundalini awakening, which is inevitably part of every spiritual emergence, needs to be attended with a strong body and an ability to manage complex and powerful emotions. Since our conventional education in church and school does not prepare us for this event, those going through the awakening usually need the services of a doctor, healer, spiritual teacher, and/or psychotherapist for assistance.

The Search for True Spiritual Experience

Over the past thirty years, some people who have been drawn to transpersonal realms have wanted more companionship in their spiritual experiences and more inspiration than the conventional religious formalities offered. They have shifted their allegiances to psychospiritual groups that offer a dynamic path to self-exploration and the rise to transpersonal levels.

Ed, fifty years old in 1970, was a member of a conventional church, yet had no place to explore spiritual experiences within that institutional setting. He went outside his church for spiritual companionship, but unlike Julia, who moved away from her church shortly after her out-of-body experience, Ed chose to retain his ties to the Episcopal church for twenty years. He also had many ties to his community as a father of five children, president of the Young Republicans, and a cub master for the Boy Scouts. He had been a subdeacon at the church, had taught Sunday school, and had given communion.

> But I sensed there was more to spiritual life than my church involvement had to offer. My distress about the war in Vietnam and my sympathy for the farmworkers who were being so abused began to make me more aware of my feelings of unity with other people outside my community.
>
> As a result, I attended a lecture on mind dynamics, where I saw a man use telepathy to heal another person 3,000 miles distant. This was a living example, and a dramatic one, of what I had read about in the Bible but never before witnessed in the church. I was very excited.
>
> That same night I woke with a powerful vision. A purple orb covered everything in my room. From purple it changed to gold—seated in a huge eye. The vision seemed to last an eternity and take up all of space. I was terrified! I recited the Lord's Prayer, trying to save myself from what seemed to be pagan forms. But I also felt overwhelmed with positive feelings. I didn't know why. It was very confusing.

Ed decided to get more involved with mind dynamics. He learned more about deep meditation, healing, remote viewing. He explored the occult: channeling, exploration of past lives, contact with people who had died, etc. He also returned to graduate school and earned a Master's degree in transpersonal psychology. His wife and fellow parishioners thought he had "gone off his rocker." They worried about him. The pastor of his church tolerated his new interests but did not support them. There were two other ministers, friends of Ed's, who were questioning the limitations of the faith but didn't feel they could speak about it publicly. In them he found some companionship, but it was shrouded in secrecy.

In 1989, twenty years later, Ed has recently modified his relationship with the Episcopal church. The formalities and the dogma are not a central part of his worship although he continues to enjoy the comradeship of the other parishioners. He does attend services at Unity Temple, where the faith is wide-based and inclusive of Christianity, metaphysics, and mysticism. He finds the temple to be more involved in the spontaneous experience of the spirit, and healing through prayer.

> I was never rejected by the church. That was helpful because I needed my close relationship to formal religion as I explored my own potentials as a healer and a visionary. The formalities were necessary at the beginning stages of my spiritual growth. But the more I *experienced* the spirit, the more unique my spiritual life became. The way

someone else defines spirituality is just not as vital as my own experience anymore.

Ed now enjoys a deeply personal relationship with Jesus Christ, who is "a manifestation of pure love" for him. Ed meditates daily, assists in a networking group to facilitate communication between healers, and has a small healing practice himself. He says that he enjoys empowering other people to experience divine energy inside themselves. Most of the techniques he uses he has learned in psychospiritual growth groups.

Perhaps one of the reasons for the rise of interest in "psychospiritual" groups like the mind dynamics group that Ed first became interested in is that they offer a technology that accelerates spiritual growth. Both the secular intensive workshops (like *est* and Lifespring) and spiritually oriented study groups (such as A Course in Miracles study groups and 12-Step programs: Alcoholics Anonymous, Adult Children of Alcoholics, Overeaters Anonymous, Al-Anon., etc.) intensify self-revelation. What is this technology used to accelerate spiritual growth? How is it different from conventional religion?

All these groups encourage a *life review.* This helps you gain some objectivity about your early life. What was your true experience at home? What feelings did you have? Were you valued for your uniqueness, your personal feelings, your need for love and encouragement? Were you abused? What were the effects of that emotional, physical, or sexual abuse?

The life review helps us to confront the conditions of our past. Then we realize more fully we do not have to repeat the conditions of our past in our relationship to friends now, or in our relationship to God. Like Jenette, Ed, and Julia, we can choose an alternative that lets our authentic spiritual life unfold *inclusive* of our individuality. Most formal religions do not demand this kind of personal confrontation. They rely more on the parishioners' desire to be safe, not to expose their personal lives, to believe that the church must be able to attend to all their spiritual needs, and to make a habit out of church attendance.

The leaders of psychospiritual group intensives offer an experience of dealing directly with one's immediate inner life. For example, an exercise in deep emotional sharing with another person in which you are taught how to listen and in turn tell about yourself teaches you the value of spontaneous personal connection. Practicing meditation together provides social sanction for the value of going deeply within yourself to experience God. Many formal religions focus more on outer symbols of faith than inner experience.

In psychospiritual groups, a conceptual framework is offered that supports dealing directly with one's inner life. Most such groups encourage you to think things like "Live in the present moment, One day at a time, one minute at a time, Love is letting go of fear, Change is the only constant, It's all right to love yourself." If you can't really love yourself, how can you love someone else? Nonverbal communication, what you say in your gestures and the feeling you project, has more impact than your words. Most formal religions take an authoritarian approach to inner life supporting self-control, self-discipline, and social action while *denying* the value of spontaneity, trust, and letting go.

In many psychospiritual groups, community support is offered to sustain the individual in moving into a new way of thinking and relating to the world. A strong model for this is evident in the 12-Step programs. All members are offered total anonymity and privacy. Their attendance at a meeting is not spoken about outside the meeting. The meetings are free and usually open to all. Each member can have a personal sponsor on request. This sponsor is someone who has been a member of the group for a period of time and can guide the new person in putting the new concepts into action. The sponsor's guidance is available between group meetings. The program is psychological, educational, and spiritual in nature. No attendance fee is charged. Group meetings are available every day at different times to accommodate different work schedules. Each meeting begins and ends in the same way. This ritual supports bonding between people and the group and is grounding. Conventional religious community members rarely see a value in individuals committing themselves to deep personal work. Such a commitment is often interpreted as a sign of mental illness.

An agenda for letting go of the past and forgiving oneself and others for harmful acts is suggested in many psychospiritual groups. Each person is guided in how to "let go and let God." In the 12-Step programs, this involves a time-consuming process of taking moral inventory and communicating directly with people you have hurt to make amends. Some psychospiritual groups encourage letting go through various kinds of group processes or individual bodywork, which both promote catharsis and self-healing.

Spiritual Emergence in Churches: A Vision

What if conventional religions took advantage of the techniques for spiritual growth offered in these psychospiritual groups? Perhaps some of the clergy would be trained as psychospiritual growth facilitators? The churches might also become more vital as "spiritual communities." What would that look like?

I imagine that each parish and temple would have a transpersonal educator. This person would be well-versed in psychology and could define the path of spiritual emergence. He could demystify spiritual growth, making the process more human. This educator would offer a conceptual framework in which people could understand the difference between spiritual emergence and emergency in themselves and others. If a young person had a spiritual experience, like the out-of-body experience that scared Julia, he could go to the church and find immediate counsel with the transpersonal educator.

People would be encouraged to do a form of body discipline (such as yoga, t'ai chi, aikido, etc.) and perhaps have bodywork (deep tissue work, structural integration, and so forth) as part of their spiritual practice. It would be understood that spiritual emergence involves purification of the body, which can be gently accelerated through bodywork. There would be rooms specifically designated for body-work on the grounds of the church. Jenette, and other people who had been conditioned not to esteem the body as part of spiritual life, would thus find it easier to accept that the body is a friend to religious life. Perhaps monastics would be the first to be trained in bodywork.

As a result of seminary training, I imagine the clergy would be able to identify when a parishioner, or clergy member, needs to work on psychological issues as part of spiritual unfolding. Therapy would be valued in a positive framework, not only as healing of mental "dis-ease" but as a technology to accelerate psychospiritual growth. A referral network to transpersonal therapists would be readily available to the religious community through the church. A person like Ed could go to psychospiritual growth groups as part of regular church activities. There would be rooms designated for therapy and healing within the church. Perhaps those like Ed who decided to work as healers would then work within the church community

There would be a contingency group within the community trained to work with anyone in spiritual emergency. When a church member was going through a spiritual emergency, his clergyman would refer him to the spiritual emergency contingent in his church. They would make house calls, or provide a place for him to stay, if needed. Members of this contingent would talk with the family to reassure them and give them confidence during this stressful and unusual time.

Community would be strengthened and grounded through ritual celebrations as well as traditional religious events. The value of these traditions in noting the seasons of our inner lives, and external circumstances (birth, death, marriage, etc.) would endure as a powerful reason to gather together.

An Innovative Spiritual Community

Following is a description of a spiritual community that illustrates many aspects of the foregoing vision. I have chosen Ananda Cooperative Village because it is in the United States and has enjoyed real success in terms of being financially viable as well as supportive of spiritual and creative work. It has also integrated both Hindu and Christian ideologies, both East and West. There are of course a wide variety of spiritual communities, some with more focus on a specific spiritual practice, like Auroville in India, and some with a broad spiritual focus, like Findhorn in Scotland.

Ananda Cooperative Village is a Christian/Yoga community in Grass Valley, California. It also has centers in major cities in the United States and Europe. It was founded by Kriyananda, an American student of Parmahansa Yogananda. Yogananda was an East Indian who followed both Hindu teachers and Christian wisdom. The aspiration for spiritual growth, to live a spiritual life, as reflected in the lives of both Christian and Hindu saints, is the bond that keeps the community together. Its concepts of the path of spiritual growth are derived from traditional texts, both Christian and Yogic. Kriyananda is a magnetic leader who personifies the creativity, compassion, wisdom, energy, and dedication to service of one who has been awakened.

The mode of practice at Ananda is strong, consistent, and well grounded. Each member practices daily meditation, energization exercises, chanting, prayer, and community service. The self-revelation that comes with spiritual practices happens regularly in small doses, and is thus easy to integrate in daily activity. Simple cabins are made available for people who request silence and solitude from time to time. Meals are brought to them. They are relieved of community responsibilities for a week or so, as appropriate. Sunday services, open to all people in and out of the community, punctuate their week. Small interest groups, organized according to one's level of commitment and involvement in the community, meet during the week. Everyone who can takes off the same week every year for "Spiritual Renewal." During this time, there are special activities that promote community bonding and deepening of spiritual practices.

As in any religious community, sometimes people arrive at the door in terrible shape, looking for rehabilitation. A minister at Ananda, Asha Praver, speaks about how the community responds when faced with the care of someone in a psychotic state or a spiritual emergency:

> We try to help the people we can. We know there are some people who are just not helped by staying with us. They need another

kind of care. We tell those people to leave—but that happens very rarely.

There are some professional psychotherapists in our community, so if we need a professional opinion about a disturbed person, we can get that advice from someone who also has experience with people in the context of spiritual problems. But usually the people who don't belong with us just leave on their own. They don't want to, or they can't, keep up with our steady practice. They don't want to do the work. They aren't grounded enough.

When someone at Ananda has problems related to her spiritual growth, she has many resources for help. Such individuals can get guidance directly from Kriyananda. (Ananda is still small enough so that Kriyananda can be personally accessible.) They can talk to one of many ministers and counselors. They can work with a wide variety of laypeople in the community who do bodywork and healing. If they are having an authentic experience, people at Ananda seem to be able to recognize their need and help them however they can. Because everyone there is deeply committed to spiritual growth, all of them have had related problems and developed empathy for others who also suffer in this. Sometimes it is the minister's job to decide if someone is having an authentic awakening that needs special attention or if the person is just caught in a cul-de-sac, avoiding something that is personally difficult. Asha said:

> A true spiritual experience always brings about an increase in love, compassion, and harmony. It's not necessary to have the fireworks of spiritual crises to grow spiritually. Self-revelation, an expanding sense of reality, groundedness, and inner harmony are evidence of growth. That's what we go by.

Ananda Cooperative Village is a strong structure for people looking for a community that supports spiritual growth. Its regulations and adherence to tradition seem to support the living spirit. Its newness and exploratory nature allow for spontaneity and creativity. Its very structure gives limits and boundaries while remaining true to the ever-changing flow of life, which constantly seeks new expression. Its members have originated innovative music, books on yoga, natural foods, and community living, an elementary school system, and wonderful organic farms, among other achievements. Its weekend retreat programs and rural retreat facilities have been widely used and appreciated by people from around the world from many different religious traditions. It is an exemplary religious community drawing on many techniques for enhancing spiritual growth.

Both conventional religious institutions and New Age spiritual groups are heading in the same direction—to allow us the safety of support while we open to our own relationship to the Divine. Where conventional rituals often do not allow room for spontaneous spiritual experience, they do offer the security of the known, the community, and tradition that has lasted through time. Where New Age psychospiritual processes allow room for spontaneous opening to spiritual experience, they do not always offer the consistent community support needed to integrate the openings. Hopefully, we will be able to draw from each in the future to have spiritual communities, with appropriate leadership, where people are free to open to spiritual experience with all the psychological, spiritual, and physiological change that implies, as well as to have consistent, integrated support when they need it.

The pace of most religious institutions is slow in accommodating change. The administrators of these institutions are inconsistent in their view of spiritual experience as part of spiritual growth. The conventional religious establishment is similar to the conventional medical establishment, which is so ambivalent about the reality of spiritual experiences that it doubts their validity altogether. Individual doctors, psychiatrists, and clergy explore alternatives to this rigid view. However, the conventional medical establishment prefers to see all so-called spiritual experiences as traceable to chemical events in the brain responsible for regressive, psychotic phenomena, capable of being controlled by modern medical technology. We will explore how body chemistry actually interfaces with spiritual experiences in the next chapter.

6
Physical Stress

Although athletics, childbirth, and illness seem worlds apart from spirituality, the intensity born of the physical stress in each of these can stimulate spiritual experiences that are profound. States of ecstasy, Causal level experiences, mental telepathy, out-of-body experiences, feats of extraordinary strength, spiritual healing, clairvoyance, clairaudience, and other psychic phenomena can manifest when the body is strained. Conventional physicians tend to attribute all of these experiences to changes in body chemistry. In this chapter, the relationship between transpersonal experiences and the interface of physical stress and body chemistry will be illuminated.

Athletics

Athletes in training put themselves in a similar position to yogis who are intensely involved in spiritual disciplines. Both of them subject themselves to rigorous physical and mental demands. Both must focus attention for long periods of time. Peak performance demands a certain detachment from the goal. Whether that goal is enlightenment or winning a race, an ability to quiet the mind and be in the present moment is essential. Both yogi and athlete are exploring human limits, testing their individual limits. Utmost commitment is mandatory. This intensity accompanies both yogi and athelete night and day. Through dreamlife and waking states, each one draws on his creative abilities to improve the practice and integrate new ways of improving performance. These parallels have been explored by Michael Murphy and Rhea White in their book *The Psychic Side of Sports.*[1]

Sports, like a spiritual discipline, demand that a person give up old patterns of functioning and acquire, or open to, new skills and inner resources in order to perfect performance. This opening up to new aspects of the self can bring an exhilaration—a sense of renewal, or rebirth. It may also be sufficiently disorienting to trigger a spiritual emergency. Mike Spino, a distance runner, had such a crisis:

> In the winter of 1967, I was training on dirt and asphalt, paced by a friend who was driving a car. I had intended to run six miles at top speed, but after the first mile I was surprised at how easily I could do it. I had run the first mile in four and a half minutes with little sense of pain or exertion, as if I were carried by a huge momentum. The wet pavement and honking horns were no obstacle at all. My body had no weight or resistance. It began to feel like a skeleton—as if the flesh had been blown off of its bones. I felt like the wind. Daydreams and fantasies disappeared. The only negative feeling was a guilt for being able to do this. When the run was over, conversation was impossible, because for a while I didn't know who I was. Was I the one who had been running or the ordinary Mike Spino? I sat down by the roadway and wept. Here I was, having run the entire six miles on a muddy roadside at a four-and-a-half minute pace, which was close to the national record, and I was having a crisis deciding who I was.[2]

What does an athlete do with such an experience? Undoubtedly, many chalk it up to the glow of fitness and the pleasure of exceeding a limit—it is simply part of the sport itself. Without another conceptual framework, these athletes do not incorporate the profound meaning of these peak moments into the rest of their lives. Former quarterback John Brodie describes this problem:

> Football players and athletes generally get into this kind of being or beingness—call it what you will—more often than is generally recognized. But they often loose it after a game or after a season is over. They often don't have a workable philosophy or understanding to support the kind of thing they get into while they are playing. They don't have the words for it. So after a game you see some of them coming down, making fools of themselves sometimes, coming way down in their tone level. But during the game they come way up. A missing ingredient for many people, I guess, is that they don't have a supporting philosophy or discipline for a better life.[3]

Living in a spiritual context is a way for athletes to find a place for peak experiences in their ordinary life. Then the highs do not come just from sports. Athletic activity is simply one of many ways of opening the door to this dimension of experience. The peak moments, like the one Mike Spino had, would be seen as part of a spiritual emergence process. Such a context would give Spino's crisis meaning as a high point rather than a breaking point. With a philosophy that recognizes the true self as beyond the ego, Spino would have rejoiced to have touched that higher self and its powers. He would have seen the experiences as a glimpse into his full potential as a human being, suggesting a direction of his life.

Without an ongoing alignment with the spiritual emergence process, peak moments have no home in which to grow. They are relegated to memory. Thus, the full benefits that are potential in these peak moments may be lost. Saint John of the Cross wrote:

> He who interrupts the course of his spiritual exercises and prayer
> is like a man who allows a bird to escape from his hand; he can
> hardly catch it again.

Of course, there are some athletes who are able to understand the possibilities that have opened for them and use it to their advantage, both in sports and in their ordinary lives.

> . . . a well-known long-distance swimmer who prefers to be anonymous [said] that whenever his physical body is exhausted during a marathon competition, he relaxes it by floating overhead in his double while continuing to swim. When he reenters his body, he feels refreshed and can go on for quite a while without fatigue. The man added that athletes in other sports also go out-of-body during competition, but they don't talk about it.[4]

Charles Lindbergh, a dedicated Christian and the first man to fly solo across the Atlantic Ocean, reportedly had out-of-body experiences as well as visitations from beings of higher intelligence during his flight.[5] These experiences happened while he was in a solitary environment, as well as engaging in a physically and psychologically demanding activity. Lindbergh's prayerful dedication to Higher Power undoubtedly helped him maintain his centeredness and not lose himself completely during these extraordinary transpersonal experiences.

Childbirth

Childbirth always occasions intense altered states of consciousness, except when impeded by drugs. The altered states may include episodes of kundalini awakening phenomena. Many women report feeling ecstatic during childbirth; sometimes feeling an exquisite spiritual communion with Higher Power and/or angelic forces. However, some women feel very troubled by spiritual experiences during childbirth. Having these awakenings at such an intense time can be very traumatic for women who have no context to understand them.

Betsy was a research biochemist in her late twenties when she gave birth to her first baby. During labor, when she was being wheeled on a gurney into the birthing room at the hospital, extraordinary vibrations of energy began streaming through her body. Her whole body was shaking. She felt as if she were losing control of herself. She realized she was moving into a very unusual state of consciousness. She worried, "Am I losing my mind?" She asked the attending nurses and physician to explain what was happening to her. They had no explanation. Betsy saw that they were also concerned about her.

Betsy's education in biology and chemistry had also not given her any understanding of the possibility of cosmic energy moving dramatically in the body. Her only way of understanding the experience was that it must be symptomatic of some pathology. She was therefore terribly frightened for her life and the life of her child. Bracing herself in fear about the birth, she was surprised to find her baby healthy and her birthing smooth. Tests were done after the birth to establish if Betsy had an organic problem. No pathology was present. Still, for ten years Betsy worried that some as-yet-undiagnosed disease, the cause of her childbirthing trauma, would manifest in her. Her fears were not put to rest until she learned about kundalini awakening during a psychotherapy session. She then realized that the increase in intuition and extraordinary peacefulness in church that had come to her in the last ten years was probably linked to the kundalini stirring in her at childbirth.

The lack of understanding about kundalini awakening in hospital childbirth can have more dramatically negative results. One woman, Samantha, was separated from her child after birth because the attending doctor interpreted her kundalini experience during the birthing as symptomatic of psychosis. Not only was she separated from her child, Samantha was given medications to stop the flow of breast milk, as well as antipsychotic medications. She left the hospital physically healthy but terribly worried because her physician had diagnosed her as psychotic. Along with her family, she asked herself, "Am I fit to be a mother? Is the child safe with me? Will I get out of control unpredictably? Is it possible I could be schizophrenic?" It took five years of worry until she found guidance to help her understand her kundalini awakening as positive and an opportunity for growth.

Another woman, Ann, in 1954, had a near-death experience during childbirth in which she talked with a disembodied being of higher intelligence who told her "he" would be caring for the baby after it died several days after birth. Ann did not initially talk to her physician about her experience. Most hospital personnel would have considered her story crazy.

Near-Death Experience (NDE)

Near-death experiences can happen during any severe trauma in which a person hovers close to death. They typically involve a pattern of experiences where people feel drawn down a dark tunnel into an expanse of light. Typically, they are then "met" by beings of divine intelligence and old friends. It is a blissful, liberating experience. People who live to tell about it, like Ann, above, have no doubt in their minds about the reality of their inner experience of this sacred territory. After recuperating, "NDErs" (people who have had a near-death experience) typically discover unusual healing ability, inner peace, a desire to serve others, no fear of death, and spiritual feelings about all of life. Kenneth Ring, Ph.D., in his book *Healing Toward Omega*, notes that these effects are the same as the effects of kundalini awakening.

How was Ann's near-death experience handled by her doctor and friends? Because the birthing had been long and hard, her baby was cared for mainly by the nurses in the hospital in order to give Ann time to recuperate after childbirth. Although the baby had appeared to be healthy at birth, it died in the nursery of cerebral hemorrhaging four days later. Ann did not grieve in the regular way, because she had an inner knowing that her baby was in the care of a divine being. When Ann told her husband and doctor, they knew that something "real" had happened to her to give her this feeling. However, her minister was unable to accept the reality of her experience.

> [He] pronounced this experience as an hallucination common to persons undergoing great stress. There was no such thing as leaving this life, going to another, and coming back here again. It was a psychological defense mechanism, he said, and I would be better off to simply forget all about it, so that my natural grief period could begin, and [be] gone through, so that my life could get back to "normal" again. . . . This conversation with [my] minister almost wiped me out . . . but I obeyed him without question—or tried to at least. In a matter of months, I had not been able to forget it and was well on my way to thinking myself to be some kind of freak. It would have been easier, I think, to try to forget my own name, than to forget that wonderful feeling, surge of sheer joy I had felt when [the divine being] took my hand, and told me he had come for *my* child. That was the greatest moment I've ever known.
>
> I still don't know who he was, nor do I care! I know he exists at least.
>
> Well, I soon realized that my acceptance back into this world depended upon "pretending" to forget, and "pretending" to grieve the loss of my baby. So I did this for everybody else's sake—except my husband, who believed me, and gained some comfort from it, secondhand. . . . [I know now] Our separation [from our daughter] is only temporary and very short, compared to all of eternity.[6]

The explanation that spiritual experiences—including those near-death ones—are hallucinations or psychological responses to stress has been accepted by both medical professionals and those who follow the medical model. The Christian Church doctrine gives no mention of experiences such as kundalini awakening having any bearing on spiritual development. Most clergy members choose an explanation for spiritual experiences predicated on conventional medical thinking. What is our current knowledge of how our chemistry effects extraordinary transpersonal experiences? In the following sections, we will consider the chemistry involved in traumas such as those we've just reviewed and those of people seriously ill or injured.

Our Own Chemistry Makes Us High!

The purely physical aspect of the high that athletes and some women in childbirth report during the most strenuous part of their activity is attributable to the release of endorphins. These chemical pain-relievers created by the body function like medications such as morphine. The endorphins block or weaken the transmission of pain stimuli, thus numbing the pain. Severe stress on the body, like marathon running and childbirth (for both mother and child), always catalyze the release of endorphins. The result is a release from the normal sense of limitation, and in some cases a sense of exhilaration.

The release of endorphins seems to be nature's way of allowing us in some circumstances to concentrate on a goal without having to be overwhelmed by distracting pain.[7] The runner will describe feeling "lighter than air," "a feeling of being able to run forever—almost like flying," and sometimes, "a sense of oneness with everything in nature and in myself." A woman in childbirth may have extraordinary resources of energy, a sense of light in her body, or a feeling of being at one with the universe. This sense of unity and ecstasy is truly a spiritual experience, a glimpse into a higher Causal reality, which many athletes relish as one of the real rewards for their efforts.

Besides being the body's way of helping us tolerate pain, endorphins are also, perhaps, one of our initiators into spiritual dimensions beyond ego. It is in those situations of life where we rise above our normal limits—where we go beyond ourselves—that we come to realize our true selves, selves not limited to this body or the concepts of this intellect, selves that can go to a realm that words cannot describe, a space/time of complete peace. In such a state, we are not distracted by a sense of separation from anything, but instead feel a unity with all.

Brain Chemistry and Transpersonal States

Could it be that, along with the release of endorphins, brain chemistry also shifts as a result of these high physical stresses? Could our transpersonal experiences simply be a result of this new chemistry? Some may think so.

Dr. Arnold Mandell, a brain chemist and professor of psychiatry at the University of California in San Diego, proposes a neurochemical mechanism to explain transcendental states of consciousness. In physical distress, one neurotransmitter, serotonin, is sometimes inhibited. Serotonin normally quiets brain activity. When it is inhibited, the brain's temporal lobes and limbic system (the emotional center) boost their electrical discharges. Old memories and perceptual stimuli are processed as if "new and fresh and full of meaning." Dr. Mandell reports that "affectual and cognitive processes characteristic of religious ecstasy and the permanent personality changes associated with religious conversion" are the result.[8]

The function of the *temporal lobes* is certainly relevant to paranormal experiences. Through the temporal lobes in the brain, we perceive not only our "sense of self" but our identity in time and space. Time and space include the cosmic now, past lives, and infinity; also the floating sensations of OOBE, flying dreams, or moving down the tunnel into light in the near-death experience. The temporal lobes are involved also with our overall sense of movement, especially spinning and floating. These are often reported as a part of the inner experience of paranormal events, especially out-of-body experience.

Olfactory sensation is intimately tied to this part of the brain. Thus, a stimulating smell may induce altered states of consciousness more quickly than a stimulating taste, which is not so connected to the temporal lobe. Perhaps this is one reason incense is used in churches and on sacred occasions—it goes directly to the part of the brain that perceives transpersonal experiences!

Two smaller structures within the temporal lobes also relate directly to transpersonal experiences. The *hippocampus* is known as the "gateway of memory." It may have a place in the process of accessing karmic experiences and recalling past lives, even recollecting skills from previous lifetimes. The *amygdala* is the seat of our passions and fears. This part of the brain relates to our will to survive, to reproduce, to share intimacy, and also to our fear of loss, separation, and death. It is also the area where we process the longing for union with Higher Power.

Michael Persinger, head of the neuroscience lab at Laurentian University of Sudbury in Ontario, has found that stimulating the temporal lobe effects mystical states of awareness. He has replicated paranormal experiences, including out-of-body and near-death experiences and the presence of Higher Power in subjects. Using an electromagnetic signaling device that penetrates the temporal lobes nonsurgically at a controlled, specific rhythm, he found that with repeated small amounts of stimulation, "mini-bolts actually alter the biochemical structure of the neurons until sending them down the ME (mystical experience) pathway requires almost no stimulation at all." These minibolts might come from his signaling device, a mantra, magnetic forces high in the atmosphere or deep within the earth, or an emotional response to a life-threatening situation.[9] These minibolts may also come from the loving touch of close friends.

The transpersonal experiences Robin Inman had during her coma may in part be attributed to "minibolts" of energy coming from holding hands with her family and friends as well as her own anxiety and sleeplessness. Robin is forty-five, an artist and organizational consultant. Her physical crisis came in 1988 as a result of an acute pancreatic failure:

> It seemed I was perfectly healthy. Then, suddenly, I was struck with severe pain unexpectedly. Within hours I was in a coma that lasted for two weeks. Each day the doctors would report to my parents that I probably would not make it through the night. My vital signs were reflecting that my body was just too weak to go on.
>
> People came to visit me. I was told later that even in my unconscious state, I would reach out for a hand of a friend and grasp it tightly. I was literally feeding on the vital energy of my friends. One day my father and my brother just sat and massaged my feet. We've always been a very physically affectionate family. I think it's this kind of care and attention from my loved ones that pulled me through.
>
> The nurses told me that I didn't sleep for the two weeks that I was in a coma. I was in a somewhat animated state—awake to some of the pain and aware of where I was. My inner sense told me I was in "the land of death." It was a place of deep inner peace. It felt very close to being in my normal state of consciousness, but it was also a world apart.
>
> When I awoke, I carried this sense of inner peace with me. That everything is perfect. Our successes. Our apparent failures. Our problems. Everything! It is all part of a perfection. It has a logic to it.

Robin told me that her coma experience had helped her understand the near-death experience she had had ten years previously as a result of almost dying from hemorrhaging after a hysterectomy. She felt there was a similarity between the two experiences.

> [Both times] I did the classic thing. I went down the tunnel into the light. It was absolutely wonderful. Peaceful. Joyful. Easy. But it was not my time to die. So, I was revived . . . thanks to modern technology and the grace of God (whom I now call the Cosmic Mother

or Goddess). My NDE taught me to have no fear of death itself. From it I knew beyond doubt that there is Higher Power. Also, that there is a reason I am living my life.

If these transpersonal experiences are simply a result of a chemical event that takes place only under the stimulation of physical stress or electromagnetic pulsations, why do they have such a profound psychological impact, which lasts a lifetime? Could it be that the chemical event is linked to physiology and psychology, in such a way that new pathways for brain activity and understanding perceptual experience are initiated in the brain? This could explain Robin's life-changing experiences. It gives us insight into out-of-body experiences, too, but does it explain them completely?

Larry, a college student, had to endure unbearable pain and have complicated surgery and a long period of hospital confinement after a car accident. Perhaps the stress resulted in a shift in brain chemistry that led to his having out-of-body experiences. However, these experiences distinctly took him beyond his body.

> I was traveling home from a music festival out of state. It was late at night. At a crossroad a drunk driver ran a red light and collided with the front of my car. My right leg was all but severed in the middle of my shinbone. I broke twenty-seven bones.
>
> I was taken to an emergency ward. Unconscious. They didn't think I was going to survive. I woke up in the surgery room. But I was not in my body. I was on the ceiling, looking down at my body and listening to the conversations between the nurses and doctors. I could see the dust in the lamp on the ceiling from my perspective. I could never have seen the dust from below because the lampshade was like a bowl suspended around the lights from the ceiling. I also left the surgery room—going through the walls and out in front of the hospital. It was very freaky, but humorous in a way. I remember my attention being drawn to a red sneaker that was on the windowsill of a room on the fifth floor—the fourth window from the western end of the building. Why I was drawn to look at that shoe I don't know. You would think I would have a more important venture to do while I was flying around.
>
> They tried to sew my leg back together again. Then they set my bones and put me in a body cast. What a mess I was.
>
> I didn't come back into my body until I was out of surgery and woke from the anesthetic in the recovery room.
>
> The next day I told one of the nurses who had been in surgery with me what had happened when I had been out of my body. I told her what the topic of conversation was between the surgeon and nurses during surgery. She said I was right—but she couldn't explain how I could have heard it. She agreed to check for the dust in the

surgery room and for the sneaker in the fifth-floor window. Later, she actually brought me the shoe to show me I had been right. We were both amazed!

Larry, like others who have been out of body, obviously produced proof of his OOBE that cannot be explained as an hallucination or delusion.

Conventional Psychiatry and Transpersonal States

Conventional psychiatry and allopathic medicine, the bastions of the Western medical model, would explain away transpersonal phenomena (including out-of-body experiences and near-death experiences, traveling to the realm of death, etc.) as hallucinations due either to the stress, anxiety, and exhaustion of illness; or, in the case of athletes and women in childbirth, the body's chemical defense system combined with hyperventilation. Conventional medicine would say there is nothing intrinsically "real" in the experiences themselves. This thinking leads nurses, hospital administrators, doctors, and counselors to be highly skeptical of patients describing mystical or transpersonal states of consciousness. Clairsentient and clairvoyant abilities, newly acquired abilities to "see" more clearly, are explained away as mere coincidence. A patient who is wrapped up in the novelty of a mystical experience may be put under special watch, as if she is predisposed to a degenerative psychosis.

In looking for the source of transpersonal experiences, we must consider whether these experiences are generated because we are indeed capable of perceiving other dimensions, like the angelic realm, and awakening new powers, like clairvoyance, or whether the transpersonal experiences are simply projections of our brain cell activity, the effect of endorphins, electromagnetic pulsations, and chemical response to primary anxieties. Perhaps both explanations are true. Out of our desire for God, we create an image of Higher Power—which actually has reality, although it may be perceived in different ways by different people according to the neurochemistry of their particular brain!

Yet, if it is just chemical, how do we explain Larry's ability to see the dust in the lamp above the surgery table or the sneaker on the windowsill of the fifth floor during his out-of-body experience? He was unconscious when he reached the hospital and when he was taken into surgery. He was in no position to walk through the hospital, or view the hospital with binoculars, when he was first received there. It was a completely new place to him. Yet somehow he "knew" these bits of odd information as if he had been on the ceiling and peered down into the lamp or been outside the building and close enough to see the shoe on the sill of the fifth floor with his own eyes. If he had been flying around, outside his body, that would explain his ability to see these things.

Our scientists have no way of validating this realm of experience to comply with traditional testing methodology. Psychic phenomena have been studied and validated by researchers in our most respected research institutes. One book that highlights this research is *Higher Creativity* by Willis Harman, from Stanford University and Stanford Research Institute, and Howard Rheingold, a columnist.[10] Scientific inquiry into spiritual emergence phenomena that arise from physical stresses, especially NDE and out-of-body experiences, have not delivered comparable legitimacy. But those who have the experiences seem to have no need for scientific proof; the direct and emphatic knowing bears no need for outside validation. What these people do want is acknowledgment, recognition that they aren't crazy, and the companionship of others who know what they have experienced is real.

Counseling in Hospitals

Hospitals are generally not prepared to answer this kind of need in their patients. Hospital staff are trained more specifically to address physical problems only and not get involved in any kind of "spiritual" questions. But what resources do patients have if they are confined to the hospital, confronting their mortality, looking for help in understanding their lives, and promoting their healing? What resources for support do people have who unexpectedly have a kundalini experience while birthing a child, a near-death experience while being resuscitated, a psychic opening while under anesthesia (see chapter 9), a shamanic journey while in a coma, an opening to life myth while confronting the decision to have a surgery that they might not survive (see chapter 4)? As our resuscitation technology improves, many more of us will be having NDEs and OOBEs in hospitals. We will need help integrating them, or, like the bird flying out of our hands, they will be lost to us.

What we need are counselors in hospitals who can help patients to understand both the physiology of their spiritual experiences and the territory of reality it may present. Information about endorphins and brain chemistry is certainly relevant. The map of transpersonal states of consciousness, much like the one discussed in chapter 1, will also be relevant. I asked Robin, "Can you imagine what might have helped you carry the inner peace you found during your experience of the realm of death into your life after your hospital experience?" She replied:

I would have liked to have had some kind of transpersonal counselor who would have understood what I had been through and could help me integrate it into my daily life and the healing process. Someone to give me techniques to maintain that peace. Now, a year later, I am turning to some spiritual practices of ancient religions. I feel a need for more ritual, more recognition of living in accord with the seasons and with natural cycles.

In the hospital staff, including my doctors and nurses, there was no one with whom I could talk about my inner experience. Some nurses were wonderful—cheerful, funny, uplifting, and gentle. That was essential to my healing process. My doctors were kind as well as excellent technicians and very knowledgeable. But there wasn't one of them who was interested in what I had experienced in myself.

I got the personal support I needed to integrate my spiritual experiences mainly from friends who had some similar experiences. Reading books by Raymond Moody and Elizabeth Kübler Ross has helped. I have also taken a lot of classes in psychology, done personal therapy, and am now taking up art. It has been important for me to incorporate all the aspects of my life: the physical, psychological, creative, and spiritual, like completing a circle, encompassing all.[11]

We need counselors who can help people find a relationship to their own experience, without too quickly cutting it off as bizarre, or crazy, or a chemical reaction. Otherwise, people who have these experiences will not be able to harvest the fruits they bear—increased self-acceptance, less fear of death, more interest in being of service to others. At the very least, counselors could offer explanations, alternate ways of looking at material reality.

Alternative Modes of Healing in Hospitals

At the other end of the spectrum, perhaps we could be more open to alternative ways of healing that specifically address the Subtle and Causal level experience. Larry's healing process might have been enhanced by someone acknowledging his transpersonal experiences and actually working with this capacity as an aspect of healing.

For the eight months I stayed in the hospital, I was in intense pain. I was so sensitive that I felt pain when someone came within three feet of me, as if at that distance they were penetrating my aura, which needed to remain whole to protect my healing. Several times I again left my body and would hover outside of it. When I was out of my body, it was the only time I didn't feel pain. It was such a relief!

I yearned for the out-of-body experience because it gave me a relief, but I also felt afraid of it. I had always identified solely with my body. I had never before realized that I was whole and complete, in a way, outside of my body. I could see, feel, hear. I could travel without being impeded by walls.

Larry had a palpable experience of the Subtle body by his ability to feel pain when someone approached him without even touching his physical body. This is true of many people in a highly sensitized state. What can we learn from them about what the body needs to heal itself?

> During my healing process, my concept of reality shifted dramatically. Since I experienced being out of my body, I came to believe unhesitatingly in my Subtle body. It was more highly tuned than my material body. It could "see" more clearly. I could pick up feelings and thoughts in other people that were not said. It helped me to develop more love and compassion for other people. It gave me a new perspective on life—I identified more with the spiritual aspect, of wanting to love well and be a healer.
>
> I wish there had been a nurse or doctor who had understood what I was experiencing. I tried to explain it to them, but they thought I was having hallucinations as a result of being delirious with pain. I gave up talking to them. I did continue to take the morphine they gave me.

The only real healing that Larry experienced—other than the relief from pain he experienced after taking prescribed painkillers—came from a master healer who visited him in the hospital.

> He worked with my Subtle body directly. He gave me a homeopathic remedy to strengthen my Subtle body. He prayed with me. He acknowledged and called forth the deepest power within me. As this came forth, he showed me how to use it to heal myself.
>
> Today I can walk. I am pain free. I feel buoyant and happy as I never did before.

Kate also attributes her recovery to the guidance she received from a health care worker who was knowledgeable about the effects of spiritual forces on physical health and was not on the regular hospital staff. Kate was cared for by a nurse who worked independently in people's homes. This nurse had schooled herself in alternative methods of healing as a supplement to what she had learned in nursing school.

At twenty-nine, Kate was diagnosed with a fast-moving degenerative arthritis. For six months she lived in bed. She could not walk. Her body was so sensitive, even the sheets moving across her skin caused her terrific pain. She was terribly frightened she would never recover. The doctors offered her no hope.

> Under the guidance of a nurse, I switched my focus from allopathic medicine to healing therapies that worked more directly

with my psychology and spirituality. These helped me come to terms with my emotions, my hurts, and my aspirations. I discovered that the more deeply I went into my own truth, the more the pain from the arthritis retreated. When I finally became a member of a spiritual group three years later, the pain was completely gone.

As Kate opened to her psychology and her spirituality, she made changes in her life to integrate her insights. She became more involved with her spiritual growth. Her husband would not support her new direction, and so they separated.

This full-spectrum nursing care that Kate received is necessary in hospitals where people most need care that supplements the medical model. Someone has to be able to answer questions such as, How do I maintain the insights I have received? How do I integrate this ability to see, or this compassion for others?

A Reason for Medical Emergency

I have come to believe that the medical emergencies I have had were nature's way of helping me come back into balance with my spiritual life. I had not been a peaceful person. I was materialistic, anxious, really not in line with my deep inner life. Now, I am more at peace, more loving, more compassionate, more service-oriented, and more creative. I also have much less need for sleep.

—ROBIN

I regard the accident and the months of pain as an intervention from higher forces who wanted me to learn about my Subtle body. It has been a gift for me.

—LARRY

Having the disease actually helped me connect to spirit. I felt I could commune with some aspect of myself I had never been aware of. . . . The healing from arthritis and the spiritual emergency were times of purification. Through them I was able to let go of parts of my identity that were keeping me from being closer to God. . . .

—KATE

My kundalini awakening was a great shock to me. It opened me to the realm of spiritual emergence and the phenomena that happen in the body as a result of spiritual emergence.

—BETSY

Kate had been an administrator, an executive in a gray flannel suit, working in downtown Manhattan—twelve- to fifteen-hour days—before her illness. "I was a real yuppie! My husband and I had plenty of money. He was a research engineer. We lived in a great place. We didn't have kids. We just worked and had fun. We were thinkers and doers." When the doctors diagnosed her and told her she would soon be restricted to a wheelchair, she was shocked.

Larry, Betsy, and Robin were also shocked by their medical emergencies. They were all active, intelligent people who suddenly became incapacitated. Betsy was a suburban housewife and research biochemist who had no knowledge of kundalini awakening.

Physical stress, particularly in those cases where spiritual emergence phenomena are present, may be considered a crisis of purification; a way the body seeks to balance itself with mind and soul, an intervention from higher forces. This would be as true of peak experiences for athletes and mothers in childbirth as for those in medical emergencies. Perhaps the people who experience these things have a destiny that demands they become more involved in their spiritual lives.

After Kate had physically recovered and was more fully involved in her spiritual life, she had a dramatic spiritual emergency that made her very clear about her life purpose. It was radically different from the materialistic goals that had been her focus in her earlier adult life.

> I was letting go of one life. It was a kind of death. I was also celebrating being in a new life. Within six months of joining a meditation group, based on surrendering to God's will, I had a spiritual emergency. It lasted five weeks. I had more energy than I knew what to do with. I would wake up in the middle of the night and have to get up. I felt very close to God, as though he was right over my shoulder, talking into my ear. It became so intense I became virtually absorbed in simply being open to his voice. I could barely eat. I never wanted to read. I was terribly frightened at the beginning. I cried a lot. It felt as if my life was changing too fast. I felt I was changing dramatically—as if every cell in my body was changing. But I knew it was all for the good. I was becoming a happier, more loving person.
>
> Now that the intensity is over, I am working as a consultant, using my business background to enable me to study the healing arts. I want to be working more frequently as a body therapist. My spiritual life is the main focus in my life. I feel my life's purpose is to give love, even to those people who can't love me back. I feel deeply connected to higher spirit. This has given me the ability to really "see" into the essence of people, the truth of people. That kind of seeing is what makes me especially good at my work.

Thus, the transpersonal experiences that come during physical stress may be a call by the body to balance and wholeness. The physical stress creates an island of reflection in a busy life. Suddenly, the door opens to new emotions, insights on the past, and spiritual revelations. Spiritual experiences, as in the cases of Kate and Larry, become a call to study the healing arts and metaphysics. Robin was inspired to go back to school and become more involved in artistic expression. Betsy began a quest to understand energy beyond biology and religious experience as she had known it. She returned to school for a Master's degree in transpersonal psychology. All of these people found their lives had been enriched by their spiritual experiences. In various ways, each had found an increase in peace, access to resources for self-renewal, increased enthusiasm for life, and emotional well-being.

Just as physical stress may catalyze a search for wholeness in the body, so emotional distress inspires a search for well-being in the heart and spirit. How emotional distress brings us to spiritual emergency is the subject of the next chapter.

7
Emotional Distress

Judith's life was full and easy. At twenty-five, she was happily married and financially secure. She had three children and loved being a mother. One morning, when she went into her baby's room to bathe and dress him for the day, she found him still and silent. There was no medical explanation for his death.

> The bottom dropped out of my life. I was thrown into a deep despair and depressed for several years. This was the first thing in my life that seemed irrevocable. It threw me into a crisis of seeking. The Christian beliefs available to me seemed like superficial platitudes. I needed firsthand experience of the truth.

Mary was overweight, hated her job, and had an intense fear of maintaining an intimate relationship with her lover. As a child, Mary had been abused physically and sexually.

> As a child, I went out of my body up into the corner of the room on the ceiling and looked back at my father hitting me. That way I didn't have to feel the physical pain—or the emotional pain.

Joan was on a camping trip with her family and friends. They had just settled in for the night.

> Suddenly, I heard an eerie whistling noise in the woods in back of us. It was like nothing I had ever heard before or [have heard] since. It went on for minutes. As it came closer, I got the feeling that whatever this was was extremely sad, lonesome, and full of longing.

Three days later, when Joan returned home, she found that her father, whom she hadn't seen for two years, had died the very night that she heard the whistling.

Judith, Mary, and Joan all discovered spiritual dimensions of life through their deep emotional distress. Loss, abuse, emotional deprivation, loneliness, are all catalysts to spiritual awakening—just as they can also be catalysts to emotional pathology. The spiritual emergencies that come as a result of emotional distress appear in any of the six patterns referred to in chapter 3. Judith was opening to her life myth. Mary was having a psychic opening with her out-of-body experiences. Joan was on a kind of shamanic journey, becoming aware of entities in the natural world that communicated directly to her heart. Opening of a karmic pattern, possession, and kundalini awakening may also erupt during times of emotional distress. Whether these experiences enhance growth or lead to a debilitating emotional pathology is a matter of finding appropriate support from friends, a counselor, or a bodyworker, plus one's own abilities to manage emotional intensity.

What causes emotional distress? Usually, it involves a loss: divorce; separation from a loved one because of illness, a move, or death; loss of status by losing a job. On a more diffuse level is the loss we all feel due to social fragmentation: the breakup of families; the frequency of moving our homes; lack of community and social or religious tradition, and the ensuing fracturing of identity. This social fragmentation is felt acutely by children or spouses who become scapegoats for family tensions, those who are abused or emotionally deprived of love and affection.

How is it that emotional crises lead to spiritual experiences? Intense emotional experiences open us to the profound mystery of life itself. Whether it be through listening to emotionally charged music or sitting with a dying relative, we become lifted up out of everyday concerns into a realm where awe, overwhelming grief, fear, or rage are present. The visible order that had defined our world is suddenly gone. It is as if the ship—our personal identity—has burned, and we are suddenly submerged in the powerful ocean of our raw emotions and unconscious forces. We realize how much we need some structure to buffer us from the extreme, uncontrollable conditions at sea. We need a boat—a companion, a social role, an affilation with a church, or some such container for comfort. Still, as we ride the waves, we also become aware of new aspects of ourselves—the capacity to be at one with all of life, the ability to see parts of life previously invisible, the knowledge of how to surrender and trust in Higher Power. Our own unconscious, no longer restricted by an externally imposed structure, reveals to us a deeper level of order through Subtle and Causal level experiences.

There are many stories in this chapter that illustrate how emotional stresses have led to spiritual emergence processes. The difficulties inherent in bringing spiritual experiences back home are also discussed, as well as the role of therapy in catalyzing spiritual emergence.

Emotional Distress Due to Loss

Joan's personal history involved a great deal of loss, even before she experienced the "whistler" at the time of her father's passing away. When she was seven years old, her older brother and sister left for boarding schools, leaving Joan alone at home, suddenly an only child. At thirteen, Joan too was sent several hundred miles away to boarding school. When she was sixteen, her parents separated and sold the family home. With her brother and sister both married and living far away, there were no longer family gatherings, no meeting place, no place to touch home. "I felt I was completely on my own, without really being ready for it. I felt very lonely, and I had no one to turn to."

Still lonely at seventeen, she turned to philosophy to answer questions about the meaning of life. She found words and ideas, but no place to call home. Friends offered her a heartfelt meeting place. But Joan's longing for answers was only satisfied when she began to meditate, turning within to find home. There, she found a stability that no one could destroy, an intimate relationship with Higher Power, truth, love. Devotedly, she practiced her meditation. As a result, she gained a deep sense of communion with nature. She became more intuitive, more aware of Subtle level phenomena.

When the whistler came to Joan's campsite at the time her father died, she was able to accept the extraordinariness of the experience. Psychic phenomena were not strange to her. However, she had never known that disembodied spirits would actually contact her in such a physical way.

> I couldn't awaken my husband. My dog didn't awaken either. That was strange. Then, with the whistling, there were footsteps coming down the hill, but they were wider than a human being would make, maybe ten feet apart. I could hear the brush crackling underfoot. The footsteps stopped about thirty feet behind where our campsite was. Then I heard him breathing long, slow, deep breaths. I sensed he and I were talking telepathically through feelings. . . . I sensed he knew me and cared for me, as if he wanted to touch me. After ten minutes, the whistler retreated back into the woods. Again, the long step and the eerie whistling. Then, a silence.

Joan and her husband were traveling with a Native American shaman at the time. She went to the shaman in the morning to ask him if he had heard a strange noise in the night. He had heard it. He called it the "whistler." She asked her friends in camp if they had heard something strange. No one else in camp had heard anything. Joan then realized her new challenge was to accept that she could hear spirits and communicate with them telepathically. She had never done this before. It scared her:

> Will I always hear the spirits when other people don't? Will I have to talk to them? Will they hurt me? Can I trust them? Can I trust that they are real? Can anyone tell me if they are real or not? Am I alone with this? Will I lead a very different life from "normal people" because I can talk to spirits?

This was a spiritual emergency for Joan. Her fear deepened when she found out that her father had unexpectedly died the very night the whistler had come to her. He had not been very old or sick. He died after falling down a flight of stairs in a freak accident.

Like many people who experience loss, Joan was opened to new spiritual dimensions. The opening was hard and somewhat frightening for Joan. Not only did she have to deal with her opening to spiritual dimensions, but also with her grief at not having seen her father for so long, and then even missing the funeral. She had been in the wilderness, out of reach of telephone or any means of communication to the outside world.

For others, such openings through loss can be exciting, a relief. Many individuals, especially women, around the time of their partner's death go through a particular pattern of experience. They feel a strong sense of connection to their life partner prior to death. Then the sense of connection continues through the death and indefinitely beyond that. Many who are left behind can "converse with" the partner who has passed on, receiving messages telepathically; they feel the presence of the spouse as if he were literally in the room, and sense a deep abiding love passing freely between themselves and the deceased. This love seems even deeper, more unconditional, than the love shared in life. Men and women who have this experience report feeling ecstatic for months in the light of this magnificent love and the realization that life continues after death in a state of love. "Love seemed to be everpresent," one woman told me. Months later, the recognition that the physical relationship with the partner has ended becomes more important. Eventually, a grieving over the loss of the physical contact becomes primary, and each individual begins to think of sharing a day-to-day relationship with someone else. However, the sense of connection to the partner who has passed on and to the reality of the spiritual realms is never lost. As time goes on, this connection simply takes on a different position of importance. Joan said of her father's passing:

The whole experience shook me profoundly. It made me really believe that there is a part of each of us that is immortal. It made me want to connect more with the part of me that is immortal—that has this power to travel in other dimensions. It made me really search to understand the relationship between the spirit each of us is and the physical part of us that is more limited.

Thus, death in the family is often a time of initiation into spiritual realms for those left behind. New capacities for interacting with spiritual dimensions are brought forth and need to be dealt with. Profound questions arise that must be answered. Often death of a loved one is the first time people stop to really question the meaning of life and begin seeking an answer.

Before the death of her baby, Judith had not been particularly involved with any church or philosophy of life.

It threw me into a crisis of seeking. Now, I wouldn't accept the surface of life anymore. I wanted answers to profound questions. Why should a six-week-old die and others live to be ninety? The Christian beliefs available to me seemed like superficial platitudes. The priests who gave my baby's funeral did not reach me. I wanted answers that would really touch me on the deepest level. I knew I needed firsthand experience of these answers. I wanted to pierce through the normal way of living and perceiving life. I wanted to become enlightened.

These profound questions lead some people back to the church they feel most familiar with. Others, like Judith, realize that the conventional church cannot give them what they need. This itself is a death, marking the end of an old identity and birthing them to a highly individualized spiritual quest. This is intensely involving and emotionally stressful in itself. In Judith's case, it led to change on every level of her life:

My husband and I decided to move to Los Angeles in 1961. There were lots of groups that thought they had answers there. I learned how to meditate; I sat with the Self-Realization Fellowship and with several Zen Buddhist teachers. At one time I experienced God as a circle of light in my meditation. This vision and other meditation experiences helped me out of my depression and provided a gradual deepening of my contact with my higher self.

However, my husband did not join me in this personal seeking. He thought I was crazy. He thought he could let go of his personal problems through drinking and working. Soon our marriage was on the rocks. There was a terrible court scene in Los Angeles where he tried to convince the court that I was unfit as a mother. He lost his case. We lost our marriage. This left me alone with three children to raise. I was twenty-nine years old, back in school, away from my parents, with very little money and none of the security that my marriage had given me.

Spiritual pursuits can upset the status quo of family life—especially when they introduce a time-consuming need that was not previously there. The upsetting times are not easy, but the rewards do come. In Judith's case, she not only had to endure her own grief for the loss of her baby and take on an impassioned quest for meaning, but she also had to assume the stresses of being alone with a family to support after her husband, alienated by her new life direction, left her. Judith's awakening spiritually after the death of her baby catalyzed these changes, ultimately taking her to a new identity. Later in life, Judith harvested the rewards of these material sacrifices. She has found her own deep inner peace and communion with Higher Power. For seventeen years, she has been happily married to a man who shares her inner quest for enlightenment.

Profound questioning like Judith's, coming from a grieving heart, has also led others to endure sacrifices and make a substantial spiritual commitment. Sean O'Laoire, forty-two years old, had inconsistent contact with his natural parents when he was a child. His grandparents raised him in the Roman Catholic tradition. As he grew up, Sean was preoccupied with a sense of loss and questions of why he didn't have what other children had. He developed a special understanding of the plight of the poor, the underdog. He couldn't understand why, if everyone is equal under God, we don't all have the same amount of money and food. "This has been a large factor in my becoming a priest and a missionary working in Kenya," he said.

The heart imploring "Why me, Lord?" and opening to its own grief and longing for peace creates one of the most powerful settings for spiritual growth. I have witnessed this time and again with my clients. I see it most dramatically with people whose mothers have recently passed on. It is inside our mothers, in the womb, that we first experience a sense of unity in the physical body. We are one with her, yet we are ourselves at the same time. This memory of and desire for unity are amplified when the mother dies. How then are we to find that deep peace, wholeness, unity? From this point, finally separated from the mother, our only answer is in becoming "one" with Higher Power. Only the divine creative element in the universe, which the Hindus call *Shakti*, can satisfy this yearning. She is that energy within us that calls into wholeness all the parts which have been fractured by loss, urging us toward spiritual emergence.

Social Fragmentation

Since the 1960s, Americans have changed homes more frequently, divorced more frequently, and seen more of the world. It is typical for us to move our homes every three years. With this lifestyle, we become less involved, less identified with our communities and family roots. With the divorce rate rising to almost 65 percent over the last twenty years,[1] we have become more accepting of, or inured to, families moving together and apart. Children growing up with their parents separated are becoming a norm.

The emotional stress this puts on single parents can be overwhelming. This new role in itself demands that people seek every resource of energy within themselves for help. Judith recalls:

> I will never forget one night in particular. I was in absolute terror, knowing I had to raise three children by myself. I cried all night. I thought I was losing my mind. I just couldn't gain control of myself. Then, at 6:30 A.M. I spoke with a friend on the telephone. He gave me the Unity prayer, which I repeated like a mantra all morning:
>
> > May the presence of God surround me.
> > May the love of God enfold me.
> > May the power of God protect me.
> > Thy will be done.
>
> At 11:00 A.M. I went for a walk by myself down to the creek in the trees. I was still crying. I sat down on a rock. I knew I couldn't do everything I had to do in life with my limited self. Soon I heard a voice, an all-pervasive voice that seemed to be coming from everywhere. "You are totally secure," it said. The sound that came with it was "the heavenly choir." The message penetrated my whole being. I really got it.
>
> I began crying for joy. I was full of energy and floating on a cloud. All the words of instruction I had gotten from teachers—Christian, Buddhist, Hindu—seemed superfluous. The *experience* was overwhelming and ecstatic! But, it was just a glimpse of the peace that comes with total self-knowing. It was just a taste of the unchangeable, totally secure God-self that is possible to realize. I have spent a lot of time deepening the experience I had through meditation and prayer, because it did not stay with me in all its initial intensity.
>
> However, the experience was central in helping me become more relaxed about life and more trusting. I now have an inner sense that all events carry perfection within them as well as the experiences I need to become more conscious and compassionate.

Judith's emotional stress as a single parent catapulted her into a profound experience of Higher Power that has been with her over twenty years. It resulted in her finding a way to actualize a fuller spiritual life in the world and function under a tremendous amount of pressure.

Although Judith did not align with a particular religious institution or teacher, she did draw from spiritual practices and spiritual communities to manage the stresses of social fragmentation and loss of her baby and her marriage. With the help of spiritual communities, the Unity Church, meditation, and a mantra, she grew into Subtle and Causal levels of her psyche. She found a way to move toward her own enlightenment, beyond the platitudes that had not sufficiently answered her life questions. Her despair had become a gateway into a richer spiritual life, awarding her deepened faith in the love this universe has to offer.

I would wish this kind of success on all the 8.93 million single parents with children under eighteen who compose 26 percent of our population of families with children.[2] I'm sure they also have their nights of terror. How many cut through their veil of tears? How many strengthen their spiritual awakening, as Judith did? How many fall into despair or emotional pathology, becoming unable to bear the strain? And what happens to the children who grow up in this situation where families and communities are splitting up?

Emotional Trauma of Childhood: Divorce, Physical, or Sexual Abuse

Children separated from one or both parents, through divorce or the complexities of an abusive relationship, characteristically feel a great deal of emotional distress. They are being deprived of something that seems essential to survival—dependable, loving contact from both parents. Some children who grow up without positive contact with one or both parents are catalyzed into a lifelong quest, as we saw with Sean. Fortunate children will find a life path that compensates for their early losses and nurtures their spiritual growth. For most children, this effort to find a life path is a desperate one. Many choose to escape the pain they feel through drugs, alcohol, or some other addiction.

Ted, a twenty-four-year-old research chemist, described a time in his adolescence when he was living with his father and stepmother. They argued a lot, and often saw Ted as the main reason their relationship was not going smoothly. His stepmother was particularly blaming and vocal about it. She was not a positive replacement for his biological mother, who had been very nurturing. Unfortunately, his own mother lived two thousand miles away, and he hardly ever got to see her. Ted's father had custody of him.

There was nothing I could do until I was eighteen and free to leave his house. So I went out for swimming from the age of ten to eighteen. Swimming practice helped me work out my sadness and my frustration.

When I swam long distances, I felt like I aligned with my spirit. My mind would go blank. I wouldn't be thinking about anything— there were no more words. I felt very centered in myself. Calm. You would call it a spiritual experience.

I think I would have been suicidal without it. Things around home were pretty bad. So, I know how to align with my spirit now. It's a great comfort to me and helps me recognize my path through life.

Ted worked with his emotional pain in a healthful manner. He found some respite from his sadness in the altered state of consciousness he reached exerting himself physically. He was part of a swim team at school, and developed a positive close relationship with the coach. He placed in both State and National competitions, to boot. The benefits were physical fitness, increased self-confidence, and the ability to concentrate. Ted had engaged his spiritual emergence process, increasing his ability to act with body and soul moving together.

There are so many other young people, however, who turn to drugs and alcohol to anesthetize the pain they feel when their parents are not dependable or lovingly present. They find comfort in decreasing their connection to the world of other people, and even their own body. (How substance abuse interacts with spiritual awakening is the subject of chapter 9.) Through drugs these young people fall out of contact with themselves and their pain. Although they may have Subtle and Causal level experiences at times on drugs, with no means within themselves to integrate the "drug high," it is not much use. When children have emotionally separated themselves from one or both parents as a result of being physically or sexually abused, the confusion and emotional instability is compounded. Yet the abuse itself, attended by grief and fear, can be a gateway for unusual spiritual experiences.

Children who are being abused, like Mary, whom I introduced at the beginning of this chapter, often have spiritual experiences during the abuse. All the female clients I have worked with who were physically or sexually abused as children have unusual psychic abilities that developed during the time they were exposed to the trauma.

How can anyone tolerate loving someone, being totally dependent on this person, and yet being scared to death of him—without going mad? One way children do this is by leaving their bodies and looking down at the scene from a "safe space." How do children tolerate living in a home where they might be abused unpredictably? One way they survive is by developing clairvoyance or clairsentience, an increased sensitivity to the visual cues and subtle vibrations that indicate an impending threat. Thus, many children develop Subtle level perceptions, such as knowing what others are thinking, being telepathically in touch with the parent who is the abuser, and sensing companionship from higher forces. These sensitivities often carry on into adulthood, when the child is no longer in a situation of being threatened. However, these sensitivities manifest in different ways, sometimes allowing a more expansive relationship with life, sometimes undermining relationships and paralyzing movement in the world.

Mary was just thirty when she came to me for therapy. She complained of depression, being overweight, lack of pleasure in her job, and an intense fear of maintaining a relationship with her lover. Mary had been emotionally neglected as a child, and physically and sexually abused as a teenager. But she had figured out a way to "escape."

> When I was out of my body, I didn't have to feel the physical pain.
> My body just went numb all over. But I did watch what was going on.
> I could sense what was going on with my father. He wasn't thinking.
> He wasn't feeling. He was just kind of out of himself.

Mary not only found a way to comfort herself in the Subtle level experience, away from the source of her pain, she also found in it a way to develop powerful perceptive abilities. However, these abilities did not save her from further abuse in her life. Her cousin molested her, demanding sexual favors of Mary when she was nearing puberty. Mary found some comfort in smoking marijuana almost daily for a few years in high school. When she was seventeen, she was raped by one of her father's friends. Although her father was informed of the rape he never said anything to her about it; in fact, he continued socializing with his friend. This meant to Mary that her intimate family, her source of support, was not caring for her. One result was that she began having severe panic attacks. She could no longer function at work or drive a car by herself.

When she was hospitalized for observation in a psychiatric ward for six weeks, Mary found that she could "see" what was happening on a psychological level with other patients. Her clairvoyant abilities were becoming more evident to her, but they also frightened her. She did not know how she could know intimate parts of strangers' lives without their telling her about them. This was her spiritual emergency. She had no control over the Subtle level, which had opened to her as an abused child, and she didn't know how to deal with it now.

Mary only began to understand her abilities when she was in therapy with a psychotherapist who identified them and affirmed the value of clairvoyance. However, Mary had to take care of some psychological tasks before moving ahead with her spiritual growth. First, she had to learn how to identify and feel her feelings without leaving her body. As she did this, she regained her energy and emerged out of the worst of her depression. Then she had to learn how to communicate the truth of her experience and what she wanted in life. As she finished this task, she went back to school and changed to a better job.

It was also important for Mary to set limits on when her family could contact her. This demonstrated to her her own power to provide a safe place for herself in her life as an adult, and resulted in her no longer having immobilizing anxiety. At this point, she was able to settle into a committed relationship with her partner. Only after these psychological tasks were complete was Mary able to work with the Subtle level abilities she had and devoted some energy to her ongoing spiritual emergence. She took massage training and worked with children at a local hospital. She also began a regular meditation practice. This helped her gain control of her emotional reactivity.

Mary's course from abuse through therapy to spiritual practice is a model for children who have spiritual experiences as a direct result of losing positive contact with a parent and being unwittingly catapulted into spiritual emergence. They need help in first feeling their own feelings, expressing them, speaking their own truth, taking control of their immediate environment, developing tools to work out relationship difficulties in a positive manner. The emotional distress needs to be attended to before the young person is ready to move onward with spiritual growth. However, identifying the parameters of spiritual experiences is useful and affirmative throughout the psychotherapy. Otherwise, the stigma that spiritual experiences are indicative of emotional disease can still infect the psyche with guilt, fear, and shame.

Emotional Distress Due to No-Self

Mary had to build a sense of self. That was her task in therapy. Before therapy, despite her spiritual experiences, she was out of contact with herself: her feelings; her desires; her right to safety, self-expression, and love. Tremendous stress goes along with maintaining life out of contact with the center of one's self, modeling oneself to fit the surrounding social environment. Often this stress is unconscious, becoming conscious only when there is an immediate need to be in true connection with oneself. Mary tried to make herself invisible and nonthreatening, a nonperson, so as not to become an object of her father's abusive behavior. However, her efforts finally resulted in extreme panic, because she did not know how to be herself, psychologically and spiritually, when she was finally in environments where that was appropriate.

Ann was an accomplished, well-to-do woman who experienced a spiritual emergency when her seven-year-old daughter was terminally ill. The young girl had an unidentified disease that was making her skin fall off. Ann consulted over fifteen physicians. None agreed on a diagnosis. None of the people she had assumed to be authorities gave her satisfactory advice. Even the prescribed drugs seemed to be making the little girl sicker. For the first time, Ann stopped assuming that the supposed authorities could be depended upon for help. She began to look inside herself for direction.

She began to focus on her own gut feelings about the problem. Ann questioned her own inner resources. She agonized, "If my child asks me about where she will go at death, do I have the appropriate answers?" Ann was forced to think, "Can I handle life without my daughter?" For three months Ann stayed up every night, holding her daughter so she wouldn't scratch herself and further irritate her skin. One evening, Ann realized she had to let go and let her child die. Shortly afterwards, on that same night, she discovered that she had been using too concentrated an amount of laundry detergent on the child's clothing. It turned out that her daughter's main problems were initiated by her strong allergic reaction to this special biodegradable soap. When she no longer had contact with the soap, the girl began to regain her health.

The child survived, but Ann soon fell terribly ill. After her daughter's crisis, she was "physically and emotionally devastated." It began with influenza and depression. She no longer ate. She couldn't hold anything down. She rapidly lost weight. She was slowly dying.

> For two months, all I could think of was that I must be going crazy. Suddenly, I couldn't help but see deeper truths in life. I could tell what people were really feeling and thinking even though they couldn't even identify it in themselves. I realized how much we usually hide the truth. It made me feel dizzy! I also realized for the first time how terribly alone and hurt I had felt in my marriage and in childhood. I let myself feel the pain. I was consumed with it. I felt uncomfortable in groups, so I stayed alone in my home as much as I could, removed from friends and family.

One day, weak and very vulnerable, she arranged a meeting with her previous yoga instructor. With her help, Ann realized that there was a part of her that she had always pushed away prior to her daughter's illness. She now needed to treat that part as if it were a baby, spending time with it, being gentle with it, nurturing it, cherishing it. These were the spiritual and deeply feeling parts of her that were awakening. Ann was referred to professional transpersonal counseling. She also attended workshops focused on connecting with her inner life. She needed connections with people who were awakening spiritually. She needed a bridge into a life that would support her in giving birth to her spiritual self and helping her find resources to regain her health.

While both Ann and Mary awakened to their higher selves through emotional distress, their avenues of approach were very different. While Ann, with a well-developed ego, had to pass through emotional stress to find her higher self, Mary had to *claim* her personal self before she could *cultivate* a full relationship with her spiritual self.

Feast after Famine: Intensive Workshops

In the process of spiritual emergence, everyone experiences an initiation that sets him more firmly on his path. Judith had her initiation in the meditation groups she attended. Sean was called to the Catholic church after being exposed to Roman Catholicism by his grandparents. Joan relied on a shaman to help her deal with her spiritual experiences. Mary was initiated in psychotherapy. Intensive workshops designed to encourage people to open to their human potential often catalyze spiritual emergence phenomena which serve as initiations.

Sarah grew up outside of New York City in an Italian-Catholic household. Two families, with attending grandparents, parents, and children, lived under one roof. Sarah was married at twenty-four, in 1954, to Randy. She moved to California with her husband in 1962, believing her life would be like her parents' and ancestors. "I would be happily married, have lots of beautiful children, never be alone at any time in my life." That picture began to change after the birth of her sixth child, when her husband told her he was having an affair.

> It broke me apart. At the same time, it opened me up. First, I wanted to smash all the windows in our house (and we had a lot of large glass windows and doors). My husband stayed with me, so I got hold of myself. Still, I went on a rampage. I ripped up my mother's picture. I didn't know why then. With help from a psychiatrist and friends, I realized that I had been holding in anger all my life about all kinds of things. I just had to get it all out now.
>
> The day after Randy told me about his adultery, a priest happened to come by the house to ask why our children were no longer in catechism. I got really angry with him. The church had not allowed me to think for myself as a child. I didn't want my kids to have that experience. I literally threw the priest out of the house. I thought, If the church hadn't molded my way of seeing life, maybe I would have seen that Randy was having an affair. I want to see the truth! So I did

more exploring of my own thoughts and feelings, including beginning hatha-yoga.

Realizing her role as wife was not inviolate and that her passive position in the church did not serve her in finding the truth, Sarah opened to wider vistas in her inner life. Sarah left her family for the first time for a week to attend an intensive workshop led by Carl Rogers, a humanistic psychologist.

> The week was full of peak experiences for me. For the first time I was writing poetry. My mind had expanded. I saw how unlimited my capacities were. I became very telepathic with people. I also fell in love with everyone there. It wasn't sexual, but a profound joy in all that each person was. We were all equal, and all divinely different.
> The most amazing part of the week was literally seeing a globe of light that stretched about ten inches out from my body from my heart. I saw it for days. No one else could see it. But it was totally real to me. I know it was connected to my feelings of really appreciating myself as an individual and realizing my real feelings of heart connection to others for the first time.

Sarah went back home after the workshop (and her psychic opening and kundalini awakening), and began living her life from a new perspective. She wanted to stay in honest emotional contact with people, including her husband and children, to continue to share her light, to continue to have the experience of her spiritual life—not just to passively act out a conventional form of religious life. She left behind the conventional role she had tried to fit at home and in church and began to live more spontaneously, being herself, opening to all of who she was.

Bringing yourself back home after a transformative experience is often stressful. You may need time to integrate the new experiences you have had. You may have left behind all the people with whom you shared your experiences and thus have no friends who understand the transition you are making. Your family may have mixed feelings about accommodating changes you have made. Sarah suffered with this:

> When I returned home, it was very hard to maintain my ecstasy. My children had grown accustomed to my always accommodating their needs before my own. They whined and complained when I sometimes put my needs before theirs. It was very tricky to not fall back into the old pattern of denying my worth all the time. But I committed myself to finding a way to live with my loved ones that allowed me to also have my own inspirations, and my own emotional life independent of theirs.

Unfortunately, Randy did not like the personal changes I was making. He married me because I would be a conventional wife, and that's what he wanted. He wanted to be king in his castle, to be first all the time. Basically, he did not want me to esteem my own thoughts, feelings, or spiritual growth. These emerging differences in values ultimately led to our divorce.

Sarah's story has been repeated for many others who tried to bring their spiritual emergence process back home. As Judith began to commit more of her time to meditation and to seeking a deeper truth, she also struggled within her marriage because her husband thought her change in value system was crazy. He also wanted a more conventional wife, one who was not so absorbed in transpersonal levels of growth. He accused her of being involved in crazy ideas, of being now no longer fit to be a mother. He continued this challenge in divorce court, trying to take full custody of the children. Joan, who was visited by the whistler, chose not to talk to her family about the experience she had had for fear they would think her crazy. She chose to keep her new knowledge to herself rather than risk the kind of rejection that Judith experienced.

Breaking open can be earthshaking for both the participant and her family. Alice, a psychologist from New Jersey, wrote to me about an experience she had several years ago. In the intensity of a large workshop that promised breakthroughs, Alice had an energetic experience that overwhelmed her. She was having a kundalini awakening and opening to life myth. Her consciousness was profoundly expanded. It was a classical spiritual emergency pattern: less need for sleep, ecstatic state, continued ability to maintain connection with people. She was full of creativity and love, living life from a mythic place, believing in the positive nature of her experience. She was in a state of rapture. Her energy was very high. But no one in her community could understand in a positive context what was happening to her.

There were no doctors or therapists in her small community who understood the nature of her experience. The day after the workshop, the leaders of the workshop were gone. Unfortunately, Alice was hospitalized against her will by her family, diagnosed as "manic," and given psychiatric drugs to stop her "symptoms."

Now, ten years after the experience, Alice looks back and realizes that she had a spiritual emergency. It was an emergency, rather than an emergence, because she did not have the personal support or the sanctuary she needed to go through the process that had been started. She needed some more personal help from someone with a perspective that was congruent with the purposes of the workshop. She needed a helper who knew how to assist her in going through all of her experience, rather than inhibiting the symptoms through drugs and preventing the process from unfolding organically. She needed help integrating her more expanded state into her work life and personal life. Without that kind of bridging, she became precariously ungrounded.

Therapists and spiritual teachers who go into communities for an intensive weekend—then leave town—need to take into account the problems participants have in integrating experiences after an intensive session. It seems essential to me that the teachers make available to workshop participants a list of therapists in their locale who have the appropriate training to help them integrate their experiences when the leaders are no longer available. This would certainly be significant in case of a spiritual emergency situation. When workshops are attended by people from distant locations, there also needs to be some provision made for their integrating the intense experiences after the workshop.

The challenge of integrating the feast after famine are magnified in people who attend events from cultural perspectives that are not their own, a Native American purification ceremony, for example. Within the space of several hours, in an environment completely strange to you, you may have confronted profoundly disturbing aspects of your unconscious, been through an extraordinary catharsis, and/or experienced unconditional love for the first time.

Tolerating this feast after famine creates its own kind of stress. On an emotional level, the malnourished psyche is suddenly given a banquet. How does a person digest the rich food? Maintaining supportive connections with people who share intensive weekends or religious retreats can be very helpful. This social network can assist you working with what might otherwise be overwhelming to manage on your own. Then you will not have to carry your fear, your excitement, your questioning, by yourself. The support network can sanction your incorporating your new experiences, yet bear some of the burden of the unfamiliar. Judith, Joan, and Mary developed an ongoing connection to a helper so they could gradually integrate the psychospiritual changes they were making. Sarah developed her yoga practice and went to graduate school to be with other people interested in psychology and human potential. At fifty-six, Sarah now teaches hatha-yoga.

> Now, I can share my light with a broader community. I also have the time and space to stay in touch with my deepest truth, my higher self. It's a much more dynamic, affirming kind of spiritual life than what I was taught as a child. My way lets me be myself, which includes the God aspect of me very fully. It brings me a lot of joy.

The Role of Emotional Catharsis in Spiritual Emergence

When the body expresses the inmost feelings completely, there is a congruence between the body and mind, a unity of motion. This is the threshold we need to construct before entering into transpersonal states. Emotional catharsis often is the builder of this threshold, particularly in people who have been habitually repressing their feelings. Jessica, who is a martial arts teacher and healer, had her first kundalini awakening during a psychotherapy session when she was expressing anger:

> I was letting out some anger toward my grandmother, who had always been very dominating and too involved in my life. She was highly critical, a real disciplinarian. I was beating the pillows with my fists, when suddenly I had this rush of energy up my spine. It stopped in my head. In fact, I felt like I could barely lift my head, it was so heavy. I had this picture that my head was now huge and rested on a tiny body, like an embryo.
>
> This happened at a time when I was teaching judo at the university. I had never missed a class, so I went that day as usual. I remember "throwing" a student, intending to bring her to the floor without hurting her, as I usually do to demonstrate self-defense. To my amazement she went "flying" across the room. She wasn't hurt, but it scared both of us. I stopped class right then. There was so much energy in my body. My body was humming. My perceptions were very sharp. I felt I was in the stream of a profound universal energy I didn't yet know how to handle.

Jessica experienced a very immediate spiritual opening in the midst of her emotional catharsis. The timing of when emotional letting go moves a person toward transpersonal levels is not predictable. Each person is different. One may need to be in psychotherapy for months, letting go of repressed emotions, before he or she feels any sense of peace, let alone Subtle level experiences. You may have a spiritual experience quite soon after being given the freedom to really feel all your feelings.

If emotional catharsis is so intimately tied to catalyzing transpersonal levels of awareness, why aren't we using this as part of religious practice? Evangelicals and charismatic Catholics seem to be the only Christian sects that promote emotional expressiveness within the Church rituals. Many shamanic cultures have practices that catalyze emotional expression. Subud, an Indonesian religion, has a meditation practice designed to allow emotional catharsis. By and large emotion is an unusual part of religious practice in modern society. We seem to believe that feelings are not a fitting part of the religious life.

We miss the point that emotional catharsis in balance with other av-enues of expression can bring about congruence, an integrity within an individual, which helps her toward wholeness and unity.

One of the most dramatic demonstrations of the productive rela-tionship between emotional expressiveness and spiritual growth oc-curs in *holotropic breathwork*, developed by Stanislav and Christina Grof.[3] To the sound of evocative music, participants are asked to breathe more fully than is normal for them. The resulting rise of en-ergy in the body catalyzes the release of repressed emotions, sponta-neous visions, physical sensations, insights, and transpersonal experiences. Within these sessions, lasting one to three hours, it is not unusual for an individual to move through a powerful emotional catharsis and then on to a dramatic spiritual opening following any of the six patterns of spiritual emergency. The Grofs do this work in a group format where each participant is attended by a "sitter" who is available for emotional support if needed in any part of the process. This is an extremely powerful technique, and should not be done without guidance of a trained facilitator. Follow-up work with a transpersonally-oriented counselor is also strongly advised to help in-tegrate the experience.

All of the health practitioners who work with the relationship between emotional catharsis and spiritual experience know that one of the most important things to do for individuals in a spiritual emer-gency is reassure them they are not alone, to let them feel the com-monality of the spiritual experience they are having. This can be practiced by any friend to someone in emotional distress. Jessica summed up the physical aspect of this:

> Hold them. Breathe with them. Hold them in a way that is nonsexual, but hold in a loving way that communicates acceptance and trust. One of the most terrible aspects of having a spiritual opening in the midst of emotional distress is feeling alone and unable to handle all of the different sensations in your body. It feels like there is just too much to hold in yourself alone. Being held by someone else is a great relief. It helps bring you back to yourself. It gives you the sense that it is all manageable.

Reassuring touch helps a person feel safer in an emotional crisis, in the midst of emotional catharsis, as well as in the process of spiritual emergency. This contact may be the catalyst helping a person feel at one with herself, body and mind in unity. Thus, the quality of touch and comforting reassurance can ease emotional distress and even transform it into a spiritual emergence process.

Just as nonsexual touch is a comfort for someone in emotional distress, sexual touch is a stimulant that can also serve to bring body and mind together, taking individuals over the threshold into transpersonal states of awareness. This is discussed in the next chapter.

8

Sexual Experiences and Spiritual Emergency

Making love is a model for living. Live as if you were making love every minute. Make love to this moment, to the car as you drive it, to the book as you read it, to the food as you eat it, to the bed as you sleep in it, to the clothes as you wear them.

Make love with the world and it makes love with you.

—D. A. RAMSDALE AND E. J. DORFMAN,
Sexual Energy Ecstasy

Making love is not only "a model for living," but a spiritual practice in itself. If approached by both partners with the right intention and focus, it is a process to enhance spiritual awakening. What a different idea this is from the conventional concept that sex belongs to the realm of purely physical desires and is thus a distraction from spiritual awakening. These ideas, endemic to many religious traditions, make the body an enemy of the spiritual life. When sex becomes part of spiritual emergence, your body and your lover become allies on your spiritual journey.

Intense sexual experiences are always central to spiritual emergence. These experiences with your partner may happen after you are both engaged in your spiritual path, acknowledging that your sexual relations are part of your sacred journey. Or they may happen as a surprise—opening you to the notion that healthy sexual relations are a natural part of spiritual unfolding, and that spiritual unfolding is a natural part of wholesome sexual relations. Intense sexual experiences without a partner can also be part of spiritual awakening. They may occur within a passionate experience of nature or divinity in some other manifestation, perhaps a dream.

This chapter describes many kinds of sexual experiences that can be part of spiritual emergence and/or emergency. There are guidelines for helping people who are in spiritual emergency as a result of sex. There are suggestions for enhancing sexual experience. In conclusion, I have included reflections on sex as a spiritual practice.

To describe what is possible, what spiritual/sexual experiences can be, I will tell the story of a man and a woman, mature partners, who are using their sexual life as one spiritual practice they share together. Their experiences may be a model, to demonstrate not only what may happen in this realm, but also how the intensity can be handled so that it enhances all of life.

High Sex

Ellen and Roger were both middle-aged and divorced when they met. Each had adult children who were now independent. Both Ellen and Roger had work in the world which was satisfying and lucrative. They had individually chosen spiritual paths in life and were dedicated to their practices and to purifying themselves of old patterns of thinking, perceiving, and behaving that obstruct spiritual awakening.

Ellen has been a member of her spiritual community for over thirty years. Within the tradition, she has made many retreats, fasted for purification, and led a life punctuated by meditation and prayer. Her intention is to "follow the will of God." Toward this end, she has also invested ten years in psychotherapy. For fifteen years, Roger has studied how energy works in the body through the ancient systems of acupuncture and yoga.

When they met each other, they were strongly attracted. Ellen recalled:

> I had decided I wanted to be with a soul mate. Either that—or forget it. I no longer wanted to play around or to share myself with anyone less than someone who could match me at every level—body, mind and spirit. I prayed for help in this direction.

This intentionality was part of the foundation that helped kindle the fire of shared spiritual experiences. Their longing and commitment, acknowledging all parts of the self while connecting to the transpersonal aspects of their lives in prayer, created a shared space where they could build a profound intimacy together. This intention is always present in partnerships that have a strong spiritual element.

The bond was strengthened during lovemaking. Not only were

both satisfied physically, but they had spiritual experiences that demonstrated the strength of their connection in other dimensions.

> Once during intercourse, I had a vision that Roger and I had made an agreement before this life to be together and to bring out the extraordinary in each other and empower each other in world service. The connection we had, the powers we had, were already there in our lives. We just needed to awaken them and manifest them.
>
> I also "saw" that I needed Roger to take me to spiritual dimensions I had no access to by myself . . . despite my spiritual practice. He needed me for the same purpose.

Visions were not unfamiliar to Ellen. She had cultivated them in her spiritual practice and was familiar with psychic phenomena and her own karmic patterning. Roger too was comfortable with his ability to "see" clairvoyantly into the past or the future. Thus, they were able to travel together in these Subtle realms without feeling uneasy.

What *was* unusual for Ellen and Roger was that they found they could spontaneously *share* visions and dreams without talking:

> One day, while we were lying close to each other, not talking, we saw ourselves in a castlelike place. We could look out over the whole planet with 360° visibility. It was a sweet and beautiful place. But the shades were drawn. I knew that if the shades opened, we would be able to see the whole universe. What was more—we could send healing vibrations from there that would touch anything we wanted to touch. We only knew we had shared the same vision when we talked together after it had happened.

In this way, Ellen and Roger as a couple were opening to life myth. Their visions, daydreams, and dreams at night about their relationship took on a mythic, archetypal quality. The metaphorical language of these visions included symbols of kings and queens, gods and goddesses, castles, stars, and planets. They used these visions as a way to explore the archetypes. For example, Ellen came to be more familiar with the male side of herself as "maleness" was shown to her in her own visions. Likewise, in his inner life Roger became more familiar with the feminine sides of himself. Each explored acting out these sides of themselves in the relationship. Ellen became more assertive. Roger became more receptive. Each was becoming more whole.

Opening to other dimensions is seductive, but can be forbidding for one person alone. For Ellen, an intimate partnership offered protection, permitting her to go deeply into transpersonal levels and become absorbed there, knowing she had a lifeline which would help bring her back to external reality.

> We were on a trip together to Canada. In our lovemaking one night, I went way, way out into a gigantic space. I felt I had no lim-

itations. I could see far. Many truths were available to me. It was beautiful and blissful. I saw many connections that make up the fantastic interweaving pattern of this life. I didn't want to stop being in this inner space. I felt I was in the flow of the Tao, at the center of truth. This continued for over twenty-four hours.

After this experience, Roger became worried because Ellen was acting strangely. She was talking very little. She was dropping things. She was wandering off. He didn't want to leave her alone with the luggage in the airport. He kept asking her, "Are you all right?"

> I hardly answered him because I was so absorbed with the state of consciousness I was in. I was tracking things—finding connections on an archetypal level that I had always longed to see. I was very busy.
>
> Then I came back down to earth to go to work after the weekend. The transition was not difficult for me. But it concerned Roger at the time.

Ellen was lucky that Roger knew that even though he was scared by the changes in her, he needed to support her, to allow her to be deeply engrossed in her process, even though it was inconvenient for him. Through his own spiritual experiences, Roger had learned to trust the process of spiritual opening, to know that at times there would be very unconventional experiences that were important to go through and not suppress. The special care and attention that Roger gave Ellen, even though he was somewhat afraid, helped her move more deeply into her own transpersonal growth. Ellen came out of the dramatic opening with more resources to share in the relationship.

Ellen and Roger's sexual relationship has enriched not only their own lives, but their entire world. The sense of wholeness that has resulted has made them more productive in their work, more interested in the well-being of others, less afraid of having loving feelings toward all people, and more physically healthy. And in line with their intentions, their sexuality has become a spiritual practice for them.

When sex becomes a spiritual practice, intercourse is a template for your relationship to God, the symbol for the highest state of consciousness. Can you let yourself go into it, become one with it? Sexual union is a place to practice surrendering to a Higher Power, to let yourself be swept away and simultaneously remain conscious. It is a place of the most profound heart intimacy, of "I" and "Thou." When sex is a spiritual practice, it is a means to have the energy of love fill your whole system. Physical sensation, the heart and spirit, become one. This unity is the foundation for moving into transpersonal levels. This unity is an invitation for the kundalini to rise.

As in all spiritual practices, if sex is to be part of an individual's spiritual emergence, it must be dedicated to God. This dedication is a setting of intention: "May the fruits of this love benefit all sentient beings"; "May the joining of our bodies and spirits assist us in becoming one with God." Ellen describes it this way:

> We use our sex life as a sacred act, a prayer to the Divine. Our sexual life is a spiritual practice, a way we access transpersonal levels of consciousness. It is also a way to praise God, to love God. We work with each other through physical touch and talking—to clear out problems each of us have which keep us from being more attuned with Subtle levels. We breathe together, opening to the harmony between us and between us and the natural environment. We pray for world peace and the health of our friends. We give each other the opportunity to enter into oneness with God. We express deep gratitude for the richness we have found in our lives together.

After an intention is set, it should be carried through the course of lovemaking. Remember what you have said. Do not "walk on your prayers" say the Lakota Sioux. If your sex is to be part of your awakening to Atman, do not begin by becoming drunk with wine or marijuana, which dull your consciousness, or lose awareness in the midst of intense sensations.

Sex demands attention, wakefulness—just like all spiritual practices. It is a mirror in which you can see into yourself, into all of who you are. But you cannot see anything if you are too distracted or drunk to look. The quality of your attention will be interwoven with the quality of your sex. The two encourage each other. What a wonderful incentive to improve the quality of your attention if it improves the quality of your sexual experiences! The more awake you are, the more aware you are of subtle energy, the more you can include these subtle sensitivities into your lovemaking. Bringing love through the quality of your touch can elevate your partner. It is a much different experience from just stimulating sexual feelings through touching the "right" places.

When sex is shared as an embracing of subtle energies, it also becomes an act of purification. It is similar to meditation in this way. Describing the meditation process, Philip, a teacher of transcendental meditation, told me:

> When you first begin to meditate, using your mantra to focus, you will experience all kinds of mental and emotional garbage arising. Many people get very sleepy. Giving in to these feelings is part of purification. It's like peeling off layers of an onion—where the center will be God-consciousness. When you are on the first layer, you will want to sleep. Let yourself. If you then return to the practice—after you have done all the sleeping you need to—you will find a new layer. Maybe it is a stream of thoughts. A laundry list. Worries about your job. Just let it happen—and continue to say the mantra as you

sit. The thoughts will wind down by themselves. Then comes another layer. Maybe a strong feeling arises—fear, grief, jealousy. You let yourself feel it, be with it. Let it move in your system. It will eventually play itself out. Then the next layer. Maybe strong physical movements, muscular spasms that arise spontaneously. Surrender to them. Let them be. Eventually, underneath it all—if you continue to practice your awareness—you will arrive at the center. You will become absorbed in a state of God-consciousness.

Sex, as a spiritual practice, can be a very similar experience when practiced with awareness. As the experience becomes more intense, you may feel sleepy, or have a strong feeling, or recall a memory that absorbs your attention. Eventually, when all this has cleared, you will find spiritual experiences. In the beginning, you need to surrender to all of the other things that can happen.

There are not many people who have prepared so fully to accommodate the intense experiences that Ellen and Roger had. Most of us have neither a conceptual framework, nor an emotional preparedness, nor the spiritual readiness to manage this kind of intensity so gracefully. Most likely, you won't go into spiritual experiences in this realm unless you have some grounding and a way to manage the experience. However, just as a child can have spiritual experiences without first having a mature sense of self, older people can have profound spiritual experiences without intending to. What happens to those who unexpectedly fall into *high sex experiences*?

Falling into High Sex

Within the comfort of being physically close, with affection, personal boundaries dissolve. We let down our guard, our defenses. When we become open and vulnerable, it becomes possible to feel "at one" with our partner. Conflicts melt away. At the high point, maleness as opposite from femaleness has little importance. The world of duality takes on a dreamlike quality. The softness of love colors the world in harmony. This sense of "oneness" is a template of the unity experience of the Causal level. It may even provide the threshold for entering the Subtle or Causal levels.

Phil and Celina had been lovers for about one month. Being together physically was very satisfying for both of them, and it seemed to be getting better and better. Celina sensed that Phil was a loving guy with a very big heart.

> I remember one night during intercourse. We were both absorbed in a very passionate, physical way with each other. The focus was on our genitals. Suddenly, it seemed as if his heart became like a penis penetrating into my heart. My heart became like a vagina—opening to

receive the new thrust of energy from my partner. Then, I felt my actual heart pulsate and throb as if in orgasm, followed by a tremendous release of energy. The only word for it is *ecstasy*.

Phil did not have the same experience Celina had, but he shared her joy. He was glad to be opening into this new territory. In fact, they began exploring this potential with more intention.

> During sex, we would sometimes focus on cycling the energy we generated in a circle moving from his penis into my vagina, then up into my heart and into his heart and down again to his penis. Or the other way around. This focus added a dimension to our sex life that brought us closer together, and opened up our hearts to other people as well. It was the start of an extraordinary transformation in both our lives.

Phil and Celina had not been involved in *Tantric* spiritual practices before this experience. (Tantric practices derive from a form of Buddhism focused primarily on the energetics of spiritual awakening that are both physical and Subtle.) But after their openings in sexuality, they began growing in the subtle energy aspect of their lives together.

Celina was fortunate that Phil was open to her experiences. It can stimulate a real crisis in the relationship when one partner gets high and the result is that the other feels his or her sexual identity is being threatened and gets defensive.

Angelica had been doing hatha-yoga for several years. She had begun to feel the flow of energy in her body and wanted to explore that flow in sex. She wanted more intimacy with her husband, Mark. She wanted to share more of herself with him. She trusted that if she let go more, she would be able to get closer, even though Mark didn't share her interest in Subtle energy experiences.

> Well, I did let go more: I began to be multiorgasmic. Sometimes, I would become deeply absorbed in the energetic experience, the bliss that moved through my whole being. He never had this kind of thing happen to him. Mark began to feel left out. He didn't know what was happening to me, he couldn't understand it. When I explored being on top—with him beneath me on his back—I had even bigger experiences of orgasm because he touched my "G-spot" with his penis. But he hated the power of my experiences. They intimidated him. He interpreted them as meaning that I was more powerful than he was, an attack on his sexual identity.

Right around this time Mark began to have an affair. Several years later, Angelica found out who the woman was. She appeared to Angelica to be someone who likes to be with a man who is always the one in control.

Angelica and her husband eventually divorced. Mark never developed an interest in the high level energy experiences Angelica wanted to have with him. Together as a couple, they did not have the resources to handle the spiritual emergence processes that Angelica was exploring.

Sex as the Experience of Mystical Union

> I had just come back from my psychotherapy session and felt really in touch with myself. My partner happened to be at home, and we decided to make love. As I became excited, my whole body began to undulate as if it were one big wave from the top of my head to the tip of my toes. I felt I was soul-to-soul with my lover. There were no boundaries between us at all. We dissolved into oneness.
>
> —FRANCESCA, thirty-eight

As suggested by Francesca's story, in the experience of unity found through lovemaking each person may have a Causal level experience. Any of the six patterns of spiritual emergence described in chapter 3 is also possible prior to or following the peak Causal level experience.

If the couple has the resources to adapt to the unusual circumstances that happen as a result of spiritual experiences, the events will be part of their spiritual growth as individuals and as a couple. This is illustrated in Ellen and Roger's opening to life myth together. If the two do not have the personal resources to support each other during the spiritual opening—as in the case of Angelica's husband being scared by her extraordinary energetic experiences in their lovemaking—the result may be a spiritual emergency, in which either partner or both become overwhelmed with fear and can no longer be available to an intimate relationship. Counseling and education may ease this kind of crisis. Chapter 11 has suggestions on helping someone in spiritual emergency.

Following is a brief synopsis of how the other forms of spiritual emergence may be experienced in the love relationship.

Shaman's Journey

> I was sitting outside in the lap of my lover one day, after we had been making love. We had an extraordinarily close relationship. As we sat quietly, not talking, enjoying the closeness, a wild hawk (one of my personal spiritual allies) came out of the sky and landed on my knee. It sat for a full two minutes, then flew off. This was a powerful example to both of us of our kinship with nature and how our physical closeness brought us to be more involved in that world.
>
> —LINDA, thirty-two

Especially after making love, you may feel "renewed," with a sense of feeling closer to nature, in tune with your partner, more sensitive to your environment. When these feelings are magnified, you may actually feel reborn, full of childlike wonder, vulnerable, and at one with the natural world, telepathically in communication with your partner, sensing many of the minute shifts in vibration in your environment. This is the time that the natural world that you have special kinship with may dramatically enter into your awareness. For Linda, who is quoted above, the hawk sitting on her knee was an affirmation of her special connection with nature that she was allowed to feel in the special relationship she had with her lover. A hawk had never come to her alone. There was something about her being so close to her lover that gave her the opportunity to be in closer contact with wildlife. This unity with nature helped her let go of her old concept of self as separate from nature, and give birth to a self-concept that was at one with the natural world. Thus, it was part of her shamanic journey.

Kundalini Awakening

In the story of Phil and Celina, we saw an example of kundalini awakening. The rush of energy Celina felt in her heart when she felt penetrated by Phil was pranic energy. Other manifestations of kundalini prevalent in sexual experiences are muscular spasms in various parts of the body, rushes of heat and/or cold, and vibrations that make the whole body "hum" or "light up" with energy. The effect is always an opening of the senses, including the heart and the intuition, to be more sensitive to other people and to nature.

As the kundalini rises, it always increases your desire for sex, and often your ability to have orgasms as well. A woman can move from being anorgasmic to having multiple orgasms with very little stimulation by opening to allow more pranic activity in the body. A man may experience more desire for sex and/or an increase of energy spreading throughout the whole body that may make multiple orgasms possible for him. This may create a big change in his sense of himself as a sexual being. It will also shift for a woman the way her lover experiences her. Ideally, she and her partner will have the inner resources to welcome the influx of energy. Men need to focus on containing their ejaculation in order to enhance sexual functioning as the kundalini awakens. With increased sensitivity to prana, men can also have multiple orgasms without ejaculating and thus move into more energized Subtle level experience through sex without depleting their energy.

One of the difficulties of kundalini awakening is that it can result in an obsessive desire for sexual activity. A transpersonally oriented psychiatrist told me about a client referred to him for mania. He had been diagnosed as manic-depressive. This doctor noted the opening-to-life-myth pattern in the man's dream-life and felt that the sexual obsession was part of kundalini awakening. Rather than use drugs to inhibit his client's impulses, the doctor attempted to persuade the man to use his increased energy level to intensify his spiritual practice. Fully allowing the process of kundalini awakening demands using some of the vitalizing energy for spiritual work.

Psychic Opening

Visionary experiences, clairvoyance, and clairsentience—all aspects of psychic opening—often accompany spiritual awakening in sexual experience. This is illustrated in the story of Ellen and Roger. They had an increase in the intensity of psychic phenomena in their lives after they became lovers. Ellen was able to move more deeply into visions that revealed archetypal phenomena in the world around her. Ellen and Roger became telepathic with each other, being able to sense what was happening to each other even though they were miles apart. As they grew closer in their lovemaking, each was able to feel more what was happening in the other, as if it were his or her own feeling. Each one also had a sense that their relationship was protected by a guardian angel, a protective aspect of Higher Power.

Opening to Karmic Pattern

Ellen and Roger also became aware of past lifetimes they had spent together as they had more intimately bonding experiences in lovemaking. Sharing these visions increased their insight into the dynamics of their present relationship. It gave them perspective on why they could establish such a strong trust in each other, and also why they have particular problems.

This facility of opening to karmic pattern through lovemaking can become natural for some people who have lived more of their lives in the Subtle realm. The increased sensitivity to Subtle realms then makes it more difficult to have just a physical encounter in sex. Junette, a forty-two-year-old woman who has been meditating for twenty years, told me:

> When I make love with a man, I immediately begin to see into his soul. I can perceive what seem to be his past lives. I get visions of how he and I have known each other before. It is exciting in one way, but it absorbs so much of my attention that I can't just relax and have a physical experience like other people can. It works better for me to have one steady partner. . . . Then, sharing about past lives becomes

one aspect of our lives, and I relax into sharing on many different dimensions: physical, emotional, intellectual, and spiritual.

As spiritual experiences become part of an intimate relationship, the intensity of the connection between two people becomes greater. It can go beyond time and space through psychic openings and openings to karmic pattern. This enriches the relationship and the bond between lovers. However, it brings with it the challenge for each person to maintain their own individuality in the midst of developing their oneness.

Possession

> When I make love frequently with my lover, I begin to feel so close to her, so bonded, that I lose touch with who I am as an individual. I love the sense of merging we get to. It's a great comfort, and it makes me high. But I really have trouble coming back to myself. It is as if I have been "possessed," as if something has been taken away from me that is precious to my very survival as well as my growth. When I begin realizing how absorbed I have gotten in our oneness together, I usually feel very threatened. Then I find something to get angry about, or I withdraw. That helps me come back to myself. Then I no longer feel possessed.
>
> —JEREMY, a sculptor, forty years old

This is a spiritual emergency: There is a unity experience in lovemaking, then an incapacity to manage the feelings that result, an inability to integrate them into life in a way that is wholly positive. Instead, this man (and it could as easily be a woman) experiences bliss intermittently with anger or isolation. This is a frequent manifestation of spiritual *emergencies* related to sexual experience.

The fear of being taken over, of being possessed, which is stimulated by the unity experience, can have even more devastating results if you are not sure if you are homosexual, heterosexual, or bisexual. One aspect of the unity, which Ellen and Roger describe, is becoming more aware of the androgyny of each person. If a person who is already insecure in his or her sexual identity (and this is especially under scrutiny in adolescence and in mid-life crisis) opens to the inner archetypal realm of being both male and female, the opening can catalyze overwhelming confusion.

What do you do if your partner is having a spiritual emergency as a result of sex?

Spiritual Emergency in the Bedroom

There are four elements for helping someone in spiritual emergency: catharsis, providing sanctuary, grounding, and education. What do these look like "in the bedroom"?

Catharsis: Having sex often stimulates emotions. The presence of love and attention also acts as a purgative. Suddenly, the sadness connected to having had sex in the past without love is felt. This may be involved with family or romantic relationships. There may be crying in fear, or joy. Marie, a forty-year-old businesswoman, said:

> One day, while making love, my partner dropped into a level of deep pain connected to his mother not being there for him as a child. We disengaged from genital sex and I held him as a loving mother would. I encouraged him to feel it all. He must have sobbed for three hours. After that, he felt open, vulnerable, and much less bound up in a childlike fear that I would leave him. From that day, it seems as if he laid claim more fully to his adult male sexuality.

Marie and her partner Ben, had had some introduction to Tantric sex practices before they had this experience. Thus, they felt somewhat at ease with surrendering to the strength of the feelings and the need for expressing them. Their story illustrates how it is more important to go through the feelings, feel them, express them rather than just analyze and objectify them. The emotional catharsis brought each of them more into the moment, more aware of the power behind their love — both personal healing power and connection to Higher Power.

Both Marie and Ben could be a support for the other. Ben also had times of holding Marie when she felt the pain she had been carrying: feeling that something was wrong with her being a woman, or being a sexual being, or having sexual energy. She needed to cry, to rage, to contract in fear at different times during the lovemaking they shared together. Her body was letting go of the trauma she had experienced in being molested as a child. This catharsis was part of her releasing old patterns of thinking and behaving to give birth to her mature womanness. In experiencing all these feelings, Marie healed and awakened to more fullness as a mature woman. Marie had been unable to have orgasms. The cathartic healing she and Ben shared was essential to Marie becoming orgasmic for the first time in her life.

The deep trust they shared also allowed each of them to discover new aspects of their own capacity to give love. Marie said:

> While Ben was crying, I felt I was the archetype of Divine Mother. I felt loving, unconditionally loving, toward him and the whole world. I dropped all expectations of the way I wanted him to be with me. I

dropped all consciousness of time going by. I was just there for him. It was a beautiful experience. It helped me realize my own capacities for loving. I never before knew how well I could be there for another person.

This kind of experience of love only happens when both partners feel safe, so that they can open up to themselves and each other. Catharsis and holding loving attention on a partner in catharsis ultimately results in a bond that is clear and energetic. Marie said, "The clear energy carries over to every other facet of my life. I have felt in meditation that every cell in my body was close to orgasm!"

As you build intimacy with your partner, you become a sanctuary for each other; you provide a safe place to be yourself with another. The partnership is then a special safety zone and a place of unity.

Sanctuary: Time together to let go to real feelings when needed—in an atmosphere of acceptance and respect—is a sanctuary. It is a sacred space of coming together in yourself and in your partnership. Of course, time to yourself in solitude, when needed, is also an important sanctuary.

Engage yourself fully with the present moment: "What do I need right now in order to feel good about myself?" Surrender to yourself, your deeper self. There is no goal here other than to be yourself. How can you serve this goal in yourself? How can you serve this goal in your partnership?

In the together-sanctuary take time to talk very directly with each other: "I am afraid when this happens. I don't like it." Or, "I like this. I want more. I just have to take it more slowly." Or, "I never dreamed this could happen. I don't know what to do, or what I should do. I feel confused." Allow time for your thoughts and feelings to be expressed. It is the holding back of honest communication that can transform a loving sanctuary into a repressive prison.

Grounding: If your partner seems disturbed because the energy in your personal sharing is becoming too powerful, or too subtle, it is usually best to pause in your sexual activity. The heights of a unity experience or the transformative perceptual changes of spiritual experiences may make you feel strangely out of touch with yourself for a period of time. Marie illustrated this:

Since exploring my sexuality with my partner, I have become orgasmic and had many spiritual experiences during sex. I have had memories of myself as a baby. I've had past-life recall. I have had energetic awakenings so that energy was flowing more completely throughout my whole body. At times I have felt overwhelmed by the intensity of the experiences themselves.

If the intensity is overwhelming, rest. Relax together. You probably aren't in bed unless you like each other. Talk, cozy up in the covers—as if they're swaddling clothes—or hold each other. Breathe together gently. Listen to music. Allow the energy you have shared to spread throughout your bodies, rather than be concentrated in your sexual organs, heart, or some other part of you.

If one of you is upset, he or she may well need to take some time away, to take some space to be alone to reestablish grounding. If this is the case, disengage gently. Let your partner know you need time to yourself. Walk around. Be in nature. Dance the movement of your true feelings . . . stretching in new ways, or being still and small. Move in ways that are congruent with your real feelings. This will help you allay your fear. When you objectify your experience by talking about it, praying about it, or moving with it, it will become less frightening.

Education: At some point, you will both feel the need to talk about your experience together, to understand it. Each will want to have some concepts to think and talk about what happened. Marie and Ben together explored new attitudes: reading, discussing, and trying things out physically.

Since there are so few of us who have knowledge of the transpersonal aspects of sexuality, we may need to be educators for each other. It was Marie's finding out about the G-spot that allowed her to open up to full orgasm. The sacred spot is an area on the interior wall of the woman's pubic bone that is especially sensitive and holds the key to profound sexual energies. After stimulation of the G-spot many women ejaculate, and have a higher frequency of orgasms.

> I am an example of a person who had physically closed down as a result of the conditioning I received as a young person. I was really uptight. I was not very aware of energy in my body. I paid a lot more attention to what I looked like—my hair, my facial expression, my weight. I loved to make love, but it was more of a physical experience for me rather than a heart experience or a spiritual experience.
>
> When I found out about the G-spot, also called the sacred spot, it changed my whole way of thinking about what was possible in sex. Before finding out about this, I was not orgasmic—only clitoral orgasms infrequently, never uterine orgasms.

Finding techniques to bring new energy into sex vitalizes marriage. A commitment to monogamy becomes the ground on which to structure a relationship that offers an oasis of unity—psychologically healing, sexually exciting as it keeps growing, and spiritually expansive. There is no limitation to the fullness that can be experienced in this kind of marriage. The relationship keeps growing into fuller experiences of love and divine energy. It also enhances each individual's own self-realization.

Those of you who are interested in using your sexual activities as a form of supporting spiritual emergence will be interested in the following section, which offers guidelines.

Spiritual Emergence and Sex

Conventionally, the act of making love (or having sex) is oriented toward achieving the goal of orgasm for both parties. However, there is a different way of making love that can lead partners into greater awareness of self and spiritual emergence. This has been called "ecstatic sex" or "process sex." Orgasm is not the goal; the goal is to deepen one's experience of the moment, transcend the physical, and unite with Higher Power. The act is based on surrendering to the spiritual dimension of ourselves while subscribing to the belief that the body is the temple of God, through which we can become closer to our spiritual selves. The central element for sex that includes spiritual ecstasy is a sincere heart that is willing to surrender. Only after this heart quality has been cultivated do techniques and special activities to build intimacy really work.

What is this heart quality about? It expresses itself in a longing for unity with Higher Power, Love, or God, as a dynamic intention. It expresses itself in a sense of adventure, a willingness to explore new territory, to embrace what has been hidden behind social conventions. It shows itself through the face of love, the desire to know love more fully.

This hunger for love can only be satisfied through surrender. Surrendering to yourself—the elements of your personal sexuality as well as greeting the archetypal, collective elements of sexuality. This is the realm of process sex—where sex becomes a journey of self-revelation, a practice of remaining present with yourself rather than self-forgetting. It is very different from "conquest sex"—where the goal of orgasm is primary, and the minds of lovers are possessed by techniques to stimulate erotic sensation. Process sex depends on the quality of *being* rather than *doing*.

Paulina and Michael (who had a Causal level experience described in chapter 1), described their discovery of process sex this way:

MICHAEL: When I was twenty-nine years old, in 1984, I met Paulina. She was thirty-three years old. Our sex was normal and great.

PAULINA: We were consumed with each other. We wanted to be together all the time. Then, after several months, we both felt we had to stop it, like it was damaging our relationship. We actually stopped having sex for several months until we were married. It was really hard to do!

MICHAEL: The relationship I had just come out of was very physical. It was about "conquest"—going for orgasm. It was intoxicating, but it was pushing me to exhaustion. I went for more and more of it, but it became less and less of a deeply satisfying experience.

Paulina and I had something different. We had a good relationship on the physical level, but our relationship had a lot of other dimensions.

A problem came for me after we were married. We had normal sex for about a year. Then my ability to have sex went down. I started to feel depleted. I could feel this as a weakness in certain parts of my body. There was no physical illness connected to this. I wanted sex less. This was very difficult for Paulina, because she was feeling very open and loving.

PAULINA: I felt rejected. It seemed to me Michael just didn't want to feel close to me . . . as if being close to me was hurting him. I wanted Michael to feel that being close to me was nurturing to him. I also felt that Michael was controlling my sexuality. If *he* didn't want to have sex, then what was I going to do?

I decided to let our spiritual life be my main focus. If I let my physical desires, or my psychological stuff be the main driving thing, then it was very difficult.

MICHAEL: I was realizing that I wanted to be done with that level of sexuality that is based in conflict. I didn't know what the next thing was. I was vaguely aware of Tantra and metaphysical thought. But, I was more involved with what was happening to me physically. I needed some down-to-earth information to help me on a physical level.

Fortunately, I ran across some information by Mauntik Chia, a Chinese Taoist teacher. I started doing the exercises he suggests. In two weeks, my sexual expression changed completely. I had found a way to have sex without ejaculation.

PAULINA: Our sex shifted overnight. Michael was interested in sex again. He could go on and on for hours without hesitation. It was amazing.

MICHAEL: I could now explore the relationship without getting physically depleted. It was fine to do that all the time! This kind of sex is not so much a physical exploration as a spiritual exploration. I have to be very aware of my energies, to track my energies. Otherwise, I'll ejaculate.

Without ejaculation, there is no goal to sex . . . which cuts out a lot of the obsessive thinking about when and how you are going to ejaculate, and what it will be like. Without the goal, you don't have the obsessive thinking, so your mind is open to experience more what is happening in the present. It's about consciousness and awareness, and the quality of connection with your partner. And, you know that going into it.

It's also a slower process without the focus on ejaculation. The change in rhythm also helps to increase awareness.

PAULINA: I could feel the difference. As Michael stayed in the "process," it created a space for us that was much deeper and much more open. It was wonderful. I also got inspired to explore my sexuality in a deeper way.

MICHAEL: All these changes have enriched our relationship on every level. In the process each of us has become more involved with our spiritual practices in church, as well.

Both psychological and physical techniques to support this unusual kind of surrender are necessary. You need to be able to let go of the images you have from movies, television, parents, and peers that have conditioned your thinking about what sex "should" be about and what you "should" be like during sex. This letting go will create the space for you to find who you are as distinct from what social conventions want you to be. You need to be good enough at communication to express your feelings, either being in the emotions or talking about them. Physical techniques are also tied to an ability to express feelings: Can you allow the love you feel to flow through you into the quality of your touch, the quality of your glance?

There are many ways to learn this method of sexuality. Some spiritual teachers can teach couples. There are a number of books that are helpful. Some relevant titles are listed at the end of the book. Some workshops are also available. As has been illustrated, this is an extremely powerful arena for initiating spiritual experience. The techniques are powerful and can create a great deal of fear and confusion if not practiced with care and true readiness on the part of both partners.

Charles and Caroline Muir lead workshops that educate sexual partners about the potential for spiritual emergence in sex, literally "how to" make sexual activities congruent with spiritual growth.[1] The physical environment of the workshop is like a sacred sanctuary, and full of beautiful flower arrangements. Simple rituals, like meeting the other participants in silent greeting and inspirational music facilitate heart opening. Massage and yoga are taught in a form to inspire feeling love for oneself and the divine. A strong theme is to let go to who you are and to facilitate your partner to do the same.

James, a teacher in his fifties, attended the Muir workshop ten years ago. He summarizes what the essence of what men and women need to know about physical techniques while they master psychological techniques of letting go:

1. Orgasm and ejaculation do not necessarily have to go together. Gaining physical control over ejaculation, what few men know

about, allows you to be in an orgastic state for minutes, even hours.[2]

2. Energy can move two ways. It can go out from the body, and it can come into the body. If a man lets the energy go inward, that changes the whole experience of sex. He then finds the dimension of receiving and surrendering, which is the complement of giving and asserting. If a woman lets her energy move outward, it adds a new dimension to sex as well.

3. There are different paths available to the high charge of energy in sex—not just energy moving into the genitals, but energy moving up the back of the spine revitalizing the brain, the heart, or other centers.

4. There is a fundamental difference from being in the world of duality and the world of unity. Going from twoness to oneness is the "Big Jump." You do that in stages. As you begin to know that there are these two ways of being, you realize in the world of duality the law is that opposites attract. In the world of unity, the law is that like attracts like. They are both true. One applies in one world, one applies in the other.

5. Ecstatic sex is a matter of being in touch with, literally, the unity in the other person and in yourself. You need to literally be able to touch it—bring it about in the other person through touch.

6. The next thing is how to go into unity without losing your consciousness. After having orgasm the old way, you lose consciousness after orgasm. It is better to stay awake to the tremendous release of energy and letting go during and after orgasm. Continue to be the experiencer . . . guide how you are going to let the energy flow through you without losing the unity. This is not an intellectual experience—it is an energetic and spiritual focus that subtly regulates energy. This focus and regulation is a large part of the ecstatic experience.

Sexuality as Shared Spiritual Practice

Unlike meditation, which is an individual spiritual practice, in sex you have a partner with whom to share your process as you let go of the veils that have kept you separate from your deepest self. Ideally, your partner helps you in your letting go to deeper layers of yourself. How can he or she do this?

1. **Be willing to have sex be a purification as well as a celebration.** We are usually attached to having sex be fun, exciting, and/or passionate. There is certainly no blame in that desire. However, if you and your partner see that sexual activity is a stage for spiritual

growth, then you can also be more welcoming toward the unexpected emotions, pranic activity, and spiritual experiences. This welcoming attitude will demand that you have less attachment toward sex "just" being fun, or exciting, or a physical release. You will need to let go of those pictures and, sometimes, explore sex without the goal of orgasm. Let your sexual experiences take you deeper into yourself, and share what you find with your partner.

2. **Be willing to be helpers for each other** as you purify as well as in your celebrating life. As you explore sex from this different attitude, you may find that the roles you have been playing in sex give way to new, more natural expressions of sexuality. Be willing to adventure together and help each other out—as two explorers in a new land.

3. **Cultivate ways of processing together.** You might want to enlist the assistance of your lover to help you develop insight and work through emotional and physical tensions if they arise, helping each other surrender. This will involve letting go into the experience first. Then letting go into a deeper level of yourself after that. For example: One partner may get very scared, remembering a time of being molested, feeling uptight about letting go to sexual feelings and being penetrated. The other partner could ask, "What is going on? It feels like you are scared. Tell me about it. It's okay. Feel what is going on. I'll be with you here as you go into it." The first one then needs to let go into the memory, the thoughts, etc.—to let it be. When the memory of the trauma has been allowed to express itself, it will no longer persist in holding a person from going more deeply into himself. Eventually, the lovers can return to lovemaking, entering a deeper level of intimacy.

   This is a very different approach to the "comforting love" that many of us have been taught. The expressions we are more used to are, "Don't cry. Everything is all right," or, "When you cry, it makes me feel sad, so please stop." If your partner has this perspective when you cry, you will most likely feel inhibited about letting go into your feelings and exploring what they mean.

4. **Be bodyworkers for each other.** Especially when one or the other hits a layer where there is muscular tension, it is a delight to have massage or some form of bodywork to help in letting go. Sex increases our body awareness, and brings our attention to gross and subtle body sensations of tightness more than any other activity. Having bodywork, or loosening muscular tension, during sex will make it easier to surrender to the fullness of your physical relationship and carry over to every other activity.

5. **Create ways to accelerate this process of using sex as a gateway to Causal level experience.** Charles and Caroline Muir suggest that

men see their partners as feminine manifestations of sacred universal energy (the Goddess), and women see their partners as masculine manifestations of the most sacred universal energy. This focus stimulates your awareness of how you perceive divine energy. It also will stimulate your perceiving your resistances to letting in Causal level experience. Perhaps a thought will arise: "I can't see a Goddess in her. I don't know how." Or, "People can't do that." Or, "That's blasphemy." Or, "If I see the Goddess in her, I might forget about the things that bug me about her. Then I would feel very open and vulnerable. I don't know if I dare."

Expressing gratitude to your lover certainly amplifies positive feelings and a sense of unity. See what happens when you thank him for just being himself! So often we only get appreciated for the things we do, not who we are.

6. **Do things that enhance your capacity to work with your energy alone and together.** *White Tantra* covers forms of yoga that are done by yourself to purify your body, gain more control over your energy, and enhance self-awareness. Hatha-yoga postures are a form of white Tantra. *Red Tantra* addresses Yogic practices that are done in partnership with your lover. These include guided meditations and special postures often done while the two of you sit facing one another. (The Muirs' workshops teach many forms of red Tantra. Other sources of information are books that I have noted in the references for this chapter at the back of the book.) Intoning particular sounds or chanting together often magnifies the effects of red Tantric practices. These practices will build the energy between you exponentially, heightening all of your senses and your positive feelings for each other. The result of this kind of energetic exchange with a lover is a feeling of fullness: "My cup runneth over." The excess wants to be expressed in creative work, being of service to others, empowering others to feel joy in themselves. Even though these love experiences are often built on an exclusive, monogamous relationship, they enhance each individual's desire to give love to others.

> The sacred space expands in all directions
> making the whole world an altar for worship.
> Light the incense of devotion to all life
> and watch its healing smoke spiral past
> the boundaries of the mind.
>
> —JUDITH WHITMAN SMALL, *Floodtide*

During sex you may fall into a "high," or consciously invoke a spiritual experience through special spiritual exercises. The process will probably involve surrendering into emotional highs and lows that take you to new self-awareness and new insight. If your relationship is strong, and you are willing to support purification and self-realization, you will harvest clear energy and profound intimacy with your partner as you open to the spiritual aspects of sexuality. Your relationship itself can then grow into a sanctuary that provides safety and truth in a world where it is often unsafe to be vulnerable.

This chapter looked at the "highs" available in sexual experience. The following chapter describes the "highs" available in the drug experience. Both these realms of experience include a spectrum of experiences involving the potential for self-revelation and inspiration on one end, and moral degradation and emotional bankruptcy on the other.

9

Drug Use and Spiritual Emergency

I was with my fiancé. It was my first time taking a psychedelic. In the beginning I went through several layers of letting go. Then, after about an hour and a half, I was sitting in a chair quietly by myself when I began to have a blissful experience. Suddenly, I knew God, I felt God, I was God! I was connected to everything! This incredible feeling of love was in me! I was breathless with it! I felt it deeply in every cell of my body! There was a whitish light all around me. This was the first time I ever really experienced God in my life.

—FLORA, a thirty-eight-year-old
schoolteacher

At the hospital, I was given very sensitive care. The doctors weren't sure what had happened to me because the psychosis had erupted so quickly. It wasn't the normal showing for manic-depressive disorder. They gave me stelazine, an antipsychotic. That stopped my mind from racing. Then my emotions were no longer overwhelming to me. The visions stopped. Everything slowed way down. Finally, I could get some rest.

—RICHARD, a middle-aged bookkeeper

I had to have all four wisdom teeth removed. My dentist did the procedure in his office. He gave me nitrous oxide. I went way out, losing all awareness of the dentist's office and my body. I saw and felt myself flying around the universe like a bird. I was free. It was beautiful.

—CAROLINE, a twenty-year-old student

Flora was taking a recreational drug outside of a clinical setting. Richard was given psychiatric drugs on a doctor's prescription, following a psychotic break. Caroline was given a frequently used anesthetic in a dental office prior to oral surgery. All three people found their drug experiences liberating for a short period of time. Caroline and Richard were freed from feeling physical and emotional pain. Flora found an opening into her spiritual life. This potential liberation from pain and opening to transcendent perspective is the attraction of drugs. When used therapeutically, under the proper conditions, drugs can have a profoundly positive effect. In all cultures throughout history, this, in fact, has been their use. In our own culture, morphine is beneficial as a painkiller; amphetamines are used as antidepressants. But unfortunately, these drugs are also often abused—causing moral degradation, illness, destructive behavior, and sometimes death. Drugs per se are not good or bad. How they are used is what is at issue.

This chapter focuses on the interplay of these three classes of drugs—recreational, psychiatric, and anesthetic—with spiritual emergence. Do drugs in any of these classifications catalyze spiritual emergence or emergency? Which ones undermine spiritual growth? Which ones may help you begin to integrate your spiritual experiences if you are in a spiritual emergency? This chapter does not deal with the profound emergency we face as a society in the use of harmful street drugs. The power of a particular drug to affect you is intrinsically linked to the type of *people* who give the drug to you, the *environment* where you take it, the *intention* you have in taking it—the set and setting. The end of this chapter offers ideas for a set and setting most likely to accelerate spiritual growth when drugs are being taken therapeutically. (These ideas may also be useful in setting up an environment conducive to inviting spiritual experiences independent of drug use.)

Recreational Drugs

> Everywhere and at all times, men and women have sought, and duly found, the means of taking a holiday from the reality of their generally dull and often acutely unpleasant existence. A holiday out of space, out of time, in the eternity of sleep or ecstasy, in the heaven or the limbo of visionary phantasy.
>
> —A. HUXLEY[1]

All of us like to get high. Conventional society allows us to do it daily with the uses of sugar, caffeine, alcohol, and prescription drugs. We feel our socializing would be pale and boring without our "coffee break," a drink after work, or wine with dinner. We feel that everyone needs a little help to relax sometimes—an occasional sleeping pill, or Valium. All of these "trips" are an acceptable part of everyday life.

Each of these substances also changes our consciousness, gives us a break from our ordinary mental pace of life. We speed ourselves up with coffee, tea, and sugar. We slow ourselves down with alcohol or anti-anxiety medication. We have all learned to be technicians of the mind, manipulating the quality of our consciousness. That is acceptable. Catholics, and many other Christians, seek to be closer to their God by drinking the Communion wine. The people of the Native American Church use peyote as their sacrament.

However, there are also those who step beyond conventional drugs. A large percentage of people in our society habitually use marijuana, for relaxation, recreation, sensory stimulation. A vast underground culture, including top-level executives, uses cocaine, "designer" drugs, psychedelics, narcotics, and opiates to remove themselves from the ordinary boundaries of conventional reality, to "take a holiday out of space and time," as Huxley said.

In 1986, an estimated 4.6 million adolescents aged fourteen to seventeen—one in every three—experienced negative consequences of alcohol use, such as poor school performance, trouble with parents, or involvement with law enforcement personnel.[2] American youth have the highest rates of illicit drug use of any industrialized nation.[3] Alcohol remains the most widely used drug among American youth. Alcohol is over twice as popular among college students as the next leading drug, marijuana, and over five times as popular as cocaine. Ninety-two percent of college students reported using alcohol in a twelve-month period, compared to 42 percent who had used marijuana, and 17 percent who had used cocaine.[4] The affects of this "holiday out of space and time" can be devastating. Look at alcohol, the most frequently used drug, for an example:

> Alcohol accounts for approximately 97,500 deaths in the United States annually. This includes cirrhosis and other medical consequences, alcohol-related motor vehicle accidents and alcohol-related homicides, suicides and non-motor vehicle accidents. The state of California finds that 50% of willful homicide is alcohol related, 30% of forcible rape is alcohol related, 40% of robbery is alcohol related. Of course, spousal abuse and child abuse [are] far more frequent in homes where "recreational" drugs are being used.[5]

In addition to statistics related to alcohol abuse, headlines spotlight the crazy behavior of people who are incited by drugs to go out of the bounds of any moral sense, immune to even their deepest instincts.

> April, 1989: Raymond Salcido is in the headlines of all the newspapers. He killed five members of his family, including his wife, and his

two children. He raped his two daughters before slitting their throats. Why? He was in a jealous rage. He thought his wife was having an affair with his supervisor. Raymond committed these murders after being high on alcohol, cocaine, and possibly amphetamines.[6]

In the therapy room and in support groups, we hear gruesome stories of lives impoverished because of "recreational" drug abuse:

> Beth was orphaned by her mother at age six. Emotionally and physically abused by her alcoholic father, Beth followed in her mother's footsteps and finally left home at fifteen. Her only means of survival was to sell sexual favors or drugs on the street. Often her customers wanted her to "trip" with them. This was her life until her mid-twenties—when she finally landed in the hospital, terribly ill and destitute. At thirty-five, she is in recovery, beginning to do the things she has wanted to do all her life: be healthy, enjoy friends who are not addicts, be of service to people in a way that is wholesome for her life and theirs.

The list of stories highlighting the horrors of drug addiction—the wasted lives, the broken families, the early deaths—seems infinite. Yet, despite all this, people don't shut the door on recreational drugs. The call to experience ourselves as larger than our ordinary selves, to have that vacation out of time and space, is immensely seductive. Recreational drugs may give us some sense of relief from lives that may be dull or unrelentingly painful. Some drug experiences can take us to transpersonal levels for a time opening those elements of the psyche that may never have been opened by spontaneous spiritual experiences. These drug experiences may initiate a spiritual emergency or be part of any of the six patterns of spiritual emergence. Thus, it is possible for a drug experience to be an initiation in spiritual emergence, as happened for Flora, or a downward spiral leading over time to physical and spiritual illness as happened in the first part of Beth's life.

The difference between a positive spiritual opening that catalyzes spiritual emergence and an opening to escapism and illness depends on the set and setting in which the drug, including alcohol, is being used. The Communion wine used as a sacrament in an environment designed to evoke spirituality is worlds apart from a bar. The peyote used as a sacrament in a sacred circle structured around ritual is worlds apart from an orgy centered in self-indulgence. Flora's psychedelic experience occurred in an atmosphere of love and trust. It was intended to be a time of exploration, self-revelation, and deepening intimacy. Her companions on the trip were therapists who had some real knowledge of the realms of the unconscious. Her experience was an initiation to a wider sense of self, an opening to her potential as an individual alone and in relationship:

I tried to tell my fiancé and my friend about my experience of God while it was happening. I told them how I felt and what I saw. They were able to really "get it" from my description. It was infectious.

The ecstatic feeling continued for an hour. I continued to feel high and positive for the rest of the trip, five more hours. To this day, I long to have that feeling again, but I don't want it through drugs. I want it just to be part of my everyday life. It's the real reason for my going back to become a member of a church.

Flora's drug experience served her well. She not only came to know her fears and her capacity for letting go, she was gifted with an experience of Higher Power. Her intuition also gave her a way to integrate the experience: During the height of her revelation, she tried to bring it to others, to her friends. Integrating her experience continued when she became a member of a spiritual community, her church. She did not use her high as an excuse to abuse drugs. She also never suffered any physical damage from the drug because she took so little of it.

There are no statistics that show how many people have had this kind of initiation to the Causal level through a drug trip. We do know that most drug trips with the synthetic drugs and psychedelic plants available to us will have spiritual *components*. Since people are having spiritual experiences as components of their drug trip, we should be prepared to address the spiritual questions and psychological crises in these situations just as we address the issue of the physical aspects of drug use and abuse, or the spiritual emergencies catalyzed by other, less provocative means.

Some of these elemental psycho-active plants have been used for this sacramental purpose from time immemorial in ancient cultures.[7] Our ancestors, the Greeks, are thought to have used a wine made from ergot-infected grain to produce religious ecstasy. The aged grain had psychedelic effects. East Indians used a derivative of hemp and a mind-altering mushroom for this purpose. "Magic mushrooms" have been used from Siberia to Mexico. The peyote cactus was used both in ancient times and today. It is thus more than likely that our ancient ancestors, including the esteemed elders, Plato and Socrates, who established our Western worldview, participated in the ritual use of psychedelics.

Psychedelics—psycho-active drugs—have been confused with narcotics and stimulants. Because of widespread substance abuse, all have been lumped together and categorized as harmful. With the exception of socially-sanctioned drugs—alcohol, coffee, and tobacco—all recreational drugs are considered illegal to possess, sell, or use. The only exception is peyote. It is still legal to use it in the ritual practice of the Native American Church, although that, too, is currently being challenged by federal authority. Perhaps this global attack on all recreational drug use is the only feasible antidote for the devastating abuse of drugs. (Abuse starts when drug use creates major problems in a person's life, and the person is unable to control his use of the drug.)

Unfortunately, the outlawing of recreational drugs also prevents people like Flora from having a legal opportunity to renew her faith in Higher Power, to discover or renew the spiritual dimension of her life. Despite the FDA's campaign to prove all recreational drugs harmful, including psychedelics, as of this date it has not been scientifically determined that small amounts of some of these drugs are indeed dangerous. Large amounts of LSD, like large amounts of commonly used drugs (coffee, tetracycline antibiotics, aspirin) produce chromosomal damage in human cells.[8] Moderate dosages of LSD do not cause DNA or chromosomal damage.[9] Furthermore, it has been clinically shown that small amounts of particular recreational drugs, when taken in an appropriate set and setting, are immensely therapeutic.[10]

Which drugs can be used therapeutically, and which drugs are harmful? All drugs, conventional and unconventional, have the capacity to give us new information about ourselves, from coffee which speeds us up, to LSD which takes us dramatically past the boundaries of our ordinary mind, to alcohol which reduces our inhibitions. Any of these drugs, in an appropriate dosage, with the appropriate set and setting, can be positive. Any of these drugs when abused can be dangerous. The common recreational drugs which are the most addictive—alcohol, narcotics, nicotine, cocaine, and crack—are also the most degenerative. The psychedelics are the ones most capable of catalyzing mental illness. All drugs are physically taxing.

Below is a list of recreational drugs generally used. People have different motivations for taking these drugs, as I have indicated. Some seek a rush, a thrilling sensation, or a release from anxiety and the commonplace cares. Some seek a psychological adventure or intellectual insight. Others, perhaps one in ten, quest for a spiritual experience. The motivation one has in taking the drug has a direct influence on the type of experience one will have. I describe each group of drugs focusing on their potential effect vis-à-vis spiritual emergence.

Paint thinner, glue: (the only "drugs" available to the poorest segment of American society). Sniffing these substances creates a quick sensory high. It also immediately destroys fat cells in the brain which are necessary for transmitting nerve impulses. The result is organic brain damage.

Marijuana: Marijuana is useful as a sedative and analgesic. Inhaling marijuana helps open sensory channels. Touching, tasting, hearing, seeing, smelling become amplified. Social inhibitions are reduced. Pain stimuli are more diffused and more easily tolerated. It is less toxic to the body than alcohol and nicotine.[11] Marijuana may initiate you into a larger dimension of consciousness. It has strong Subtle realm effects. Over a period of time it may decrease your motivation and skill to integrate your transpersonal experiences into your ordinary life. It is addictive for those people already emotionally prone to addictive behavior.

Alcohol, barbiturates, and narcotics: Ingesting any of these induces a state of relaxation and reduces social inhibitions. Depending on tolerance, moderate to large quantities can facilitate emotional expressiveness on a spectrum ranging from hostility to an increase in feelings of oneness with others. Spiritual experiences of the Subtle realm—mental telepathy, clairvoyance, clairsentience, clairaudience, visions, creative inspiration—may be accessible through use of these substances in restricted quantities. Both alcohol and narcotics (such as heroin) are addictive. Over time their use has a cumulatively degenerative effect on both the body and mind.

Stimulants, including amphetamines, MDA, cocaine, and crack: The strongest and most popular of all the stimulants, cocaine and crack, produce a euphoria unmatched by any other drug. Stimulants provide an experience of personal power, often translated into sexual power. The mind races. Thinking or sexual activity is more important than communication. These drugs can "steal your soul"—remove all empathy with other people, the desire to care for or serve others, and spiral away from the spiritual journey. These drugs are highly addictive.

Empathogens (MDMA, also called Adam or Ecstasy):   These are powerful drugs, the effects of which are intimately tied to the motivation of the user. This class of synthetic drugs can bring body and mind into harmony, opening the heart, relaxing social inhibitions and emotional defenses, bringing insight and profound personal self-revelation. Subtle and Causal level experiences become accessible in a therapeutic or sacred setting. In other settings, they are used as an aphrodisiac or to reduce social inhibitions for other purposes. These drugs are not addictive. They can be harmful to people with heart conditions because they contain stimulants. There is, as yet, no conclusive research indicating that these drugs are physically dangerous.

Psychedelics (LSD, psilocybin, mescaline, various plants from ancient shamanic cultures):[12]   These drugs produce powerful sensory, emotional, and/or transpersonal experiences. Any of them may be overwhelming. Hallucinations are typical. Because these experiences are so powerful, the need to integrate them is essential and challenging. Without integration, the powerful experiences may be split off from the rest of the personality and be of minimal use, or even impede personal growth. A safe environment and an experienced guide are important during the experience. Used in on-going therapy psychedelics will accelerate personal growth.[13]

With the empathogens and psychedelics, it is especially easy to open to life myth, open psychically, and experience karmic patterns, shamanic journeys, and kundalini awakening. Especially with the psychedelics, the contents of the unconscious seem to explode from their subterranean home.

Tripping into the Transpersonal

> I knew I needed to get to a friend who could be an anchor for me. I called an old friend, Frank. Luckily, he answered the phone and I could go and be with him and his girlfriend. When I got to the house and got out of the car, I fell onto the ground, holding on to the grass with my fingers for grounding in fear I would be pulled out of my body. Everything in the world, animate and inanimate, was moving, alive with cosmic energy. Nothing was solid.
>
> When Frank came out to greet me, I just looked into his eyes. This helped me feel grounded, helped me not get swallowed up in my experience, to keep part of me as a witness.
>
> —JULIA, a college student on her first
> trip, with mescaline

Any of the six patterns of spiritual emergency may be catalyzed by any of the drugs listed above. Just as the psychedelics, for example, open individuals to release from the small ego-self in transcendence, they also place people in a psychic situation that is out of their control. Julia was released from her personal sense of limitations and boundaries. This release can be exhilarating or threatening. For her, with no competent guide or trusted friend, being out of control was terrifying.

Any personal fear is of course amplified by the paranoia implicit in taking an illegal drug. Both fear and the lack of tools to integrate the expanded view exacerbate the possibility for spiritual emergency. The potential for spiritual emergency is certainly reduced if drugs are taken with the intention of spiritual growth under the supervision of a trained guide in a legally sanctioned setting.

Eva, thirty-five years old, took the empathogen MDMA, when it was still legal to do so, under the direction of a trained guide. As a practitioner of yoga and meditation for fifteen years, she was already quite familiar with her own inner life, having had many spiritual experiences. She had also studied Buddhist psychology as a way of understanding the mind. The house was completely quiet, with no interruptions from others. The telephone was off. Inspirational music played in the background. A fire warmed the hearth. Peaceful Oriental art was placed aesthetically around the room. Incense wafted through the house. This was truly a sanctuary designed to allow Eva to open to greater aspects of herself:

> On MDMA I felt a rarefied ecstasy I had only experienced after several days of a silent meditation retreat. I experienced opening to love. Love was no longer a feeling—it was a state of being. My friends and family appeared in an inner vision before me. I experienced my absolute, unconditional love for them; I saw our history together from the perspective of archetypal truth; I knew beyond a doubt that we would be connected through all time; I had no fear of death. I knew why my father had been cruel to me at times when I was growing up. I was able to feel complete forgiveness for him. This was new for me—and what a relief from the dogged resentments I had carried!

Eva's guide encouraged her to experience love as a state of being. The guide was attentive to Eva's need for reassurance and company when she was letting go to the drug experience.

For Eva, and others prepared for inner work, using an empathogen or psychedelic while being cared for by a guide in a therapeutic setting can open up new capacities in the mind. On an emotional level, this engenders forgiveness where forgiveness has seemed impossible. On a mental level, it may engender new dimensions of concentration and intuition.

> Several days after the drug trip I went to a weekend meditation retreat. This was to be my test, to see if my concentration was dulled by my recent drug experience. I was surprised to see that my concentration was the best it had ever been. I could go for much longer periods of time without moving, I could focus on far subtler levels, I could even focus on several dimensions of my mind simultaneously: my emotions, my thoughts, sense impressions of other people, clairvoyant perceptions happening all at once. My capacity for concentration had vastly expanded.
>
> Just as the MDMA trip put me in touch with my heart, it also grounded me more deeply in my body. Since I took the drug, I have more respect for my body, and I am more in tune with what I need to stay healthy.

This experience was so wonderful—didn't it make Eva want to use the drug often? In fact, it didn't.

> The drug experience was so powerfully transformative, it took me two months to assimilate it. Actually, I feel it will take the rest of

my life to really actualize all the wisdom I glimpsed in that "trip." I don't feel that doing more trips would help me to build that bridge to my ordinary life. I intuitively knew that more trips would make me feel scattered and ungrounded. I just need to recollect the power of the experience I had the first time. My guide supported this insight.

The drugs and alcohol we use for recreation—to step aside from our normal routines into a wider field of consciousness—have many purposes. Certainly, there is a broad spectrum of experience between *use* of drugs for increasing self-realization and *abuse* of drugs, where the use becomes another way of avoiding self-revelation. The dividing line between this "use" and "abuse" can be very slender. Especially because the possibility of becoming inflated with one's own power is so great with recreational drugs, the guidance of an objective, skilled counselor and respect for the laws of this country are essential.

Psychiatric Drugs

Psychiatric drugs, unlike recreational drugs, are not used for self-revelation but to stop psychological pain and to prevent people from being a danger to themselves or others. There is usually very little attention paid to the set and setting where the psychiatric drugs are taken, other than to watch out for the safety of the patient. The importance of the "bedside manner" of the attending psychiatrist, the medical "guide," is also not considered vital to the type of experience the patient will have. Conventional psychiatrists believe that the psychiatric drug itself will override the environmental factors. The psychiatric drug is seen as a chemical solution to a chemical problem.

The subtleties of the auditory and visual environment, the spiritual development of the guide, the social environment, can become lost under the significance of the medical factors of dosage and symptom control. As demonstrated in the use of recreational drugs, the set and setting in which drugs are used has a powerful impact on the course they take. An experience of opening to the unconscious can be frightening or it can be opening, depending on the state of mind and skill of the guide. This may be as true with psychiatric medication as it is with recreational drugs.

Richard was given psychiatric medication to help him come down from the psychotic symptoms linked to opening to life myth.

February 29, Leap Year night, I had what I call my "night journey." I couldn't sleep. I was seeing visions. Everything had mythic proportions. I was experiencing myself as the resurrected Christ, my lover was my "disciple." I had an incredible amount of energy—and very little sense of my own boundaries. Alone, at one o'clock in the morning, I went down into the street in my pajamas, left the front door wide open, wandered through the park, and then caught a bus. The driver took me just half a block, then let me off when he realized I was out of my mind. Fortunately, I found my way back home.

The next morning my roommates and my lover began taking care of me—sitting with me around the clock. Intuitively, I knew it was best for me to just stay in bed. I was talking a mile a minute. My mind was racing. My friends took turns listening. They thought I was manic, because manic-depressive disorder runs in my family. They fed me and made sure I drank liquids. I always felt that they were respecting me, never deriding me, even though I was acting like a child. They notified my place of work. Then they convinced me I should go into the hospital for a while. I trusted them because they were all so supportive and loving. It felt right.

Richard was attended by very kind and understanding nurses and doctors while recuperating. The psychiatric medication he was given was used to inhibit his symptoms for a period of time so he could rest and gather his strength.

I stayed in the hospital for ten days. I caught up on sleep. I took exercise classes. I received a lot of loving support from the doctors and nurses. Then I went home. I only missed three weeks of work during the whole episode. I continued on medication for two months. The side effects were bothersome. For instance, I didn't have good visual resolution while I was on Stelazine, which made me very myopic. My digestion and elimination were difficult. But the drug helped me get back to an even keel with my emotions and thoughts.

Under medical supervision, Richard stopped using the drugs when he had had the rest he needed and had renewed energy to work with the area of his unconscious that was unfolding within him. He was opening to vast resources of his own spirituality in opening to life myth, which had been initially overwhelming for him. Now, he could begin to integrate these new parts of himself at a slower pace.

Richard's experience with psychiatric medication was ideal. He had medical supervision around the drug use, but was not left with the sense that he had to depend on psychiatric drugs to handle his unconscious in the future. His doctors used medication judiciously—as an important crutch at a particular time. He was not encouraged to continue using drugs after his initial crisis, but to find a way to integrate the spirituality that had shown itself in his "psychotic episode."

Richard's friends never stopped believing in him. From beginning to end, they continued treating him with the understanding that what he said mattered. Fortunately, this kind of care continued at the hospital. This helped Richard feel less fearful and maintain his own self-respect. Richard's network of friends, including his coworkers, was wonderfully strong. No one rejected him for having experienced a psychosis. This again was an important element hastening his being able to integrate the positive aspects of his journey into his life. He didn't feel any pressure from his friends to reject the episode as bad or wrong.

Although Richard feels that the psychiatric medication he was given, Stelazine, was a great help to him overall, he also recognizes the difficulty inherent in taking the drug. All antipsychotic medications have a powerful effect on the mind, body, and emotions. People report that the effect of Stelazine is like hitting a solid wall after flying. It is abrupt and hard. Nerve impulses that had been firing very quickly in the temporal lobes and limbic system suddenly fire very slowly. It creates a dramatic shift in how people feel their emotions and how they see themselves. They feel dense and heavy. Emotions that had been spontaneous and vivid are now remote. Thinking processes are slowed. Time seems to move more slowly. Space has a density; gravity is more palpable. However, the condition does make it easier for the body to rest.

If given in doses that are too large, or over too long a time, some psychiatric medications can rob people of their capacity to complete the "journey" that has become alive in them. This may happen when a person in spiritual emergency is misdiagnosed as chronically schizophrenic and given a life prescription for antipsychotic medications. As with the abuse of recreational drugs, overuse of some psychiatric drugs (especially antidepressants, anti-anxiety medication, and antipsychotics) may close the door on spiritual awakening and seal it tight. The experiences that catalyzed the overwhelming opening then become inaccessible, because the state of mind habitually removed from authentic emotions prohibits the deep psychological processing that needs to be done in order for individuals to become whole in themselves. All psychiatric medications do not have this effect. Lithium, for example, given for manic-depressive disorder, compensates for a physiological chromosomal disorder and brings the body into balance so those with the disorder can be in touch with a balanced emotional life. (However, the side effects of Lithium, as for many psychiatric drugs, may be bothersome for some people.) Differentiating spiritual emergency from the psychosis of schizophrenia, manic-depressive disorder, or chronically debilitating personality disorders is therefore essential in determining correct medication. (Readers who want more information on differential diagnosis may refer to *A Sourcebook for Helping People in Spiritual Emergency*.)

The subtleties of this particular kind of differential diagnosis is especially difficult for psychiatrists and psychologists unschooled in transpersonal psychology. The compassionate and skillful care that

Richard received at home and in the hospital is not always the norm, nor are the people admitted to hospitals always as stable as Richard. There are many situations where people have been misdiagnosed and lived with the stigma of psychological disease and, perhaps, physical debilitating side effects of taking a psychiatric drug. People have been hospitalized inappropriately when what they needed was simply a sanctuary of care and little or no medication while they went through the spiritual emergency and the integration phase following the most acute part of the crisis.

A professor of transpersonal psychology tells the story of being hired in California to go through the psychiatric wards of a community hospital to determine who might need to be treated for spiritual emergency and who needed treatment for organic brain syndrome or psychological disease. Her being hired for this function illustrates that some hospital staff are sensitive to the fact that patients have been misdiagnosed and that some caregivers need help in recognizing the difference between dysfunctional behavior related to "breaking down" and behaviors related to "breaking through" to new levels of functioning. Lee Sannella, a psychiatrist, touched on the need for improved diagnostics in this area in his book, *Kundalini: Psychosis or Transcendence.*

At this time, conventional psychiatry has not yet reached a consensus about the validity of transpersonal states of consciousness. Diagnostic criteria to distinguish a debilitating breakdown from a spiritual emergency have not yet been accepted by medical professionals. Psychiatric drugs are often administered to people in spiritual emergency as if they were in a more typical psychosis or mania.

This lack of recognition of spiritual dynamics in psychiatry affects not only our health care systems but our judiciary system as well. Kitty was married. She and her husband had a two-year-old son. Kitty was psychic, and shared her insights about the future with friends and family members. Her brother was extremely upset by this ability of hers, and her openness about it. Her predictions about accidents in the family were often uncannily true. Unbeknown to Kitty, her brother took her letters to a psychiatrist. Because Kitty revealed in these letters that she could "talk to God personally," the psychiatrist reasoned she must be mentally ill. He had her involuntarily committed to a psychiatric ward, diagnosed as paranoid schizophrenic, and advised to take medications daily. She was in the hospital for three months, separated from her child and her husband before her attorneys were successful in having her released after several psychiatric examinations by more transpersonally oriented professionals.

Richard's and Kitty's stories illustrate the differences in diagnostic styles and care extended to those in spiritual emergency within the medical establishment. While it is possible to get excellent guidance and drug treatment in a hospital situation, it is also possible that if people in spiritual emergency enter a hospital setting, they will be incorrectly judged as "ill" and inappropriately medicated.

Supplementing Conventional Hospital Interventions

What should you do if you feel that a friend or family member is not being diagnosed, treated, or medicated appropriately in a hospital setting, and you sense she might be in a spiritual emergency?

1. Offer information to the attending physician about an alternative way of looking at your friend's condition. Tactfully ask if he has considered the problems from the perspective of transpersonal growth *in addition to* the more conventional medical approach. It might be helpful to give the physician a copy of this book, and/or the *Sourcebook for Helping People in Spiritual Emergency.*

2. If none of the caretakers are receptive to this alternative perspective, do not consider it your mission in life to persuade them. Your assuming this role will likely lead to polarizing the situation. The ethical and legal responsibilities of attending hospital staff are weighty. If the physician in charge feels that a patient is a threat to himself or others, the physician is obliged to keep the patient hospitalized and restrained. Drugs are often used as restraining methods.

It is a tremendous responsibility to care for a person in crisis. Even if you, as a family member or friend, feel strongly that your loved one has been hospitalized or drugged unnecessarily—and even if you have the legal right to take your loved one out of the hospital, be circumspect about taking over the responsibility for his or her care. It is demanding and may enlist your time twenty-four hours a day. It can be exhausting physically and emotionally.

A positive use of your energy in a difficult situation may be for you to work with your friend. For example, encourage her to write down the visions, the inner experiences, that happen to her. Simply sit and be with your loved one while she writes, draws, or tells you the story. Do not take on the role of judge, analyst, or critic, but rather that of the interested witness. This journal work and personal storytelling will help an individual integrate his experiences and give him some significant information that can be useful in later reflections.

3. If the hospital setting you are in is unresponsive to the transpersonal aspects of your friend's condition, you may be able to find a skilled helper who can work with her to supplement the kind of care available at the hospital. You may want to contact the Spiritual Emergence Network in Menlo Park, California, for a referral to someone in your community. Specify whether your friend has the financial

resources to consult a professional at regular fees or needs to work on a sliding-scale fee arrangement.

4. Encourage your friend to develop a working relationship with a helper who is skilled in transpersonal psychology.

TO THE PERSON IN CRISIS: Your becoming overwhelmed indicates a need in your life to resolve some inner psychological issues. You will need to find out what they are, to work with them on an inner level, and to make some changes in your life to accommodate the results of your inner work. Finding someone you trust to accompany and support you on this voyage is a boon, but may be difficult. You may need to rely on articles and books for companionship if you cannot find a guide or helper in your area. (See the Reference section at the back of the book.)

There are times when psychiatric medications can be useful for persons in spiritual emergency (not complicated by other psychopathology or physical disease):

If you are truly overwhelmed by the contents of your inner world and feel you may hurt yourself or others, psychiatric medications are very useful in providing a respite from intensity. Use them to modify the intensity of your inner experience so you can deal with your inner world at a pace that is manageable for you. After you have done this, you may consider easing away from the drugs.

If you are on a drug trip (or highly activated by intensive meditation or spiritual practice) and become overwhelmed, you may first try to calm yourself by listening to music which is harmonic and soothing. Remind yourself, or have someone remind you that you are on a drug trip and the effects will subside. Gentle physical activity like walking in nature or moderate stretching exercises will ease anxiety. Talking or being with a friend is comforting. Vitamin C—alone or in juices—can be helpful. Alcoholic beverages are not advisable as they might create a toxic reaction on top of the drug used. If these methods are insufficient or inappropriate, consult a physician who can prescribe a moderate anti-anxiety medication, like Valium. If this is inadequate, follow a physician's advice for stronger medication. Try to put yourself under the care of a psychiatrist who is knowledgeable about transpersonal psychology.

Anesthetics

Several types of anesthetics used in dental procedures, outpatient clinics, and hospital surgery can catalyze spiritual emergence phenomena. However, anesthesiologists who administer these drugs and attending nurses are not consistently trained in caring for people in the psychological or spiritual aspect of their experience with anesthetics. Thus, if you have a spiritual experience on these drugs, you will likely be left on your own resources to integrate them.

Caroline, at twenty, was given enough nitrous oxide (also known as "laughing gas") in a dental procedure so she would be oblivious to the pain accompanying the extraction of all four of her wisdom teeth.

> Just as the nitrous oxide wore off and the operation was over, I experienced myself landing in a small bird cage. It was barely big enough to house my real self. "I" (my soul) was crammed into it (my body). This awareness made me feel very sad. I woke up sobbing uncontrollably. Not because I was in pain. I was unaware of any physical pain at the time. I was absorbed in the feeling of having been so free and now realizing how trapped I felt in my body. I had felt myself flying around the universe like a bird—completely free.

Caroline, like most people who have a transpersonal experience in the dental office, was given no counseling to help her understand her overwhelming sadness or her vision. She was basically alone with it. The dental assistant sat with her and offered tissues as Caroline gained control of the tears. Caroline's friend Ray put his arm around her in an attempt to comfort her. It took Caroline years before she could make sense of the inner experience itself. It had been earthshaking at the time, and set her life in new directions.

> I didn't know how to talk about this with my family. I was afraid they would think I was crazy if I told them how much this vision had affected me. But the vision had had a profound effect on how I saw my world. I now wanted, more than anything, to find a way to make my "cage" bigger, also to open the door so I could "fly" again. I started doing hatha-yoga and a lot of meditation. I dropped out of college after I completed that semester. I knew that my inner life would give me the key as to how to "fly" again. Academics would not do it for me.

This was a spiritual awakening for Caroline. From the nitrous oxide she had had her first out-of-body experience, and a powerful knowing of her soul as different from her body. She had realized a new purpose and found renewed determination to find freedom. She said that the freedom was, in essence, a longing for unity with God.

> I felt unity with God when I was free, when I was under the influence of the drug. I knew it was possible for me to have that freedom. I just knew I wanted it more than anything else.

Other anesthetics promote similar kinds of experiences. Sodium pentothol ("truth serum"), stronger than nitrous oxide, also allows the consciousness to completely dissociate from the body, promoting visions and inner experiences like Caroline's. Ketamine, an anesthetic used frequently with adults preparing for heart surgery and with children, seems especially conducive to catalyzing spiritual experiences. Research by D. Rogo indicates that 12 percent of those people who take ketamine have experiences similar to near-death experiences.[14]

Following is the account of a doctor undergoing surgery after he was anesthetized with ketamine.

> I heard odd buzzing sounds in my ears. Then I fell unconscious. Then I gradually realized my mind existed, and I could think. I had no consciousness existing in a body; I was mind suspended in space. It was like I was floating in a void. I was not afraid. I was more curious. I thought, "This is death. I am a soul, and I am going to wherever I should go."[15]

After his experience, the physician reported experiencing a great deal more compassion for his own patients. Like others who have had out-of-body experiences, he found he no longer feared death as he had. He also knew that the body is a home of the soul, and he could relate more directly to people as being souls as well as bodies.

Children who have these kinds of experiences under anesthesia must also be profoundly changed. Do they think they are a bit crazy for having had an out-of-body experience? Is their awakening to this realm of transpersonal experience given a positive place in their lives? Most children keep their spiritual experiences from surgery to themselves as secrets. They pay a price for holding this secret, because often they feel ashamed or embarrassed about it. It would make a difference for these children if they could come to understand what happens to them in positive terms.

On many occasions, I have worked with adult clients around inner experiences they had as children waking up after surgery. They had carried fear and anxiety about being crazy for decades as a result of their hospital experience. Perhaps there is a way that medical attendants or counselors might help children after surgery to come to terms with any inner experiences they have had in the hospital so that they would not have to carry this kind of psychic baggage into adulthood.

It may also be a real help to adults who are deeply affected by inner experiences under anesthetics to be offered some form of counseling either before or after surgery. What a comfort it might have been to Caroline to understand that other people have out-of-body experiences as a result of anesthetics, to be given a conceptual framework to help her understand the nature of the experiences, and to know that she was not alone, or crazy. It would have helped her to know that spiritual practices and a spiritual community might assist her in finding a way to work with her experiences. Through these, she might also have been able to find the words to talk to her family and friends about what happened to her.

Set and Setting

In the use of any kind of drug, the presence of a trained guide for counseling and referral is beneficial along with establishing the intention of physical, emotional, and spiritual health and creating the environment that conscientiously supports that end. A guide, a positive intention, and an appropriate environment are all parts of the set and setting that can make a drug experience conducive to spiritual emergence. If any of these parts are missing, a spiritual emergence process may well involve a spiritual emergency.

Bad drug trips—on the street or in homes—are often attributable to poor quality drugs. Sellers of recreational drugs, also known as "street drugs," may lace one drug with another in order to use less of an expensive drug. The result is more money for the seller and a bad drug trip for the user. Hospital emergency rooms receiving people on bad trips in a toxic condition are often charged with unraveling the mystery of what drug has been taken and what additive might have been used as a filler in that drug. Without the answer, the drug to counteract the symptoms cannot be identified or administered. Life and death hangs in the balance. This problem is one directly attributed to street drugs. It does not happen in hospitals where the Food and Drug Administration has quality control over the drug company's manufacturing and distributing procedures.

Bad drug trips that overwhelm people with fear and anxiety may also be caused by an inappropriate set and setting in the street, at home, or even in the hospital. All of the drugs referred to in this chapter have the capacity to take people out of their conscious minds and into the storehouse of the unconscious. What is revealed there may be a spiritual experience—delightful and liberating (as it was for Flora experiencing God on a guided drug trip) or earthshaking and transformative (as it was for Caroline in the dentist's office). Drugs may open people to overwhelming emotional experience—freeing them to lose themselves in formerly unexpressed emotion (as with Louise in chapter 3 when the contents of her unconscious exploded) or giving them refreshing new perspective on love (as it did for Eva when she took Ecstasy). If the set and setting are chaotic, the drug trip will more likely be chaotic. If the set and setting are not conducive to integrating new aspects of people's emotional or spiritual life, the drug trip will more likely produce anxiety and fear. The setting in which drugs are taken has an immediate affect on the quality of the experience a patient will have under the influence of the drug.

The internal environment of the subconscious mind is as much a part of the set and setting as the external environment. Recreational and psychiatric drugs and anesthetics have the ability to amplify what is already in the subconscious mind—to the point where it may become larger than life.

Of course, what the social and physical environment inspires in people will determine which part of their subconscious they are most likely to meet. If you want to use drugs to clear emotional complexes, it is best to be in an environment that can truly guide you in that task. If you want to use drugs to have an experience of Higher Power, be in a place that evokes Higher Power (a natural setting or a church, for example) with people who have skill in drawing out that side of life. If you are in the dentist's chair and want to use drugs to escape the pain of the imminent dental procedures, be aware that you may be more likely to have an out-of-body experience, an escape from the body's pain that is more powerful than you expected. If you are about to have surgery and fear for your life, you may propel yourself into a profound reflection on your mortality in ways that far transcend your ideas of what is possible.

Since we know that the total ambience has such a significant effect on the quality of experience for someone taking drugs, we should use this knowledge whenever drugs are being used. We know that transpersonal experiences are a component of drug experiences. We know that integrating these experiences enhances creativity, compassion, peace of mind, and a desire to be of service in the world. Wouldn't it be a good idea to consciously enhance those environments where drugs are taken in order to facilitate transpersonal experiences?

This can be done even in the simplest of ways. Wendy, at twenty-five, was in a clinic for a minor operation.

> I lay on the table shaking with fear. I always shake with fear—as if I am chattering all over with cold. I was given a shot of a muscle relaxant. As I relaxed, I began to take in the room I was in.
>
> On the ceiling above my head was a mandala—a beautiful round picture of redwood trees. The symmetrical design was very pleasing to look at. As I looked into the picture, I could easily imagine I was at the bottom of a grove of redwoods looking up into the sky. The enormous trunks reminded me of the strength and endurance of the redwoods. The look of the branches high overhead reminded me of how a redwood reaches high into the sky. The picture helped me recall my own strength, my connection to the earth, and my ability to connect to Higher Power.
>
> I looked at the picture all through the procedure. The picture continued to give me strength. There was something friendly about it—much more humane than the sterile walls and masked faces of the medical attendants. I knew that whoever had put the picture on the ceiling was thinking of my feelings, not just my physical health. This acknowledgment helped me feel more whole, and more cared for by

the people attending me. It also made it easier to feel my connection
to Higher Power, because I often have felt inspired by trees.

Just the picture on the ceiling, a small change in the design of the
doctor's office, helped make Wendy more fully present. She was able
to shift her consciousness to become more aware of her strength and
the compassion of the people who attended her and less dominated by
her fear.

A dentist in my area uses nitrous oxide for people who are ap-
prehensive about dental work. He has a wonderful sound system and
headphones in each room. The patient is asked to bring in his or her
favorite music tape and listen to it through the headphones while
under the influence of the nitrous. Martha, a fifty-five-year-old professional woman, a dedicated member of her church for over twenty
years, uses her dental work time to feel the presence of God. She
brings in tapes that are particularly inspirational for her. She told me
she often receives insight into her practical problems while she is
under the influence of the nitrous and listening to her music.

Inspiring music and pictures are dynamic ways of creating an environment conducive to engendering transpersonal experience. The
understanding of attending medical people, friends, and/or a counselor will also assist in making a drug experience a doorway into a
sacred experience.

Hopefully, in years to come, all the environments where mind-
altering drugs are administered will be designed to elicit the peace and
the power of transpersonal experience. People who administer these
drugs will accommodate the emotional and spiritual needs of the people receiving the drugs—as well as the physical needs. Those of us
who have transformative experiences in these settings will have the
counseling and companionship we need to integrate these episodes.
Then, the technology of drugs that change consciousness can truly be
used to enhance human development in the most positive direction.
The unconscious use or abuse of drugs, which has devastated this
culture, might then become a nightmare interred in past history.

At the current time, we must fight our battle against the abuse of
recreational drugs. A few people receiving drugs get through this arena
positively. Many more are scarred by bad experiences. Some die, or
must live with the guilt of having abused someone else while under
the influence. It is a serious problem. All of our lives have been
touched by someone who abuses drugs. Most of us know drug abuse
in our own families, most often through alcohol. Most of us will have
some experience with mind-altering drugs in the course of our lives.
The challenge of how to manage the experience is one that is relevant

to everyone—whether they are taking the drug themselves or are a companion to someone else under the influence of a drug.

The following chapter discusses changes influencing our culture globally that effect spiritual emergence. Keep in mind the powerful effect that drugs have had on the quality of our lives as you read the next chapter. People have been able to experience the most sacred universal power—people who might never have had that experience otherwise. With the increased drug traffic, there has been an increase in numbers of people who have had transpersonal experiences. Keep in mind too that many people have given years of their lives to drug abuse in themselves or others. These sacrifices and the attending remorse, guilt, shame, broken dreams, broken marriages, and broken homes sometimes propel people toward spiritual opening. Alcohol abuse brought Bill Wilson financial ruin, marital difficulties, emotional turmoil, and near-death before he resurrected himself as a founding leader in a worldwide movement in support of sobriety, Alcoholics Anonymous. It was a Causal level experience he had in the hospital in recovery after delirium tremens that catalyzed Wilson's transformation. A positive impact of the drug abuse that infects our world at this time might be more people, like Wilson, who can bestow upon our culture the gifts of their spiritual emergence. But as Aldous Huxley warned:

> . . . there are moments in the course of intoxication by almost any drug, when awareness of a not-self superior to the disintegrating ego becomes briefly possible. But these occasional flashes of revelation are bought at an enormous price. For the drug-taker, the moment of spiritual awareness (if it comes at all) gives place very soon to sub-human stupor, frenzy or hallucination, followed by dismal hangovers and, in the long run, by a permanent and fatal impairment of bodily health and mental power. . . . Occasionally . . . a [drug-induced] revelation may incite its recipient to an effort of self-transformation and upward self-transcendence.[16]

10

Global Crisis and Spiritual Emergence

In 1945, the first nuclear bomb exploded on this planet. Just about the same time, LSD was first "dropped" in the United States. I was born within months of these two explosions. I came into adulthood in a world where women had the Pill, blacks and women were fighting for equal rights, gays were coming out of the closet, and "flower power" was the new rallying cry. The United States was at war in Vietnam, and United States citizens were at war with each other over it. The human population was expanding at a superexponential rate. In the 1960s, it was doubling every thirty-five years.[1] President John F. Kennedy was assassinated. So was Martin Luther King. Technology was racing along—we reached the moon in 1969, but it didn't seem to help the social chaos, the riots, the possibility of nuclear war, the increasing pollution of our air and water, and the accelerating divorce rate.

At sixteen, I looked at the world with dread. I wasn't sure I wanted to be alive. The only oasis of comfort for me was spiritual practice. I weaned myself from my fear of social chaos on meditation and transpersonal psychotherapy. No political movement, social movement, or technology was big enough to get us out of the mess we were in. Our social and political traditions got us here; I didn't believe they could get us out. I knew that our only hope was to be found within ourselves, in a place beyond our social patterns, and I was determined to find it. I felt I would die unless I found it. Fortunately, I found people who were especially wise to help me. From them I learned how to draw on the "perennial" wisdom that has been alive in many cultures of the world throughout time.

Although my personal reaction to the social crisis of the day was not shared by the majority of my peers, the set and setting of the day was shared. In America, we all faced the social chaos. We all had to find some way of meeting the challenges of living in this insecure and rapidly changing world.

What does our conventional American way of life hold for us as a way of meeting the challenges of terrorism, possible nuclear destruction, overpopulation, the information glut, the breakdown of traditional sexual roles? Over the last twenty years, these elements of life have prevailed and grown stronger. Can we defeat them through a return to traditional values: the nuclear family, the small community, the wholesome way of life based on a firm national economy, and a family-oriented pace of life?

No. That way of life is no longer available to us. Families are breaking apart. Small communities are dying as young people go to urban areas for better jobs.[2] Farming is becoming financially impossible for small farmers. Agribusiness is taking over, so that fewer people can afford to live a life in touch with nature. Our urban and suburban rat race has become so fast, many working couples have little time for parenting their own children. America is "running itself ragged" keeping up with the glut of new information that must be assimilated.[3] Alienation from nature and separation from family roots creates a fragmentation in the psyche of each individual as well as the collective. Add that to the realization that our defense system can no longer protect us from the possibility of nuclear disaster. Our national financial system is built on a fantastically enormous debt interwoven with the finances of the burgeoning Third World economy.

This breakdown of social traditions has affected all high-technology cultures, East and West. Now, we must attend to unbelievable additional new responsibilities brought on by technological advances. Television satellite linkups facilitate communication globally. We are connected to the realities of each other's lives in seconds through networks of radio, television, and telephone. There is an explosion of information exchange. Business ventures go on around the clock, crossing all time zones. We have the capacity to destroy all life on the planet many times over through nuclear warheads and chemical pollution. Through the eyes of our space travelers, we voyage over 25 thousand miles per hour, stand on the moon, observe our earth, Gaia, within the context of the universe. In our laboratories, we actively participate in the evolution of the earth. Biologists have learned how to modify genes in a cell, opening the door to the creation of completely new species. Now, new life-forms can be designed consciously and created rapidly. Scientists, with particle accelerators, are able to change some elements into others or even create completely new elements. We have created a new way of harnessing the sun's energy: the solar cell. Through improved agricultural practices and transportation we can feed all the people of the world—becoming one planetary family is a possibility in function as well as in vision. *Will* we do it? *Can* we create a safe and viable life despite the national boundaries and defenses that have separated us for centuries? *Do* we choose to live as one cooperative family? What an awesome and unique perspective we have on our life!

We continue to refine technology, to assimilate new information, to accommodate change, and now we are alienated from social traditions that have given life meaning. A social structure falling to pieces, the shadow of our high-technology advances, shows itself in the eyes of the homeless, the abused, the addicts, the poor, the lonely—the ones who do not have the resources to keep up with the pace. Where is a safe harbor away from the hustle? What is the value of material abundance for the few who benefit from the hustle? Collectively, the technologically advanced societies search for safety and a reconnection with some deep roots that help recollect the meaning of life.

True Safety in a Rapidly Changing World

Many esoteric religious groups predict that the rapid change and alienation from social tradition will be catalyzing a psychological and spiritual frenzy as people acknowledge profound insecurity. Starting in the 1990s, this frenzy will effect 75 percent of the people in technologically advanced societies. John White, author of *Pole Shift*, quotes modern researchers who believe that natural earth changes and geophysical shifts will have a significant role in catalyzing this psychological frenzy. The years between 1990 and 2010 are supposed to bring many unusual and significant earth changes.[4]

The current increase in earthquake activity, hurricanes, droughts, and unusual weather patterns substantiate these predictions. In October 1989, I experienced the California earthquake, as did all of my clients and friends. We live very near the epicenter close to Santa Cruz. For three weeks following the big quake, we experienced hundreds of small tremors, twenty measured over 4.0 on the Richter scale. The unpredictable nature of the 7.1 quake and its aftershocks, their awesome power, the loss of security and groundedness they created, plus the destruction of homes and belongings effected tremendous psychological stresses for everyone. Turning within, dealing with fear, grief, anger, and aligning with Higher Power, became a biological imperative. All of us learned that our survival demanded that each person come to terms with his inner chaos and quest for peace in order to manage the magnitude of external chaos.

The disturbances which affected our community in the wake of the earthquake may be an illustration of the frenzy predicted by esoteric traditions. What stands before us during disasters are two roads: one road would lead to either degenerative psychological breakdown, a real falling to pieces, or the other road would lead to breakthrough, strengthening our alignment with Higher Power, and dealing with our inner psychologies. The disasters crack open the doorway to the unconscious forces, both the dark and the light.

Safety from the inner chaos can only be found through finding the stable voice of Higher Power within and creating social groups which can effectively help us manage our inner turmoil. Many of our old social traditions offer us a false security because they are, for the most part, no longer viable. They only remind us of something that was stable in the past.

We will have to learn the difference between "true safety" and "false security." William Lonsdale, a scholar and teacher, says:

> False security is the deep gut need to have something in your world to hold still long enough for you to feel comfortable in relation to it. It values that which is stable, fixed, definite, and predictable. [This is what the adults had when our financial, defense, religious, social, and family systems seemed immutable for twenty years after World War II.] It is a dependable counterpoint to all the thousands of things which are constantly changing around you.
>
> True safety is a realization of your relationship to the world above you and the world below you—not just the horizontal, social level. Thus, we need to develop the recognition that we are being formed and guided by spiritual directive, or Higher Power. And, similarly, we need to realize that we are in an instinctive belongingness to the world below: the genuine, sentient intelligence of this planet. This vertical relatedness will provide the center of stability and safety that cannot be destroyed by the social chaos of the time. It gives a wider sense of connectedness.
>
> The safety depends on your not only acknowledging the relatedness but synchronizing with it. Living in this true safety is an *active* relationship, whereas false security demands nothing. You don't have to do anything, be anything, in the old system. All you have to do with false security systems is grab hold of them and they will do for you what you want them to do. This is why people like money and possessions. You don't have to be worthy of your money or possessions. They have no claim on you. They have to serve you. In true safety, there is a lining up of your being with that which is beyond you and that which upholds you from beneath in order for you to be

served by it. You can't just swig your beers and forget it. You have to be there. It won't be given to you automatically.[5]

In the true safety, we recover a source of meaning in a direct living relationship to Higher Power and to Earth as a sentient being. Through these relationships, we recollect our morality, our source of true leadership, our vision of our life purpose.

How do we find true safety? The conventional social and political institutions cannot provide the guidance. There are no "experts" who can do it for us. There are few professionals who can truly guide the transformation process. Some books contribute guidance. (See the references in the back of this book listed as References on the Process of Transformation.) But the real work must be done within oneself.

Those searching for "true safety" will find counsel with those who have attained some wisdom from their own spiritual emergence process. These people are weathering the breakdown of social traditions by creating new forms in their personal and professional lives. They are accommodating the cross-fertilization of religious and health practices in a positive way. They weather the acceleration of information exchange by incorporating gifts of many cultures to benefit their well-being. True safety will always involve an ability to be flexible, permeable, and able to appreciate other ways of finding meaning and well-being. It is when we become rigidly attached to our own social traditions and our own perception of reality, out of contact with the fundamental flow of life energy, that we are lodged in false security.

Cross-Fertilization of East and West

In traditional Buddhist cultures, reaching "true safety" comes from rising above the flow of constant change, birth and death. Particular meditations on death, sometimes in the presence of a corpse, are used to guide the practitioner on this profound path. The reality that life is in a constant state of change and flux becomes undeniable with such a focus. More important, it becomes very clear that our own lives are in a constant state of change—leading to the ultimate transformation, death. This was brought home to me during the year I wrote of in chapter 2 when many members of my family died, and again during the October 1989 earthquake. My Buddhist meditation helped me retain a sense of inner stability during those times. Whatever I was doing, the question kept turning in my mind, "What remains after the body is gone?" The question took me to a transpersonal level of awareness and knowing of the presence of Higher Power. From this perspective, a life based on something more enduring than fickle ego desires or even social structures (which also crumble easily) became essential. The insight that "change is the only constant" provided me, as it does many Buddhist practitioners, with the inspiration for a deepening desire to reach transpersonal levels of consciousness.

Thich Nhat Hanh, a Vietnamese Buddhist monk, poet, and educator, brings this wisdom to the West in his books and retreats. He tells about the time when he was only nineteen years old and was assigned by an older monk to meditate on the image of a corpse in the cemetery. He thought at the time that such a meditation should be reserved for older monks. But now he sees how relevant that meditation is for our world today:

> I have seen many young soldiers [during the Vietnam War] lying motionless beside one another, some only 13, 14, 15 years old. They had no preparation or readiness for death. Now I see that if one doesn't know how to die, one can hardly know how to live—because death is a part of life. . . .
>
> Only now is it possible to rise above birth and death, and to know how to live and how to die. [The Buddhist Sutra on Mindfulness] says that the Boddhisattvas who have seen into the reality of interdependence have broken through all narrow views, and have been able to enter birth and death as a person takes a ride in a small boat without being submerged or drowned by the waves of birth and death.[6]

More people from Western cultures are spontaneously finding their own methods to accommodate rapid change finding a new way to live that integrates the ways of both East and West. Isaac, sixty years old, transformed his life in the last twenty years by drawing from the techniques of the East. He had been trained through the Western model of science. For years, he practiced as a family doctor in a rural community. Then he happened to watch a demonstration of acupuncture by a noted practitioner. He witnessed the fact that a hand that had been cramped and completely dysfunctional for ten years could become functional by working with an acupuncture point on the opposite leg. This demonstration and others like it destroyed many of his concepts of reality, making him feel insecure personally and professionally. Everything he thought was stable and immutable was actually in process, in a flow of change. It was as if the very ground he had been standing on was trembling.

Isaac had to accept the significance of pranic energy in the body—and recognize that by working directly with that energy we can promote healing more efficiently than with many Western medical procedures. He changed his professional direction and became licensed to practice acupuncture. Isaac also wanted to develop a relationship to his own inner energetic flow, something that he had never thought about before. To do this he studied yoga and began meditating. As he deepened in his spiritual practice, he became more sensitive to himself and others. He was gifted with a greater vision about life. His compassion for his clients grew. Although there were no models for him to follow, Isaac developed a style of working with people that incorporated acupuncture, Western medicine, and his own sensitivity in working directly with the energetic flows in the body. He is now sought after as a teacher, and enjoys an exceptional degree of personal well-being.

The Breakdown of Traditional Cultures

As we draw from other cultures, we also become less identified with our own traditions, and contribute to the breakdown of our traditional culture. This breakdown and the need "to know how to live" has its greatest impact on young people who are beginning to form a sense of self and wanting to belong to their culture. Yukio is a Japanese man, twenty-eight years old. He has been maturing into adulthood just at the time when Japan has been changing. His life illustrates the breakdown of the old Japanese tradition and the difficulty of making the move away from false security toward true safety.

> Before 1979, when you graduated from college, it was assumed you would join a company. From then on it would be impossible to quit your job or change jobs. Especially the men would be under tremendous social pressure to stay in one place. Since 1979, Japanese have been wealthier—like the 1950s in America. More people can drive big cars. They can afford luxuries. They have made it to a very comfortable style of life. The Japanese have also been forced to open to the influence of other countries, other cultures. Women are coming out more, wanting to change and have more responsibility for their own lives.

Japan was the first Oriental country to not only embrace postindustrial technology but take on the computer age—and all the complexities of a modern, fast-paced, competitive, wealthy civilization vying for economic power on a global level. Traditional ways became less important—as they inevitably do in countries that begin to participate fully in the global economy. This shifting inevitably sifts down to affect the young people and their life choices. Yukio continued:

> I was twenty-two in 1983. I went to college like my friends. Then I dropped out of the traditional ways. I did not join a company. I worked in a cafeteria part time. During the rest of my time I thought about my life. I had a lot of anxiety. I had no identity. I didn't fit in anywhere.

> There was no one who was really helpful for me at this point. I couldn't go to therapy for help in finding out what I wanted to do with my life. There aren't any therapists in Japan. There are psychiatrists. If you go to a psychiatrist, people assume you are crazy. My parents were supportive of me—and they also thought I was lazy. I didn't have a connection with a religion or a spiritual teacher. I wanted to run away from Japan—to find another option for my life.

The traditional ways were no longer relevant for Yukio. This is increasingly true for other young people in postindustrial cultures. These people are waking up to the fact that their lives are not based on survival issues or maintaining conventions anymore but on finding meaning in a rapidly changing world where many old conventions are obsolete. The question inevitably arises, "What will give my life meaning and stability?" Yukio said:

> I ended up going to the United States and studying religious anthropology. I studied very hard and got the highest grades. I also found myself questioning the meaning of life and death. I wanted to find answers to these deeper questions, not just be a scholar, or work in a company.
>
> Two years later, when I returned to Japan, I collapsed—emotionally and physically. There was no medical diagnosis for my condition. I just needed to sleep and sleep and sleep—for about a year. I had no energy for relationships, studying, or working. My head felt as if it was full of darkness.

Yukio pulled out of this condition when he met Shin, a Japanese man who had successfully disengaged from the rigid expectations of the traditional Japanese social system. Yukio was impressed by Shin, who had created his own way out of the mainstream. Yukio thought that Shin had found his authentic self and thus changed the whole context of his life. Subsequently, Yukio found ways of connecting with his inmost self in various forms of meditation and movement exercises drawn from many cultures. This has helped him cultivate his relationship with Higher Power.

Today, Yukio is a man who has gone beyond the rigid boundaries of nationality identity. He has found himself as a person in change on this changing planet with an inner peace. He has acquired tools to work with his own darkness effectively so it no longer overwhelms him. He enjoys both Japanese and American cultures. He is particularly inspired by Taoist philosophy. He lives in America and is interning as a transpersonal counselor in a clinic. He wants to give what he has learned to other people who want to awaken spiritually.

What about the adolescents and young adults in America? Those born after 1965 were also immersed in a rapidly changing world. What skills do these young people need to get along in the country as it is today?

Who are the role models for our young people? Our world political leaders are visibly untrustworthy. Political scandal became big news at Watergate and the resignation of President Nixon in 1974. These scandals have continued peaking at home and abroad, through to the recent Iran-Contra arms scandal in 1988–89. Terrorism flourishes and has become a tool of international politics: in skyjackings, murders at the 1972 Olympic games, and the taking of hostages. Drug trafficking also flourishes, at schools and throughout the culture, undermining the authority of our social traditions. With family structures crumbling (see chapter 7), fewer children have consistent relationships to their parents and extended family who would normally provide role models.

Financial or religious authority has usually upheld order. Is it dependable now? We are no longer the financial world power we used to be. We are just one member in a world economy. We are interconnected with other countries for our own financial viability. Our economy is profoundly influenced by the oil cartel's price hikes, the debts of the Third World countries, the rise of industrial powers in the Pacific Rim. Like financial authority, religious authority is in question. The pope and clergy from Protestant churches are being vociferously challenged for their stand on abortion, birth control, homosexuality, and women entering the clergy. Evangelical faiths are taken to task for the hypocrisy of their leaders, who preach monogamy and practice something less.

Where can the young people find true safety? Where can they find moral values? Where and how do they develop their own ability to take authority over their own lives and find their place in the world? Cults have gained popularity, offering some relief from inconsistent political leadership, confused religious leadership, and financial uncertainty. Television is the preoccupation of mainstream culture. Old Guard Protestant churches, which defined the moral and spiritual ethos of this country, began a decline in the sixties that has shrunk membership approximately 25 percent to date.[7] "We are experiencing a reaction against modernity," says Richard Mouw of Fuller Theological Seminary. "We are getting magic and the occult and the New Age." This is the environment that affected Galen, the sixteen-year-old girl in chapter 3 who came for counseling after experiencing possession and bizarre psychic phenomena.

These young people need to find something more. Like Yukio, they need to find role models who can help them toward their own authenticity, their own strength, independent of the structures of social conventions that may be obsolete. From there they will find inner authority and, eventually, their place in this world.

Contacting the adults who can be role models for these young people may be problematic. They are not generally part of the mainstream culture. Books and articles may be a source of guidance. John White, writer and teacher, in his article "Liberation Literature," suggests a seminar for young people on the literature of spiritual emergence.[8] Books in relevant chapters of this book may also be of use. National Outdoor Leadership School and Outward Bound are two organizations that conduct trainings, in many locations nationally, designed to help young people enrich their relationship with the earth and their own inner resources through survival training. Innovative school programs, like Nizhoni School for Global Consciousness in Galisteo, New Mexico, have originated school programs for young people that give them tools for spiritual emergence and caring for nature. Contact addresses for these programs can be found under Resources at the back of this book.

Although role models may be difficult to find, there are people who have achieved some degree of true safety who will probably be available to our young people from time to time. They will be sources of inspiration, as Shin was for Yukio. They will stimulate thinking by demonstrating a way to live which springs from the authentic self, beyond ego. These people are part of the "Wisdom Culture," discussed under a subheading later in this chapter.

The only consistently present authority in our world today for people of all ages in the energy of the Higher Power and Earth herself. Cultivating a relationship to these Higher Powers is the best way to adjust to the breakdown of national and family boundaries. Grounding in a deep caring for Earth rooted in a sense of belonging to her is the best way to achieve stability. Balancing between these higher and lower worlds, in a global consciousness, is ultimately the only way to find safety and wisdom. The shift to this consciousness is an essential part of the spiritual emergence process for all people on this planet.

Global Consciousness

I have been in love with the sky since birth. And when I could fly, I wanted to go higher, to enter space and become a "man of the heights." During the eight days I spent in space, I realized that mankind needs height primarily to better know our long-suffering Earth, to see what cannot be seen close up. Not just to love her beauty, but also to ensure that we do not bring even the slightest harm to the natural world.

—PHAM TUAN, a Vietnamese who went out into space in 1980[9]

Global consciousness is a recognition that each human being is a living part of a larger sentient being, Earth, which is constantly changing from within. It is the realization that this earth is a very small jewel suspended in an unpredictable, constantly changing universe charged with universal energy. Our thoughtless consumerism is putting Earth under stress. As a result, she is losing her mantle of oxygen-giving trees and the mantle that protects her from burning ultraviolet rays.

"On a Subtle level," says Reverend Joseph Martines, a noted Filipino healer, "Earth is dropping veils that have kept her insulated from direct relationship with cosmic energies."[10] The esoteric side of global consciousness is the recognition that all life on Earth is now being charged with universal energies that are accelerating spiritual growth throughout the globe itself and all her people. This may be the reason for the increased interest in spiritual emergence. Conceivably, Earth is also evolving—going through her own spiritual emergence process—dropping the boundaries that have kept her from being one with the highest spiritual energies in this universe.

Recent scientific discoveries support the idea that "the planet Earth functions as a single living organism and that we, as part of the planet, are life *within* life. The Earth produces and renews its parts, including the thick atmospheric boundary through which it exchanges energy with its environment."[11] This is the *Gaia* (Greek for "mother of all things") hypothesis. The writings that are seminal to this hypothesis can be found in the works of Sahtouris, Lovelock, and Margulis in the references at the end of this book.

Now, think of what we are doing to this mother of whom we are a part. We bore into her, extracting her insides—minerals, gases, oils—as if she has an infinite supply. We pour toxins into her waters and her air. Even her atmosphere is becoming polluted. By harvesting the trees and jungles, we further devastate her potential for giving us clean air. We rip away the ecosystems that support whole species of life. We tear holes in the ozone layer that protect all life from ultraviolet radiation.

Are the unusual droughts, flooding, earthquakes, climactic changes, and other natural disasters Gaia's language to tell her children to stop the polluting and uncontrolled plundering of her body? Is she calling to us in her physical distress, "Wake up, wake up"? Is her physical illness (and our psychological and spiritual distress as cells of her body) becoming our wake-up call?

In the past, Earth was revered as a goddess, a force more intelligent than mortal human beings. It is time for us to revere her now, again. In an active way we need to treat her as the mother she is to us. We need to respect that her resources are not constantly renewable. She has finite resources. She cannot always find balance and health in the face of all that we do to her. James Lovelock, a scientist and theoretician, writes:

> Individuals interact with Gaia in the cycling of the elements and in the control of the climate, just like a cell does in the body. You also interact individually in a spiritual manner through a sense of wonder about the natural world and from feeling a part of it. In some ways this interaction is not unlike the tight coupling between the state of the mind and the body. Another connection is through the powerful infrastructures of human communication and mass transfer. We as a species now move a greater mass of some materials around the Earth than did all the biota of Gaia before we appeared. Our chattering is so loud that it can be heard to the depths of the Universe.[12]

There is no positive logic to our depleting the earth's regenerative power and nonrenewable resources. It is suicide. We must find a way to recollect, to live through, our love and interconnectedness for the earth. We will find this only when we turn within.

Many American-Indian cultures use the Purification Ceremony to renew their kinship with "Grandmother," the Earth. They set up a small lodge covered with blankets and tarps so tightly that no light can enter in. In the center is a pit for rocks that have been heated in a fire. When the participants in the ceremony have entered the lodge, the rocks are brought in and the door is shut. The heat and darkness demand a profound surrender. In this "sweatlodge," we are, metaphorically, back inside of Grandmother's womb in a safe place with our brothers and sisters. The heat draws out our fears, anger, and repressed feelings, along with the realization that we have these bodies, these feelings, just for a short time. In turn, each individual lets go and prays for the help she needs on a spiritual level in order to be true to her inmost soul purpose. We feel how dependent we are on Grandmother Earth. We feel how we want to become the beautiful people God put us on Earth to become. We rekindle our desire to treasure Earth and all sentient life.

The crisis on the earth, like the heat and darkness in the sweatlodge, catalyzes a transformation in consciousness. We are forced to become aware of the preciousness of life and our connection to both Earth and Higher Power. Our survival instincts, deep in our own biology, have direct knowing that to move to transpersonal levels of consciousness is the only way to effectively address the crisis. Only in these realms will we find our potential for health, and world peace, and creative answers to our problems. There, we will generate a more refined experience of happiness that is not at Gaia's expense. The veils that have protected us from communicating with the rest of our universe fall away. We realize our potential for managing ourselves in a space more huge than we ever imagined.

The Wisdom Culture

> Have men's minds changed,
> Or the rock hidden in the deep of the waters of the soul
> Broken the surface?
>
> —ROBINSON JEFFERS, "Night"

The people who are responding to the world crisis by embracing their spiritual emergence are creating a new culture, the Wisdom Culture. Many of these people are, like Isaac, in middle age and approaching seniority. They are committed to Self-realization. They have achieved a stable identity; they take responsibility for themselves. They are living on the Subtle level and growing toward the Causal and Atman; in so doing, they have realized the "perennial wisdom." These people are more "global," less identified with local, state, or national boundaries and more identified with the issues of maintaining this planet as a whole. A relevant motto is, "Think globally, act locally." These people realize their soul connection with others and their own soul purpose. They are souls who have transcended the personal identification with personal desires. They are dedicated to evolution—wisdom is revered above possessions and money. They are inspired by compassion and a desire to serve—as the stories in this book have illustrated. These are the people who can give assistance, vision, and motivation to people struggling in their personal darkness. They hear the souls of the people screaming for real guidance and preparation for the world as it is changing, and want to be of service.

The people who comprise what I am calling the Wisdom Culture have found their alignment with the upper and lower worlds. They have the tools to continue awakening, and are now more accessible to those beginning to wake up. They are initiating new school programs, training seminars, alternative healing hospitals, and community-based projects to strengthen community and wellness. Their work is becoming more and more visible.

The dawn of this Wisdom Culture coincides with the aging of America. Americans are living longer, and the older generation is healthier, more vigorous, and more influential than any other older generation in American history. A decade ago, the birthrate in the United States plummeted to its lowest point ever. It has been hovering there ever since, and it's not likely to change.[13] The great population of elders is not being offset by an explosion of children. The Population Reference Bureau, a nonprofit demographics study group in

Washington, D.C., has projected that by the year 2025, Americans over sixty-five will outnumber teenagers by more than two to one. According to the Census Bureau, by 2030 the median age is expected to have reached forty-one.[14] More and more of these people will have near-death experiences and the accompanying spiritual awakening, as a result of improvements in resuscitation technology.

Monsignor Charles Fahey, a prominent religious leader and gerontologist, suggests that the older years offer the opportunity for increased awareness and personal growth. "We know that even with the best of care, overall fitness will decline gradually with the years. While the strength of the senses is weakening, what if the powers of the mind, the heart, and the spirit are rising?"[15] Erik Erikson (a psychologist well known for conceptualizing the stages of life) also suggests that the later years are the time naturally centered on drawing together the loose ends of life and achieving personal wholeness and wisdom. This later part of life, less hurried and more reflective, allows the further development of the interior life of the intellect, memory, and imagination, of emotional maturity and of one's own personal sense of spiritual identity. It is a period of giving back to society the lessons, resources, and experiences accumulated over a lifetime.[16] As quantitatively more of our population focuses on this quest for wholeness, there should be more wisdom in circulation, available to those beginning to awaken. As more of us grow older, and stay older longer, we may have a wisdom-oriented culture replacing the youth-oriented perspective of the fifties and sixties.

As the post–World War II "baby boomers" are just reaching their forties, there is a cultural fad of health through diet and exercise. Now is the time for the Wisdom Culture to take a more prominent position—when there is increasing energy in more people interested in maintaining well-being during middle and old age.

What does the Wisdom Culture have to do with spiritual emergency? People of the Wisdom Culture are in a natural position to be helpers to those in spiritual emergency. They can be role models. They are personally acquainted with the journey, and know the landscape of spiritual emergence. They are not afraid of the phenomena as are those who have not undertaken the awakening process. Those of the Wisdom Culture who are at the age of retirement especially are more likely to have the time to be with people needing companionship around the clock.

Twenty-Four-Hour Care for People in Spiritual Emergency: Models for Worldwide Use

The Spiritual Emergence Network regional coordinators maintain offices in forty locations around the world. (Their current addresses and telephone numbers are available through the Spiritual Emergence Network's central office in Menlo Park.) Like the central Spiritual Emergence Network office, they do not offer crisis care by telephone but act as a referral service routing people to resources in the larger community. Some coordinators also organize talks, seminars, and conferences to educate people about spiritual emergency. Educational materials and administrative policies are available to these coordinators from the central SEN office in Menlo Park, although the regional coordinators are not restricted to using them. In some cases, coordinators are making a dedicated effort to manage twenty-four-hour care for people in spiritual emergency, when conventional hospital treatment is inappropriate. These nonresidential programs are being implemented in the United States, Scotland, Denmark, and Germany.

Following are models for caring for people in spiritual emergency who need companionship twenty-four hours a day. Ideally, people in spiritual emergency are cared for within a familylike setting by qualified helpers. Currently, there are three models for this kind of care that are being used and can be adapted to different communities. One is a large family home where people in crisis are cared for as if they are each part of the family. The second model has the person in crisis stay in his home and a group of helpers come into the home on a rotating basis. The third model is in a hospital setting where one ward is designed for people in spiritual emergency.

The competencies of these helpers have been written about in *The Sourcebook for Helping People in Spiritual Emergency.* Briefly, these include: an open heart, the experience of integrating spiritual experiences into daily life, familiarity with one's own unconscious, groundedness, emotional stability, and resourcefulness. Clinical qualifications are also important: the ability to recognize psychosis and not be put off by someone who is in an extremely altered state and some psychotherapeutic skills for working with people in extreme states. Training for helping people in spiritual emergency is available through the Spiritual Emergence Network in Menlo Park, California. (See Resources at the back of this book.)

The essential task of being a helper is in maintaining a particular state of *being*. It is a state that goes beyond conventional models where the person helped is seen as weaker than the helper. Richard Gorman and Ram Dass express it in the following way:

> The most familiar models of who we are—father and daughter, doctor and patient, "helper" and "helped"—often turn out to be major obstacles to the expression of our caring instincts; they limit the full measure of what we have to offer one another. But when we break through and meet in spirit behind our separateness, we experience profound moments of companionship. These, in turn, give us access

to deeper and deeper levels of generosity and loving kindness. True compassion arises out of unity.[17]

Family home model: This model was drawn from traditional cultures that acknowledged spiritual emergency. Many ancient cultures have developed their own ways for managing the spiritual emergence process. In Tibet, for example, the person in spiritual emergency was kept at home. He or she was relieved of household duties and allowed to be quiet, participating or not in family activities. The disorientation of the spiritual emergency was regarded as part of the experience and not a symptom of pathology. People who had been through the same process and integrated the experience were available for companionship in the family and community. They provided an anchor point for the person in crisis. The crisis was acknowledged as a time of bridging to a deeper level of wisdom and compassion.

This model has been replicated in our culture in several experiments under the supervision of John Weir Perry, M.D., Lauren Mosher, M.D., and Alma Menn, A.C.S.W. One such experiment designed for first-break psychotics, was Soteria House. It used a large older home in San Francisco to care for six residents. Two staff members were always on duty. One or two volunteers were usually present. In all there were six paid staff members plus the project director and a quarter-time project psychiatrist. This small group atmosphere maximized the possibility of a resident getting to know and trust a new environment and to find a surrogate family in it. Structure and rules for dealing with residents who were acting out could be more flexible within such a small group. Staff and residents shared the responsibility for household maintenance, meal preparation, and cleanup. The primary focus was on growth, development, and learning—as opposed to "treating" or "curing." Medications were not routinely used but were available.[18]

Soteria House had notable success as an alternative treatment facility for first-break schizophrenics, although it was not given an adequate state subsidy to continue. Psychiatric medications were hardly ever used. After care, the residents adjusted more easily to work, living arrangements, and friendships than others who had been treated in a more conventional hospital setting with medications. The cost of this "care" in the mid-1970s was similar to that of patients treated for psychosis in a regular hospital setting.

A similar home-oriented therapeutic setting has been established at Pocket Ranch, outside of Healdsburg, California. Under the supervision of Barbara Findeisen, a marriage, family, child therapist, individuals in crisis have access to twenty-four-hour care by resident counselors, including intensive psychotherapy. The caregivers at Pocket Ranch are attuned to the potential evolutionary nature of psychological crises, and work with their clients within a transpersonal framework. Bodywork and a natural foods diet supplement the counseling as important components of creating wellness.

Rotating Helpers: This model is currently being used in community settings in the United States as well as by Spiritual Emergence Network helpers in Denmark. When I lived in the San Francisco Zen Center Community in the early 1970s, there were a few occasions in which a community member became severely psychologically disorganized. Other members would take turns sitting with the distressed person in an attempt to give the person time to work through the psychological material that was upsetting him. All of these helpers shared a similar growth model for development that included spiritual emergency processes, and all of us had become acquainted with our own unconscious through meditation practice. However, we had varying degrees of psychotherapeutic skills and comfort levels with extreme states. We rarely had access to psychiatric supervision. This detracted from the level of care we could give.

More recently, at Esalen Institute, a retreat center in California offering seminars in human growth, and at Findhorn, a similar center in Scotland, plans are under way in training a group of six to eight helpers with basic therapeutic skills to be "on call" for spiritual emergency situations within the community. These people will coordinate their schedules so they can together offer twenty-four-hour care to an individual in his or her home. The special skills of each person will be recognized by the others such that their work with the "client" will be complementary. A supervising psychiatrist will be available for consultation. The surrogate "family" will come to the client's home.

Hospital Ward: Another alternative is a hospital ward designed specifically for people in psychospiritual crises. I visited one in Boulder, Colorado, in 1988. It is on a separate wing of the community hospital.

The ward is small, self-contained, informal, and oriented toward community building. Nurses and doctors wear street clothes as one way of not setting themselves apart from (or as better than) the clients. There is room for approximately twenty beds. There is also a hot-tub room for relaxation. Bodywork is given to each client once a day. Nautilus and exercise equipment are available on the ward, as is a padded room for solitude and/or emotional catharsis. Group therapy and personal psychotherapy are available. Many of the clients also go into the community to attend 12-Step program meetings like Adult Children of Alcoholics or Alcoholics Anonymous. In this way, they are encouraged to disengage from dysfunctional family patterns, let go of old fear, grief, and anger, and cocreate a more affirmative surrogate family on the ward. The hospital staff who work on this ward are all trained in a transpersonal perspective. Questions about this hospital may be addressed to the SEN regional coordinator in Boulder, Colorado.

A freestanding independent hospital, called Sanctuary, created on the above model, is now being initiated in Santa Cruz, California. It is conceived as an alternative to the local community hospital system. Psychiatric care under the regular community system is based solely on a disease model, where psychological distress is seen as pathology and usually treated primarily through medications. At Sanctuary, staff will also be attuned to a "wellness" model, so that episodes of psychological distress are viewed as potential stepping-stones to enhanced functioning. Dietary changes, bodywork, exercise programs, rest, and becoming knowledgeable about one's inner life will be favored above drugs as an adjunct to psychotherapy. Psychiatrists and other professionals will attend to the physiological aspects of the emotional problems. Again, the emphasis is on finding true safety rather than bolstering false security with unnecessary dependence on drugs, recreational or psychiatric.

Sanctuary will hopefully be functioning by 1992. Two of the project coordinators can be reached by telephone for information regarding clinical and business details of the project. (See the Resource section at the back of the book.)

In sum, the current global situation has created a longing for true safety and the necessity for personal transformation. In response to the stresses of our time, people are catapulted into spiritual awakening. There we find true safety, renewed strength, inspiration, a desire for service, and a deeper sense of spirituality. Without this true safety, we reach out to social and political systems that are in the process of crumbling. Our spiritual emergence is the only way to find security as the earth beneath our feet trembles with change and universal energies become more accessible, accelerating our own awakening.

The concluding chapter of this book offers guidelines for friends and family members of someone in spiritual emergency. Of course, they are also relevant for anyone personally in crisis.

11

How to Help in Spiritual Emergency

Throughout the foregoing chapters, there are suggestions on how to support spiritual emergence and how to identify spiritual emergency. This concluding chapter gives a summary of the main points to remember if you are in a position to help someone in a spiritual emergency. I include a synopsis on the importance of *grounding* and the value of bodywork and transpersonal psychotherapy in that process. In conclusion, there are answers to questions most frequently asked about spiritual emergency.

The suggestions and instructions in this chapter cannot substitute for actual training. Working with people who are in crisis demands not only the desire to be of service, but skill and seasoned understanding. Although all psychological disturbances may have spiritual aspects to them, these are not necessarily all spiritual emergencies. Differential diagnosis by trained health care workers may be vital. A licensed physician, psychologist, or psychiatrist should be consulted in cases of real emergency—ideally, one who has a transpersonal orientation. If one cannot be found, the suggestions in this book may be a useful supplement to conventional treatment authorized by professional health care personnel.

Checklist for the Helper

1. First ask the person what he or she needs and what would be helpful. Does the person in crisis need to see a professional mental health worker to assess the need for therapy and/or drugs? Does he need to consult a physician to assess the state of physical health? Does

he need to have a sanctuary or a place where he can be looked after twenty-four hours a day?

If so, help your friend make an appointment with an appropriate health care worker. Look in the yellow pages for a transpersonal or humanistic counselor or psychologist. Offer your assistance in helping your friend get to the appointment/hospital/sanctuary and back home.

If you need a referral to a transpersonal therapist or place of sanctuary in your geographic area, contact the Spiritual Emergence Network in Menlo Park, California.

2. If you can, be a spiritual companion to your friend in spiritual emergency. Offer her compassion and acceptance. Verbally or nonverbally, affirm that spiritual experiences are okay. Tell a story demonstrating your ease with spiritual experiences. Acknowledge that they can be disorienting.

Stay in the present moment yourself—without getting wrapped up in apprehensions about the future or concerns from the past. Maintain your connection to Higher Power. Use your spiritual community of friends for extra support. If your friend is affiliated with a religious group, help her to make a connection to a clergy member or elder who can be supportive.

3. Help your friend to get grounded. This might mean describing the process of spiritual emergence so your friend has a map of the journey and does not feel completely lost. Help your friend feel more connected to his body and the earth. Help him take a break from the intensity and solitude of his inner life. Eat together, take a walk in nature, take your friend away from overstimulating sounds, give a neck and shoulder rub, massage his feet, listen while your friend tells his story, encourage his expression of feelings.

If there are bodyworkers or transpersonal psychotherapists in your area, you might educate your friend about the value of the kind of inner work they offer. This will also encourage more grounding.

4. Talk to your friend about her relationship to Higher Power. In doing so, you are, in a sense, evoking the presence of that power. What is it? How does she experience it? Is there a prayer or ritual practice to do that is particularly helpful in aligning with Higher Power? This might be going to a 12-Step program meeting, or meditating, or saying affirmations, reading from a spiritual text, listening to inspirational music, looking at a particular picture, etc.

5. If you feel overwhelmed, or scared, get the help you need. Almost every large city has a suicide hot line for crisis counseling twenty-four hours a day. Emergency care at your hospital is also available twenty-four hours a day. No one has to be alone in a crisis— neither the person having the crisis nor the person trying to help them.

Grounding for the Helper

Being a helper can be terrifying! You may be faced with unusual behavior, strange and new ideas, extraordinary interests, incredible stories, and overwhelming emotions, from your friend in crisis. You may be afraid that your friend has "flipped out" and will be crazy forever. You may be afraid that you will go crazy from being around your friend in crisis. Seeing and hearing your friend may remind you of parts of your own life that have always been difficult to face.

For a helper to feel some apprehension is natural. The transpersonal dimensions are extremely powerful, and demand respect. These dimensions put us in touch with the deepest, most profound mysteries in life. Being around someone immersed in a spiritual emergency will make changes in you too. The quickening of inner life in them will incite your own inner life. Just as laughter and passion are infectious, so is spiritual opening. The more I work with people in these realms, the more I need to work on my own grounding, inner processes, and spiritual opening.

There are several appropriate ways to handle your own fears. One way is to speak about them. Say, "I feel frightened by what is happening to you." This honest self-revelation might well help both you and your friend in crisis to become grounded together in the truth—you are both facing a difficult situation together. Another way to manage your fear is to get the help you need. If I have any fear in working with a person in emergency, I consult a colleague for extra support and insight. Another way is to be aware of your breath; feel the fear and continue breathing. If you contract your breath, it will increase your fear. If you continue breathing normally, and focus on the constant rhythm of your breath, it may help you to be less fearful. Maintaining your own grounding will be essential to your capacity to help. You will need to stay rational and be able to take care of details. There are basic issues that always need to be attended to.

Keep in mind that phenomena similar to spiritual experiences may happen as a result of physical imbalances. What looks like a "possession" by a negative force may actually be the result of a food allergy. An "altered state" may be the result of an organ dysfunction, fasting, drug use, a nutritional imbalance, overexposure to the sun, or even intimacy. Physical well-being needs to be assessed. Even before you take someone to see a doctor, you can pay attention to their basic functions: Has your friend had enough liquids, enough solid food? Has he or she been getting adequate rest? Is he or she warm enough, or feverish?

You need to assess your own resources in helping your friend in crisis. You need to know how much emotional energy you have to offer this person, who may need a great deal of reassurance and companionship. If you can't provide all that is needed, perhaps there is another mutual friend or family member who could step in? Ideally, you can establish a support network that is consistent.

You must also attend to your own needs, even though you are drawn to help your friend or family member. No one of us can give infinitely without also filling up somewhere. Make sure you stay grounded by receiving the support and nurturing you need as a whole human being. Although I see individuals in crisis for some period of time, I never see them by myself for more than a few hours. I always make sure there is a network of support people for myself and anyone in crisis. If I have a client in severe crisis, I speak with a psychiatrist at the hospital to alert him that I may need help in hospitalizing someone.

This need for a network of support is especially important if the person in crisis has any history of suicide attempts or self-mutilation, or is talking about them now. It is essential to find out if your friend has been considering suicide. Ask directly: "Have you been thinking about hurting yourself? Have you thought about how you would do it? Have you got the pills, gun, or other tools to carry it out? Have any other members of your family killed themselves?" Answers to these questions will indicate the severity of the issue. Although some suicidal thinking may be a cry for help, a need for attention, or an underlying longing for peace, suicidal thinking can also lead to real suicide. If there is a threat of suicide, call your local suicide prevention hot line or the police for help.

Grounding the Person in Crisis

People in spiritual emergency may feel out of touch with their body, or their emotions, or the earth, or their friends and community. Getting in touch with these elements can provide the grounding needed. However, these same elements may also be out of reach during the crisis.

The helper needs to assist the person in crisis in getting some grounding without denying the power of the spiritual experiences he may be having. One way to ground other people is in the quality of your relating to them. Tell them the truth, don't lie or pretend that there is not a crisis, and keep your own agreements. For example: "Yes, this does seem like a crisis. I want you to get some help. I feel I can't do it alone. What I can do is spend the morning taking you to see a therapist. I don't feel comfortable having you stay at home by yourself all day."

Another way to ground someone is to be in physical contact. Again, here is what Jessica, the martial arts teacher who herself experienced spiritual emergency, recommends:

Hold them. Breathe with them. Hold them in a way that is nonsexual, but hold in a loving way that communicates acceptance and trust. One of the most terrible aspects of having a spiritual opening in the midst of emotional distress is feeling alone and unable to handle all the different sensations in your body. It feels as if there is just too much to hold in yourself alone. Being held by someone else is a great relief. It helps bring you back to yourself. It gives you the sense that it is all manageable.

If the person in crisis makes it clear that she does not want to have physical contact, do not force the touch. Let your friend's desires be the determinant.

A third way to help your friend get grounded is by taking him out in nature to walk or sit. Fresh air, the sounds of birds, the scent of trees and flowers, the touch of the earth beneath our feet, are always grounding. When Galen felt possessed, her girlfriends took her out of the house and made her do calisthenics, which brought her back into her body fully.

The food we eat has a tremendous impact on grounding. Heavier foods, which are harder to digest—meat, fish, milk products, and bread—help in grounding. Foods that are easier to digest—fruit and vegetables, grains, soups, juices, tofu—will be less help in grounding. However, the very act of eating is itself grounding, because it helps the person pay attention to the body.

Other elements that will help people in spiritual emergency get back in touch with themselves more fully are catharsis, sanctuary, and education.

Catharsis

Oftentimes a person in spiritual crisis needs to vent emotions. Being provided with a safe context to have this catharsis is of great value to those who are beside themselves with strong emotions. As a helper, you can offer a shoulder to cry on or a pillow to pound on. Help people express anger or fear that has been kept inside by encouraging them verbally: "It's all right with me if you want to cry. I think it might be really good for you. You don't have to hold back your feelings. . . . When I feel angry, I lie on a bed and kick and scream for a while, it helps me get it out of my system. The important thing is not to physically hurt yourself or someone else."

If you do not feel comfortable helping your friend in this way, perhaps there is someone else in your network of family and friends who can serve this purpose. If not, you may want to consult a professional psychotherapist (see the subheads on transpersonal psychotherapy and bodywork in this chapter).

Sanctuary

Helping people in crisis more often than not includes providing them a safe place to surrender to themselves. A sanctuary is a physical place where people in crisis can be absorbed with their inner life without being a burden to anyone else. It is a place where nothing is expected of people but to be themselves. (The days of solitude Ananda Cooperative Village offers its members are one example of a sanctuary. Such days afford people uninterrupted time to meditate and rest.)

Richard's friends (see chapter 9) offered him a real sanctuary in his own home. Around the clock, they kept him company, allowing him his feelings, his visions, his inner voices, and his thoughts. They encouraged him to drink liquids and brought him his meals. They respected him for all of who he was. They also consulted a psychiatrist to obtain medication and hospitalization for Richard when he needed it.

Jackie also needed to find sanctuary with a supportive group when she found that her son was comatose and would die within weeks. For hours, she was so upset she just lay down, wouldn't talk, and hardly moved.

> My husband went to the phone and called all my women friends. He told them what had happened, and of my great need. For the next three months these women attended me in the most exquisite ways. Some brought me flowers and food, gave me a special bath salts and body massage. Others brought special religious symbols and shared experiences of grief. We talked about death and life, and I could express my deep feelings of pain and fear. The love and special support helped me out of my paralyzing despair and helped refocus my energy.

Another element of sanctuary is feeling close to Higher Power. Traditionally, a sanctuary is a place of reverence for God. You as a helper might offer to pray or sing hymns with your friend or family member. Sit quietly together. In that silence, you may want to say a verbal prayer, such as, "May you find a return to peace and well-being through the help of Jesus Christ." Or, addressing the feminine aspect of God, "Goddess"—or "Divine Mother" or "Grandmother Earth"— "please guide me to complete well-being through your divine protection." A woman who is mistrustful of men may be more comfortable appealing to a feminine personification of divine energy such as Kuan Yin, the goddess of compassion, than appealing to Jesus Christ or a masculine God. If a personification of divine energy is not meaningful to your friend in crisis, you might use the Divine Invocation (repeated from chapter 4).

I am created by Divine Light
I am sustained by Divine Light
I am protected by Divine Light
I am surrounded by Divine Light
I am ever growing into Divine Light

There are other ways of evoking Higher Power that are more secular and thus more appropriate for a person who is unfamiliar with or estranged from all forms of spiritual prayer. The terminology is very important, and should be personally meaningful to the person in crisis. A positive short phrase, or poem, that is easy to remember in times of distress will suffice. Examples of these affirmations are: "Faith and Courage carry me on," "I choose the course of Love," "I rest assured in a greater power than myself," "All things work together for good," "Forgiveness sets me free." Listening to music, especially harmonic, classical music, will also be soothing and harmonizing.

Education

If your friend is not too absorbed in the phenomena of his own spiritual emergency, it may be appropriate to offer stories that conceptualize spiritual emergence and emergency. These stories about other people who have been through spiritual phenomena can be tremendously reassuring. They may also help awaken a person to a particular manifestation of divine energy that is meaningful to them. You might refer to some of the books in the References section for chapter 5 for biographies of spiritual adepts. A description of the cartography of spiritual emergence, as outlined in chapter 1, may be a real comfort as well.

Integrating Back into Life

After people have been through the critical phase of a spiritual emergency, they will have to bring their new perspective back into their own lives. They will be reevaluating the way they have related to family, friends, and community. They might want to change the way they eat, the way they relate to friends, and what they do for recreation. They may be more interested in cultivating their relationship to the earth and their own body. They may want to explore different spiritual practices or make a career shift. This is an important process of their valuing their own uniqueness and honoring their ability to create the life they need.

This process of integration can be extremely difficult. It is less dramatic and less romantic than the phenomena of the patterns of spiritual emergency. However, it is no less significant in terms of the process of transformation to higher levels of consciousness. These people need to create a lifestyle that is enduring and practical and gracefully supports spiritual emergence.

A helper's role in this process is to support people in staying grounded and getting professional help if they want it. Psychotherapy, for sorting out the value of old ways of relating and exploring new ways of relating to themselves and others, is valuable for anyone in a process of reevaluation. Bodywork can assist people in eliminating the physical holding patterns that were aspects of old ways of being. As the body regains its natural flexibility, the body and mind become free to have new, more functional response patterns to life.

The following sections discuss the roles of transpersonal psychotherapy and bodywork in helping people integrate spiritual emergency phenomena and maintain ongoing spiritual emergence. They should be useful in choosing a psychotherapist or bodyworker.

The Role of Transpersonal Psychotherapy

Usually, we think of psychologists and psychiatrists as healers of mental disease and the impasses of thorny relationships. Sickness and life problems are their focus. We only go to a psychotherapist if we perceive something "wrong" with ourselves. Sadly, it is unusual for people to think of a psychotherapist as someone who will help nurture a side of themselves just coming to life, or help in finding balance between the personal and transpersonal aspects of life. This is a realm where transpersonal psychotherapists can be of service.

The role of the psychotherapist for anyone needing to establish a life-affirming relationship to his or her spiritual awakening is to offer grounding, containing, and connection with an appropriate community. Take Ann, for example. She was the mother referred to in chapter 7 who became deathly ill after she had confronted the threat of her daughter's death. To begin with, the therapist will *educate* Ann about the phenomena of spiritual awakening in the context of natural human development and how to maintain *grounding*. This conceptual framework will give her a way to think about the experiences she had, and help her understand that she is not alone . . . everyone has some relationship to their spiritual side. The relationship with the therapist would be the *safe container* where Ann could feel her feelings, explore her thoughts, be appreciated for her uniqueness, without any demands placed on her other than to be herself. Thus, the therapeutic relationship would function like the group that Jackie had: listening, caring, encouraging her to be herself. The therapist will also offer Ann techniques to nurture her relationship with the spiritual side of herself—for example, meditation, guided imagery, affirmations.

The therapeutic hour will be a time for Ann to come to terms with how she can incorporate her spiritual life into her home life, to *integrate* the two. Ideally, the therapist could treat Ann's awakening as a sacred process and nurture it as such—providing Ann with a model of how to care for herself. Last, the therapist will help Ann decide what kind of group would be appropriate for her to join at what time. Thus, through the therapist's *referrals*, Ann would have a way to a group that would help her contain her ongoing spiritual growth.

This model of a psychotherapist's role is actually similar to a shaman's role. The therapist, like the shaman, is a teacher of how to bridge the transpersonal world, beyond ego, with the ordinary world, defined by ego. The goal of this kind of therapy is for the individual to find a manageable way to move back and forth, gracefully participating in either world at the appropriate time. This is especially important for people having spiritual experiences around the death of a loved one, where there is an intensified possibility of becoming absorbed in spiritual dimensions. The goal is to have a strong sense of self but not to become rigidly identified in ego. The goal is to have a strong sense of one's spiritual life, but not to become rigidly identified as a spiritual being unwilling to participate fully in the world. People need to be able to take care of all the responsibilities they have in their family and community as well as continue to enter into their spiritual life with increasing fullness. The two together bring about wholeness.

Transpersonal psychotherapists, like myself, are oriented toward promoting optimal health. This always includes nurturing spiritual growth, as well as catalyzing healing of personal issues that may be the source of emotional distress. The transpersonal psychotherapist must be able to distinguish emotional disease from the phenomena of spiritual awakening—to see the difference between a debilitating psychosis and phenomena of a dramatic spiritual emergence. Therefore, a familiarity with Western psychology, which is oriented toward understanding and treating emotional disorders, is essential along with an understanding of transpersonal states of consciousness. This is obviously more demanding than just treating emotional pathology—there is quantitatively more to understand about human nature. However, after we acknowledge the reality of spiritual emergence, how could we ask for less from a psychotherapist?

In a similar vein, after we acknowledge the reality that universal energy, prana, has a pathway through our bodies that can be worked with to enhance well-being, how could we not ask for some form of bodywork in health maintenance? Bodywork can have a powerful positive impact on integrating spiritual experiences, grounding, and expanding to new states of awareness as well.

The Role of Bodywork (including martial arts, yoga, accupressure, massage, authentic movement, etc.)

> Most people come to my hatha-yoga classes for practical reasons, to improve a bad back, or get better circulation, or simply increase their sense of having some control over the health of their body. Hatha-yoga is excellent at simply addressing particular physical problems. People make improvements. So, I like my classes to flow from the needs of the people in each session.
>
> I don't usually tell people about the outer reaches of what is possible with yoga . . . for example, the kundalini awakening. Most people don't want to know, although some people in my classes know that yoga offers an opportunity to become aware of Subtle energy as well as improve physical health. Those people who are experiencing some manifestation of spiritual energy usually come to me privately for consultation.
>
> —LOLLY FONT

What bodywork can do for a person is directly linked with what that person wants from it. With a skilled practitioner, bodywork can be done to stimulate physical healing, work with emotional problems, and/or address spiritual emergence. This is certainly true of Oriental body therapies—like hatha-yoga, the martial arts, acupuncture, accupressure—and Western forms of body therapy—the neo-Reichian therapies.

What do they all have in common? Each form increases your contact with your own body, allowing you to trust the knowledge of your body to bring about healing and balance. In both passive forms, like receiving bodywork, and active forms, like the martial arts, you are being touched in a way that recognizes both your physical body and your Subtle energy body. The quality of touch enhances your consciousness of Subtle energies. Then, the bodywork technique itself helps to bring you into a deep *alliance* with your own body, replacing the authoritarian idea of the body as being the slave to the intellect and the ego. It is this same congruence *of body and mind together* that is the platform for moving to transpersonal levels of consciousness. When a person receiving bodywork is in body-and-mind congruence, spontaneously he or she will be open to pranic activity. This is the time we are most given to spiritual experiences. The more we have bodywork that brings us together, the more we increase our possibilities of having spiritual experiences. Sarah (from chapter 7), for example, feels that her heart opening at the Carl Rogers workshop would not have happened unless she had been doing hatha-yoga regularly for a year preceding the workshop.

The quality of touch from a bodyworker, or a martial arts partner or friend, can, by itself, comfort a person in spiritual emergency. This reality is the basis of our phrase *to be deeply touched*. It does not relate to the mechanics of penetrating the flesh deeply; it has to do with contacting the underlying emotional and spiritual aspects of a person. This sensitive touch provides comforting to someone who feels alone. It also helps to anchor spiritual experiences in the body, so the person receiving the bodywork is not perceived as "way out" of reality.

In the workshops I have given on helping people in spiritual emergency, the questions people ask are usually similar in various parts of the country. I list some of them here as a quick reference for families and friends concerned about someone in crisis. Of course, this list is also relevant for people in crisis themselves.

Questions and Answers

How do I know if my friend is in a spiritual emergency?

Refer to chapter 3 of this book. Read through the forms of spiritual emergency from pages 28 to 47. Relate these to the experience your friend is having. Read through the checklist for a helper at the beginning of this chapter. If you have any questions in identifying spiritual emergency, follow the suggestions for a referral in the checklist. Most likely a professional mental health worker can be found in your area through the Spiritual Emergence Network.

My friend doesn't understand what is happening to her. What should I say?

If you feel sure that your friend is in a spiritual emergency, let her know that. Giving the experience a name is usually very reassuring for the person in crisis, especially if the name is not associated with mental disease.

Let your friend know that it is an experience not dealt with consistently by ministers, physicians, or psychologists. Some of these professionals may not be knowledgeable about working with the crisis. Let your friend know that there are resources for help.

Let her know that it is the psyche's (or soul's) way of bringing about wholeness. It involves looking at parts of the self that have been outside of her awareness before, and it will ultimately provide a deeper spiritual understanding of her place in the world.

What will happen if I contact the Spiritual Emergence Network for help?

The Spiritual Emergence Network is not a crisis line but an information service. If there is not someone in the office when you call, an answering machine will take your message: You will be asked to leave a telephone number where you can be reached. When you do talk to someone from the Spiritual Emergence Network, you will be asked for identifying information: name, address, zip code, and phone number. Then you will be asked the reason for your call.

People call the Spiritual Emergence Network for a number of reasons. The Spiritual Emergence Network sells literature and sponsors workshops on spiritual emergence. Some callers want information about these offerings. Some helpers call because they want to become members of the Spiritual Emergence Network. Other people call to get a referral in their area for someone needing help in their spiritual emergence process.

If you want a referral, you will be asked; "What kind of things are happening to you or the friend for whom you want help? Do you want to speak with a helper in your area who is knowledgeable about spiritual emergence phenomena? Would you like this person to be a licensed professional?" The Spiritual Emergence Network can give you some suggestions about how to proceed in caring for your friend but cannot diagnose spiritual emergency.

You will also be told that the Spiritual Emergence Network does not endorse the people whom we refer you to. We have not met all of them. We do know some important information about them. We know that they have a transpersonal orientation, what patterns of spiritual emergence they are most familiar with, what they feel they are most qualified to work with. We know whether they are licensed by their state or not. We know if they charge by sliding scale or set fee. We know if they have resources for twenty-four-hour intensive care.

We ask you to phone us back after you have seen your referral, to let us know if it worked out. This is one way we can gather information that will enable us to qualify the people in our roster of helpers.

How long does spiritual emergency last?

There is no answer to this. It depends on what kind of patterns of spiritual emergence people are experiencing. If the experience is physically very intense, it will end when the body gets tired of the intensity. Likewise, if it is very emotional, the crisis will let up when the body tires of catharsis. All life pulsates—expands and contracts. A contraction cycle will inevitably follow an expansion. An expansion will inevitably follow a contraction.

Curiously enough, people involved with opening to life myth often take forty days to complete the cycle of their crisis. This is measured from the time the crisis starts to the time when they are ready to take up a more normal routine involving family duties and their job-related responsibilities.

The acute physical aspect of Jill's kundalini awakening (in chapter

3) lasted less than twenty-four hours, but learning to live with the changes it brought about lasted several months. During this time, Jill needed to be in retreat from the world and her regular activities. This is generally true of all spiritual emergency experiences. They may last only minutes or hours in the acute phase, but the integration of these experiences may take months. People in the integration phase need to be cared for with continued patience and understanding.

If you try to rush your friend to get through the process, you will likely stimulate some resistance. This will result in the process taking longer. It is helpful to see the process as similar to pregnancy except, in this case, your friend is giving birth to a new aspect of himself or herself. If you rush a woman in pregnancy she will get anxious and feel alienated, and the process may be disturbed. If you relax, let nature take its course, appreciate the fact that new life is taking form, the pregnancy will be beneficial for everyone involved.

Will my friend return to normal when the crisis is over?

Your friend will be changed by spiritual emergency. He or she will regain the ability to go to work, participate in family activities, etc. He or she will regain the ability to live within the routine constraints of the clock, and consensual time and space. Your friend will regain the ability to suppress emotions and to respond with appropriateness in social situations.

However, he may also reevaluate priorities in life. A job change might become important. A shift in the routine of marriage may become desirable. Relationship difficulties that had been swept under the rug for years may come out for airing. Becoming more truthful and more affectionate in all relationships may become a priority. A passion for some creative pursuit, including having a child or returning to school or making a career change or taking a sabbatical, may come to the fore. Getting in better physical shape may become important. There may be a desire to participate more fully in spiritual activities at church or in meditation. All or any of these may demand a radical shift in your relationship to your friend.

Will my marriage to this person in spiritual emergency be able to continue after the crisis is over?

There are no statistics that show what percentage of marriages fail or are improved after spiritual emergency. It depends on the flexibility of both partners in the relationship. Are they able to explore new territory together? Are they able to maintain their connection while they also explore new areas in their lives (work, play, church activities) individually? Are they able to increase their capacity for communication, intimacy, love, and respect? If so, the marriage will thrive with new energy.

If spiritual emergency happens once, will it happen again? Can you predict when?

There is no way to predict if a crisis point will happen again after a person has had a spiritual emergency. The majority who have had spiritual emergencies that they were able to integrate later long for the intensity of the experience. They remember feeling dynamically alive during the crisis and wish for that again. However, they also remember how the crisis point disturbed their lives at work and at home. Usually, this last memory helps them find a way to engage the same energies present in their spiritual emergency without the critical aspects. How? In creative pursuits like painting, sculpting, music, dance. In spiritual practices like meditation, hatha-yoga, vision quest, retreats, chanting, or religious rituals that evoke the presence of Higher Power. In community activities like working for peace and health for self, family, community, and on this planet.

Spiritual emergency is a wakening call, a call to become whole—to engage one's creativity, one's love, one's capacity to serve the well-being of this planetary life. It may be one person's style to have this once or twice in life. It may be another person's way to experience continuous valleys and peaks, a series of opportunities for spiritual emergence. It may be useful to regard the wakening call as an autonomous force that will sound whenever the time is ready for new energy.

My brother had a psychotic break some years ago, and was given medication to stop the symptoms. It looks as if my friend is having the same kind of symptoms my brother had. Does this mean my brother was actually having a spiritual emergency that was misdiagnosed?

It would be very difficult to answer that question without knowing what your brother experienced. The differentiation between psychosis, which is a breakdown, and spiritual emergency, which is a breakthrough, can be very subtle, especially in the beginning stages. How a person is treated in these beginning stages may also increase or decrease the possibility of his gaining useful spiritual insights from the experience itself (see chapter 9 sub-head, Psychiatric Drugs). You might want to talk to your brother. Offer him the concepts of spiritual emergency and see how he relates to them. Ask him if he imagines his experience with psychosis might have been different if he had been treated for spiritual emergency instead.

Should we make any changes at home to provide for the person in crisis?

The environment is the most crucial aspect of caring for someone in spiritual emergency. The physical environment needs to be clean.

Closeness to nature inspires grounding as well as uplifting thoughts and feelings. Natural sounds like water flowing and birds singing are preferable to evocative music or traffic sounds. Low light is better than strong light. Harmonic soft colors in a room are better than dramatic colors and patterns. Soft furniture is better than hard, angular furniture. These aspects of interior design all inspire an attitude of warmth, comfort, and ease.

It is ideal if the family, the social environment, can be accepting of the person in crisis. He or she will have special needs. More need for quiet, for being taken care of, for being reassured and made to feel safe physically and emotionally. People who understand the spiritual emergency process will be the most reassuring, safest people. People who are not honest, are scared or needy, or are trying to manipulate the person in crisis will be the least positive influence. Inspire trust and be trustworthy, consider the thoughts of the person in crisis as important in all decisions made on his or her behalf. Let the person be with people he feels close with.

In terms of providing food for someone in crisis, ask the person what she wants. Try to provide that. In addition, make foods available that are relatively easy to digest to provide adequate, balanced nutrition. People who are upset often have problems with digestion and appetite. *Spiritual Nutrition* by Gabriel Cousins is a good reference book on this topic.

If I am all alone and have a spiritual emergency, what should I do?

Spiritual emergency is most frightening for people when they are alone. The desire to stop the phenomena is then very strong. Somehow the process is much easier when there are other people around, as if other people diffuse the concentration of intense energy.

If you are alone, do something that is grounding for you. Walk around, focusing on your feet and your contact with the ground. You might focus on your breathing—take long, slow breaths, evenly paced inhaling and exhaling. If you have a photograph or a memento that reminds you of someone who loves you, hold it in your gaze or in your hands. You might want to eat some food or drink herb teas, which will help you get more grounded.

Do not put yourself in a situation that will stimulate your inner life unless you are prepared for intensifying the phenomena. Do not take drugs, sugar, caffeine, or any stimulants. Do not go to movies or watch television programs that give you stimulating, violent, chaotic, or sexual pictures. Listen to music that is peaceful if you listen at all. Be in an environment that makes you feel peaceful and close to what is sacred in your life.

Prayer can be very helpful. Meditation is usually too stimulating. Prayer helps you feel yourself as an autonomous entity *in relationship to* the energies of Higher Power. Thus prayer makes you more aware of your limitations and boundaries, your personal identity.

In conclusion, spiritual awakening is a natural process of maturation that seems to be affecting increasing numbers of people. Spiritual awakening phenomena are not in themselves indicative of a crisis. They are manifestations of a positive transformative process. As we become more familiar with the landscape of this process, we will be able to encourage people to move through it and to bring the gifts of wisdom they find back to enrich our culture and our communities.

Glossary

Angel: A disembodied spirit that lives between the world of full union with Higher Power and ordinary absorption in material reality. It has higher intelligence, is motivated purely by love, and has the capacity of opening human beings to increased feelings of love and compassion. Angels are said to be perceptible by some people in transpersonal states of consciousness, particularly in near-death experiences.

Ally: A friend, either in body or in the spiritual realm, who helps people to realize their full potential as they grow more skillful in accommodating the transpersonal realms. In shamanic cultures, the ally is often an animal, bird, or plant.

Archetype: The symbolic embodiment of a universal aspect of human experience, such as the clown, the king, the witch. Each archetype carries a particular constellation of energy having the power to evoke particular emotions.

Archetypal realm: The dimension of life related to universal human instincts (like the urge for power, meaning, survival, reproduction) perceived by the senses and/or manifested in fantasies and dreams. (C. G. Jung)

Atman: The level of consciousness that transcends and includes all earlier levels. Here there is complete unity with Higher Power—the witness and the witnessed, the supernatural and the mundane, are one in the same. It is a state beyond verbal description. (Wilber, *The Atman Project*)

Aura: Emanations of energy that reflect pranic activity in an organ, chakra, or entity as a whole. Specific colors in the aura relate to specific energy states or emotional states.

Boundary: A psychological term referring to one's felt inner sense of identity as unique, autonomous, and distinctly separate from others.

Causal: The level of consciousness in which one experiences union with Higher Power, or God. In the Causal level experience, a person feels perfect ecstasy untainted by distracting thoughts, desires, or moods; there is no sense of time—only eternity.

Channel: (verb) To withdraw one's personal identity and personality from the body in such a way that one's own higher intelligence or that of a disembodied spirit can use the physical body as a vehicle to communicate. (noun) A channel is a person who performs the act of allowing a higher intelligence to communicate through his or her physical body.

Chakra: (Sanskrit for "wheel") An energy vortex in the body that connects the physical system with more subtle sensory activity. The chakras are believed to have significant control over the energetic functioning and well-being of the body. When kundalini awakens, it potentiates increased activity in the chakras.

Clairaudience: The ability to perceive Subtle level impressions through inner hearing that is not necessarily connected to the physiological hearing apparatus. People who are clairaudient may "hear" the rumble of a future earthquake days before it actually happens.

Clairsentience: The ability to perceive information about others through sensation in one's own body. A person who is clairsentient may "feel" the emotions, disturbing thoughts, or disease of someone else in his own body.

Clairvoyance: The ability to perceive accurate information about the past, present, or future through inner visions. These visions may relate to physical activity, biological health, emotions, thoughts, or spiritual experiences. A person who is clairvoyant may "see" the essence of his or herself or another in a way that was formerly imperceptible through ordinary intelligence.

Collective unconscious: Universal, social, human themes that are potentially manifest in all people. They are particularized by nations, communities, and families. The contents of the collective unconscious are more accessible during spiritual emergency than at other times. The higher a person moves in her development, the more differentiated she becomes from the collective unconscious. (C. G. Jung)

Consciousness: A state of awareness. One's level of development defines the quality of that awareness.

Déjà Vu: (French) Refers to a sense of witnessing something as if it has already been seen or happened previously.

Delusion: A belief that has no basis in consensual reality.

Deva: A disembodied being that holds the essence of manifest reality. For example, every place or plant species has a deva that is its overlighting spirit. It emanates higher intelligence. They are sometimes perceivable to people who are open to Subtle levels of consciousness.

Ego: The central organizing and regulating principle of the personality. The authority of the ego is transcended as a person reaches levels of the Subtle, Causal, or Atman.

Essential Self: That part of the soul that is in direct connection with Higher Power, the unity experience, or God.

Exorcism: A ritualized process of ridding the body and mind of negative disembodied influences that are interfering with autonomous action and thought.

Extrasensory perception (ESP): The ability to perceive events beyond the limits of physical hearing, seeing, tasting, feeling, smelling. ESP often refers to intuition, direct knowing, clairvoyance, clairsentience, and clairaudience.

Hallucination: The perception of sights or sounds that are not visible or audible to others, and thus believed to be meaningless and fictitious. The word is commonly used to refer to a pathological state of mind.

Higher intelligence: That part of intelligence that is not under the control of personal desires or personal will. It is motivated by love and compassion. It offers a perspective about oneself or another that is grounded in wisdom and loving-kindness rather than judgment or criticism. Higher intelligence becomes more accessible to us through spiritual disciplines.

Higher Power: Synonym for the ground and source of all creation, of which we all are a part. In 12-Step programs Higher Power can be anything that transcends the authority of individual ego—community, for example.

Karma: (Sanskrit) Refers to the law of cause and effect. We are responsible for our thoughts and actions and their results. Thus, our lives do not unfold randomly, and we have real control over the creation of our destiny. The results of past actions create circumstances that give us the opportunity to learn the lessons we need.

Kriya: (Sanskrit) A release of pranic energy evidenced by shaking, vibration, and strong emotional states.

Kundalini energy: (Sanskrit) The life force that is the fundamental power of creation and the primary consciousness of the universe. After human life is created, the kundalini energy typically lies dormant close to the base of the spine. Prana subsequently activates the biological functions. As an individual experiences spiritual emergence, the kundalini is said to "awaken," activating potential for union with Higher Power and instilling a desire for full self-realization.

Mature ego: This developmental stage is reached after a person has integrated the various parts of his or her personality. The person can then differentiate from the ego to seek a higher order of unity in spiritual growth. (Wilber, *The Atman Project*)

Mythic realm: Pertains to dimensions of personal experience that relate to archetypal experience. People in spiritual emergency often are absorbed in perceptions of reality that have mythic proportions.

Near-death experience (NDE): Refers to being clinically dead for a period of time and then revived. The majority of people who have had an NDE report experiencing a certain set of Subtle level events while "dead," such as seeing the white light, and then undergo radical personality and value changes after their NDE, often becoming more loving and compassionate. (Ring, *Heading Toward Omega*)

Out-of-body experience (OOBE): A period when the soul is disengaged from the body, when consciousness travels independent of physical functioning.

Possession: The experience of being dominated either by a part of one's own personality that has been repressed or by another being.

Prana: (Sanskrit) An electrical-like energy flow in the body that essentially activates the mind and the entire physiological system, through the sympathetic and parasympathetic nervous systems. It is a grosser form of energy than the kundalini, and is always active. Prana is intimately tied with the breath, and may be manipulated through breathing exercises, thus activating more conscious awareness and control of the mind and organic body. When Kundalini awakens, the pranic activity increases and may elicit muscle spasms, vibrations, and sensations of streaming energy.

Psi phenomena: Forces beyond the physical world that are perceived by senses beyond taste, sight, hearing, feeling, smelling. Thus, they include ESP, precognition, clairvoyance, etc.

Psychedelic: A chemical compound that facilitates direct knowledge of the mind when used in the appropriate set and setting.

Psychokinesis: Movement of objects without a physically perceptible material catalyst. Psychokinesis is a psi phenomenon.

Psychosis: A state of emotional turmoil including at least one of the following: incoherence or loosening of associations, delusions, hallucinations, or behavior that is grossly disorganized or catatonic. The personality is disorganized and there is no stable center of consciousness—the awareness moves chaotically from one focus to another.

Samskara: (Sanskrit) A behavioral tendency or condition brought into this life from a previous life, or acquired during present life conditioning.

Satanism: A cult that honors Darkness and the Powers of Destruction, set against the Power of Light, Love, and Creativity (symbolized by the major world religions in their figureheads—Christ, Buddha, Brahma, Allah, etc.).

Shadow: A term from analytical psychology referring to those aspects of the self that are not yet consciously identified with. We often defend our sense of self from overly negative or overly positive parts of the shadow by believing they belong to someone else. For example, since it is not customary to be angry or to feel one's closeness to Higher Power in public, many people prefer to believe they don't have these capacities in their own shadow.

Shakti: (Sanskrit) The powerful activating energy that is the partner of pure consciousness. Together they are essential for manifestation or for any activity to take place. Shakti is an East Indian goddess, often portrayed as a female figure who accompanies Shiva, the symbol of pure consciousness. Shakti refers to the universal nature of energy and, as such, may refer to either prana or kundalini.

Shaman: A woman or man who knows the techniques of creating ecstasy, including unusual trance states. He or she may use these techniques in healing, manifesting miracles, communicating with disembodied beings, and/or with embodied souls telepathically, or exercising social and political power.

Siddhis: (Sanskrit) Powers that become available to an individual as he or she attains access to the Subtle level of consciousness. These powers may include the ability to regulate the heartbeat, heal by laying on of hands, be clairvoyant, etc. These powers become more extraordinary the more the individual dissociates herself from dualistic thinking. In shamanic cultures, these siddhis include the power to transform into a bird or other animal at will.

Soul: The central guiding aspect of the whole person, including aspects of the personality, past samskaras, and the impulse towards self-realization. The soul as a palpable entity resides in the unconscious until a person begins to master the Subtle level, when it then becomes more conscious. It is distinct from but temporarily coexistent with the body during life.

Spirit: The essential part of a person that is completely one with Higher Power and thus devoid of personality and past samskaras.

Spiritual emergence: The process of awakening to dimensions of consciousness that are beyond ego.

Spiritual emergency: Critical turning points in the process of spiritual emergence punctuated by disorientation and absorption in inner life. During spiritual emergency, the way of perceiving and experiencing the world that is based on ego is expanding to include transpersonal modes of perception and experience.

Spiritual illness: One form of illness in which a person readies himself to enter the Subtle and Causal realms. While these illnesses may appear to be only organic, they function to purify a person and give her more access to Subtle level experiences. Spiritual illnesses often occur in children whose destiny is to become a shaman.

Subtle: The level of consciousness beyond the normal capacities of the gross body/mind, wherein a person experiences psi phenomena, occult knowledge, beings of higher intelligence, and profound inspiration. As consciousness matures and differentiates itself from the mind and the body, Subtle level perceptions become more available. (Wilber, *The Atman Project*)

Unconscious: (adj.) Relates to aspects of ourselves we are not yet fully aware of or willing to accept. These aspects may be part of our social selves as members of the human race or part of our individuality. They may be positive or negative in nature. (noun) The unconscious is that realm of the mind that contains energies, perceptual capacities, and memories that the ego is not yet ready to manage.

Vision Quest: A prescribed time in which a man or woman seeks definition of his or her personal power and connection with spiritual allies. It is an important part of training to become a shaman. It is a time of dying to one's conditioned social self and being reborn in the deeper realization of one's essential nature.

Resources

National Outdoor Leadership School (NOLS)
P.O. Box AA
Lander, Wyoming 82520

Nizhoni School for Global Consciousness
Route 3, Box 50
Galisteo, New Mexico 87540

Outward Bound
384 Field Point Road
Greenwich, Connecticut 06830

Pocket Ranch
3960 West Sausal Lane
Healdsburg, California 95448

Spiritual Emergence Network (Central Office)
c/o Institute of Transpersonal Psychology
250 Oak Grove Avenue
Menlo Park, California 94025

Spiritual Emergence Network (Rocky Mountain Office)
c/o Rebecca Browning
4301 North Broadway
Boulder, Colorado 80302

"Sanctuary"
150 Felker St. Suite "G"
Santa Cruz, Ca. 95060
Business details: Gary Haraldsen, Esq.
Clinical details: Bob Newport, M.D.

Notes

Chapter 1

1. Ken Wilber, *The Atman Project* (Wheaton, Ill.: Theosophical Publishing House, 1980).
2. Wilber, *The Atman Project.*

Chapter 2

1. Andrew Greeley, "Mysticism Goes Mainstream," *American Health*, January-February, 1987.
2. Andrew Greeley, "Mysticism Goes Mainstream."
3. For Near-Death Experience: see Kenneth Ring, *Heading Toward Omega* (New York: William Morrow, 1984). For Kundalini: see Gopi Krishna, *Kundalini: The Evolutionary Energy in Man* (Boston: Shambhala, 1971). For shamanism: see Michael Harner, *The Way of the Shaman: A Guide to Power and Healing* (New York: Harper and Row, 1980). For Creativity: see Willis Harman and Howard Rheingold, *Higher Creativity: Liberating the Unconscious for Breakthrough Insights* (Los Angeles: J. P. Tarcher, 1984).
4. Arthur Abell, *Talks with the Great Composers* (Garmish Partenkirchen, Germany: G. E. Schroesder-Verlag, 1964).
5. Abell, *Talks with the Great Composers.*
6. G. N. M. Tyrell, *The Personality of Man* (London, 1946).

Chapter 3

1. Ken Wilber, *The Atman Project* (Wheaton, Ill.: Theosophical Publishing House, 1980).
2. Stanislav Grof, M.D., and Christina Grof, "Spiritual Emergency: The Understanding and Treatment of Transpersonal Crises," *ReVision* 8, no. 2 (1986).
3. Carl G. Jung, *Man and His Symbols* (New York: Doubleday, 1964).
4. The Findhorn Community, *The Findhorn Garden* (New York: Harper & Row, 1975).

Chapter 4

1. Joseph C. Pearce, *The Magical Child: Rediscovering Nature's Plan for Our Children* (New York: E. P. Dutton, 1977).
2. Erik Erikson, *Childhood and Society* (2d ed.) (New York: W. W. Norton, 1963).
3. Erickson, *Childhood and Society.*
4. National Institute on Alcohol Abuse and Alcoholism, "Sixth Special Report to the U.S. Congress on Alcohol and Health from the Secretary of Health and Human Services," DHHS Publication No. (Alcohol, Drug Abuse, Mental Health Administration) 87-1519, (Washington, D.C.: U.S. Government Printing Office, 1987).
5. American Association for Counseling and Development Foundation, letter to members of A.A.C.D. (December, 1988).

6. Arthur Hastings, "A Counseling Approach to Parapsychological Experience," *Journal of Transpersonal Psychology.* 15, no. 2. (1983).
7. Hastings, "A Counseling Approach to Parapsychological Experience."
8. David Lukoff and Howard Everest, "The Myths of Mental Illness" *Journal of Transpersonal Psychology* 17, no. 2. (1985).
9. Erikson, *Childhood and Society.*
10. "Most First Marriages Doomed, New Study Says," *San Francisco Chronicle,* (13 March 1989).
11. U.S. Bureau of Census, *Statistical Abstract of the United States: 1988,* 108th ed. (Washington, D.C.: Washington U.S. Government Printing Office, 1988).
12. Andrew Greeley, "Mysticism Goes Mainstream," *American Health,* January-February, 1987.
13. U.S. Bureau of Census, *Statistical Abstract of the United States: 1989* 109th ed. (Washington, D.C.: Washington U.S. Government Printing Office, 1989).
14. Eric Neuman, *Amor and Psyche* (Princeton: Princeton University Press, 1956).
15. Robert Bly trans. *The Kabir Book: Forty-Four of the Ecstatic Poems of Kabir* (Boston: Beacon Press, 1971).

Chapter 5

1. R. Fulop-Miller, *The Saints that Moved the World* (New York: T. Crowell, 1945).
2. R. Fulop-Miller, *The Saints.*
3. Teresa of Avila, *The Interior Castle,* trans. K. Kavanaugh and O. Rodriguez (New York: Paulist Press, 1979).
4. Gopi Krishna, *Kundalini: The Evolutionary Energy in Man* (Boston: Shambhala, 1970).
5. Gopi Krishna, *Kundalini.*
6. Gopi Krishna, *Kundalini.*
7. Matt. 4:1–11.
8. St. John of the Cross. *The Dark Night,* in *John of the Cross: Selected Writings* (New York: Paulist Press, 1979).
9. R. Assagioli, "Self-Realization and Psychological Disturbances," *Mandalama,* August 1981.
10. The Vipassana Community, "Psychotherapy and Meditation," *Inquiring Mind* 5, no. 1 (Summer 1988).
11. Gopi Krishna, *Kundalini.*

Chapter 6

1. M. Murphy and R. White, *The Psychic Side of Sports* (Addison-Wesley: Reading, Mass. 1978).
2. Murphy and White, *The Psychic Side of Sports.*
3. M. Murphy and J. Brodie, "I Experience a Kind of Clarity," *Intellectual Digest* 3, no. 5 (1973).
4. H. Greenhouse, *The Astral Journey* (Garden City, N.Y.: Doubleday, 1974).
5. C. Lindbergh, *The Spirit of St. Louis* (New York: Scribner's, 1953).
6. K. Ring, *Heading Toward Omega* (New York: William Morrow, 1984).
7. R. Ornstein and D. Sobel, *The Healing Brain* (New York: Simon and Schuster, 1987).
8. T. Clifford, "Anatomy of Ecstasy," *American Health* Jan./Feb. 1987.
9. Persinger quoted by Dennis Stacy, "Transcending Science," *Omni,* Dec. 1988.
10. W. Harman and H. Rheingold, *Higher Creativity* (Los Angeles: J. P. Tarcher, 1984).
11. R. Moody, Jr., *Life After Life* (Atlanta, Ga.: Mockingbird Books, 1975) and E. Kübler-Ross, *On Death and Dying* (New York: Macmillan, 1969) and E. Kübler-Ross, *Death—The Final Stage of Growth* (New York: Simon and Schuster, 1986).

Chapter 7

1. U.S. Bureau of Census, *Statistical Abstract of the United States: 1988,* 108th ed., (Washington, D.C.: U.S. Government Printing Office, 1988).

2. U.S. Bureau of Census, *Statistical Abstract, 1988*.
3. S. Grof, "New Perspectives in Psychotherapy and Inner Exploration," *The Adventure of Self Discovery* (Albany, N.Y.: State University of New York Press, 1987).

Chapter 8

1. Charles and Caroline Muir can be contacted at the following address for information about their workshops and cassette tapes:
   Source Vacation Seminars,
   P.O. Box 330309,
   Kahului, HI 96733.
2. D. A. Ramsdale and E. J. Dorfman, *Sexual Energy Ecstasy* (Playa del Rey, Ca.: Peak Skill, 1985).

Chapter 9

1. A. Huxley, "A Treatise on Drugs," *Moksha: Writings on Psychedelics and the Visionary Experience*, ed. M. Horowitz and C. Palmer (Los Angeles: J. P. Tarcher, 1982).
2. NIAAA, *Sixth Special Report*.
3. L. D. Hohnstone, P. M. O'Malley, and J. G. Bachman, "Illicit Drug Use, Smoking and Drinking by America's High School Students, College Students, and Young Adults, 1977–87," in preparation.
4. "Drug Use Among American High School Students and Other Young Adults," 1985, Institute for Social Research, University of Michigan, Ann Arbor, MI.
5. NIAAA, *Sixth Special Report* and California Report to the Legislature, 1984.
6. K. Roderick and D. Morain, "Death Suspect's Life Was Unraveling." *Los Angeles Times*, 17 April 1989.
7. R. Yensen, "From Mysteries to Paradigms: Humanity's Journey from Sacred Plants to Psychedelic Drugs," *ReVision: The Journal of Consciousness and Change*, Spring 1988.
8. Yensen, "From Mysteries to Paradigms."
9. J. Stevens, *Storming Heaven: LSD and the American Dream* (New York: The Atlantic Monthly Press, 1987). Quoted from *Science*, 172, (1971).
10. Yensen, "From Mysteries to Paradigms."
11. L. Grinspoon and J. Bakalor, "Marijuana: Six Years of Reconsideration," in L. Grinspoon *Marijuana Reconsidered*, 2d Ed. (Cambridge, Mass.: Harvard University Press, 1977).
12. R. Schultes and A. Hofmann, *Plants of the Gods: Origins of Hallucinogenic Use* (New York: McGraw Hill, 1979).
13. S. Grof, *LSD Psychotherapy* (Pomona, Ca.: Hunter House, 1980).
14. D. Rogo, "Ketamine and the Near-Death Experience," *Anabiosis: The Journal of Near-Death Studies* 4, no. 1 (1984).
15. R. Johnstone, "A Ketamine Trip," *Anaesthesiology* no. 39 (1973).
16. A. Huxley, "Downward Transcendence," in *Moksha: Writings on Psychedelics and the Visionary Experience*, ed M. Horowitz and C. Palmer (Los Angeles: J. P. Tarcher, 1982).

Chapter 10

1. P. Russell, *The Global Brain* (Los Angeles: J. P. Tarcher, 1983).
2. R. Hornik, "Small-town Blues." *Time Magazine*, March 27, 1989.
3. N. Gibbs, "How America Has Run Out of Time." *Time Magazine*, April 24, 1989.
4. J. White, *Pole Shift* (New York: Doubleday, 1980).
5. Personal interview with William Lonsdale.
6. Thich Nhat Hanh, *The Miracle of Mindfulness*, revised edition. (Boston: Beacon Press, 1987).

7. R. N. Ostling, "Those Mainline Blues," *Time Magazine*, May 22, 1989.
8. J. White, "Liberation Literature: A Path to Self-Transcendence," *New Realities* 7, no. 4 (1987).
9. K. Kelley, ed., *The Home Planet* (New York: Addison-Wesley, 1988).
10. Talk by Reverend Joseph Martinez, 11 October 1988, in Santa Cruz, Ca., sponsored by the Healing Connection.
11. E. Sahtouris, *Gaia: The Human Journey From Chaos to Cosmos* (New York: Simon and Schuster, 1989).
12. J. Lovelock, *The Ages of Gaia: A Biography of Our Living Earth* (New York: W. W. Norton, 1988).
13. K. Dychtwald, with J. Flower, "The Third Age," *New Age Journal*, Jan./Feb. 1989.
14. Dychtwald and Flower, "The Third Age."
15. Quoted in Dychtwald and Flower, "The Third Age."
16. E. Erikson, *Childhood and Society.*
17. R. Gorman and Ram Dass, *How Can I Help?* (New York: Knopf, 1985).
18. A. Menn and L. Mosher, "Soteria: Alternative to Acute Hospitalization for Schizophrenics," in *New Directions for Mental Health Services*, I, ed. H. Richard Lamb (San Francisco: Jossey-Bass, 1979).

References

Chapter 1

Bragdon, E. *A Sourcebook for Helping People in Spiritual Emergency.* Los Altos, Ca: Lightening Up Press, 1988.

Grof, S. *Beyond the Brain.* Albany, N.Y.: State University of New York Press, 1985.
The Adventure in Self-Discovery. Albany: State University of New York Press, 1987.
Spiritual Emergency: When Personal Transformation Becomes a Crisis. Los Angeles: J. P. Tarcher, 1989.

Wilber, K. *The Atman Project.* Wheaton, Ill.: Theosophical Publishing House, 1980.
"The Developmental Spectrum and Psychopathology," Parts I and II. *Journal of Transpersonal Psychology 16* (1 & 2), 1984.

Chapter 2

Castaneda, C. *The Teachings of Don Juan: A Yaqui Way of Knowledge.* New York: Simon & Schuster, 1968.

Castaneda, C. *A Separate Reality: Further Conversations with Don Juan.* New York: Simon & Schuster, 1983.

Durkheim, K. G. *Hara: The Vital Centre of Man.* London: Unwin Hyman, 1962.

Eliade, M. *Shamanism: Archaic Techniques of Ecstasy.* Princeton, N.J.: Princeton University Press, 1964.

Krishna, G. *Kundalini: The Evolutionary Energy in Man.* Boston: Shambhala, 1971.

Harman, W. & Rheingold, H. *Higher Creativity: Liberating the Unconscious for Breakthrough Insights.* Los Angeles: J. P. Tarcher, 1984.

Harner, M. *The Way of the Shaman: A Guide to Power and Healing.* New York: Harper & Row, 1980.

Jamal, M. *Shape Shifters: Shaman Women in Contemporary Society.* New York: Routledge, Kegan and Paul, 1987.

Nicholson, S. (ed.) *Shamanism.* Wheaton, Ill.: Theosophical Publishing House, 1987.

Ring, K. *Heading Toward Omega.* New York: William Morrow, 1984.

Chapter 3

Armstrong, T. *The Radiant Child.* Wheaton, Ill.: Quest, 1985.

Campbell, J. *The Hero with A Thousand Faces.* Princeton, N.J.: Princeton University Press, 1949.

Campbell, J. *The Mythic Image.* Princeton, N.J.: Princeton University Press, 1974.

Eliade, M. *Shamanism: Archaic Techniques of Ecstasy.* Princeton, N.J.: Princeton University Press, 1964.

Grof, S. & Grof, C. "Spiritual Emergency: The Understanding and Treatment of Transpersonal Crises." *ReVision* 8, no. 2 (1986).

Grof, S. & Grof, C. *The Stormy Search for the Self.* Los Angeles: J. P. Tarcher. Manuscript in process.

Halifax, J. *Shamanic Voices.* New York: Crossroads, 1979.
Harner, M. *The Way of the Shaman: A Guide to Power and Healing.* New York: Harper & Row, 1980.
Hastings, A. "A Counseling Approach to Parapsychological Experience," *The Journal of Transpersonal Psychology* 15, no. 2 (1983).
Krishna, G. *Kundalini: The Evolutionary Energy in Man.* Boston: Shambhala, 1971.
Oesterreich, T. K. *Possession and Exorcism.* New York: Causeway Books, 1974.
Perry, J. W. *The Far Side of Madness.* New Jersey: Prentice-Hall, 1974.
Perry, J. W. "Spiritual Emergence and Renewal," *ReVision* 8, no. 2 (1986).
Sannella, L. *Kundalini: Psychosis or Transcendence.* San Francisco: H. S. Dakin Co., 1976.
White, J. *What is Enlightenment?* Los Angeles: J. P. Tarcher, 1984.
Wilber, K. *The Atman Project.* Wheaton, Ill.: Theosophical Publishing House, 1980.
Woolger, R. *Other Lives, Other Selves.* New York: Doubleday, 1987.

Chapter 4

Armstrong, T. *The Radiant Child.* Wheaton, Ill.: Quest Books, 1985.
Erikson, E. *Childhood and Society* 2d ed. New York: W. W. Norton, 1963.
Greeley, A. M. "Mysticism Goes Mainstream," *American Health* Jan./Feb., 1987.
Grof, S. *Realms of the Human Unconscious.* New York: Viking, 1974.
Hastings, A. "A Counseling Approach to Parapsychological Experience," *Journal of Transpersonal Psychology* 15, no. 2 (1983).
Hine, V. *Last Letter to the Pebble People.* Santa Cruz, Ca.: Unity Press, 1977.
Jung, C. G. *Memories, Dreams and Reflections.* New York: Random House, 1961.
Pearce, J. C. *The Magical Child: Rediscovering Nature's Plan for Our Children.* New York: E. P. Dutton, 1977.
Sogyal, R. "For the Moment of Death," *Spiritual Emergence Network Journal* 2, (Fall 1989).
Young, V. *Working with the Dying and Grieving.* Davis, Ca.: International Dialogue Press, 1984.

Chapter 5

Ajaya, Ballentine, R. and Rama. *Yoga and Psychotherapy: The Evolution of Consciousness.* Honesdale, Pa.: The Himalayan International Institute of Yoga Science and Philosophy, 1976.
Assagioli, R. "Self-Realization and Psychological Disturbances," *Mandalama,* August 1981.
Bragdon, E. *A Sourcebook for Helping People In Spiritual Emergency.* Los Altos, Ca.: Lightening Up Press, 1988.
Isherwood, C. and Prabhavanada, trans. *How to Know God: The Yoga Aphorisms of Patanjali.* London: Mentor, 1969.
James, W. *Varieties of Religious Experience.* New York: Collier-Macmillan, 1961.
Krishna, G. *The Awakening of Kundalini.* Toronto, Canada: Clark, Irwin, 1975.
Metzner, R. *Opening to Inner Light: The Transformation of Human Nature and Consciousness.* Los Angeles: J. P. Tarcher, 1986.
Tart, C. (ed.) *Transpersonal Psychologies.* New York: Harper & Row, 1975.
Vaughan, F. *The Inward Arc.* Boston: Shambhala, 1986.
Wilber, K. *No Boundary.* Wheaton, Ill.: Theosophical Publishing House, 1981.

References to Bodywork

Almaas, A. H. *Essence: The Diamond Approach to Inner Realization.* York Beach, Me.: Samuel Weiser, 1986.
Baker, E. *Man in the Trap.* New York: Macmillan, 1967.
Grof, S. *Beyond the Brain.* Albany, N.Y.: State University of New York Press, 1985.

Grof, S. and Grof, C. *The Stormy Search for the Self.* Los Angeles: J. P. Tarcher, 1990.

Hendricks, G. *Transpersonal Approaches to Counseling and Psychotherapy.* Denver: Love, 1982.

Hendricks, G. and Hendricks, K. *At the Speed of Love.* Colorado Springs, Co.: self-published, 1988.

Johnson, S. *Characterological Transformation: The Hard Work Miracle.* New York: W. W. Norton, 1985.

Lowen, A. *The Betrayal of the Body.* New York: Macmillan, 1967.

Pierrakos, J. *Core Energetics: Developing the Capacity to Love and Heal.* Mendocino, Ca.: Life Rhythm, 1987.

Reich, W. *Character Analysis.* New York: Farrar, Straus & Cudahy, 1949.

References to Stories of Spiritual Adepts

Courtois, F. *An Experience of Enlightenment.* Wheaton, Ill.: Theosophical Publishing House, 1986.

Donkin, W. *The Wayfarers: Meher Baba with the God-Intoxicated.* San Francisco: Sufism Reoriented, 1948.

Furlong, M. *Merton: A Biography.* New York: Harper & Row, 1980.

Isherwood, C. *Ramakrishna and His Disciples.* Hollywood, Ca.: Vedanta Press, 1965.

Kapleau, P. *The Three Pillars of Zen: Teaching, Practice Enlightenment.* New York: Doubleday, 1980.

Merton, T. *The Seven Storey Mountain.* San Diego, Ca.: Harcourt, Brace, Jovanovich, 1978.

Radha, Swami. *Radha: Diary of a Woman's Search.* Porthill, Id.: Timeless Books, 1981.

Ramakrishna. *The Gospel of Sri Ramakrishna.* New York: The Ramakrishna Vivekananda Center, 1973.

Roberts, B. *The Experience of No-Self.* Boston: Shambhala, 1985.

Teresa of Avila. *The Interior Castle.* Translated by K. Kavanaugh and O. Rodriguez, New York: Paulist Press, 1979.

Tweedie, I. *Daughter of Fire: A Diary of a Spiritual Training with a Sufi Master.* Nevada City, Ca.: Blue Dolphin, 1986.

White, J. (ed.) *What is Enlightenment?* Boston: J. P. Tarcher, 1984.

Yogananda, P. *Autobiography of a Yogi.* Los Angeles: Self-Realization Press, 1946.

Chapter 6

Gallup, G. *Adventures in Immortality.* New York: McGraw-Hill, 1982.

Krieger, D. *Living the Therapeutic Touch.* New York: Dodd, Mead and Co., 1987.

Moody, R. Jr. *Life After Life,* Atlanta, Ga.: Mockingbird Books, 1975.

Murphy, M. and White, R. *The Psychic Side of Sports.* Reading, Mass.: Addison-Wesley, 1978.

Ornstein, R. and Sobel, D. *The Healing Brain.* New York: Simon and Schuster, 1987.

Ring, K. *Heading Toward Omega.* New York: William Morrow, 1984.

Ring, K. *Life at Death.* New York: Coward, McCann & Geoghegan, 1980.

Sabom, M. *Recollections of Death.* New York: Harper & Row, 1982.

Wolman, B., (ed.) *Handbook of Parapsychology.* New York: Van Nostrand Reinhold Co., 1977.

Chapter 7

Bass, E. and Davis, L. *The Courage to Heal: A Guide to Women Survivor's of Child Abuse.* New York: Harper & Row, 1988.

Lewis, C. S. *A Grief Observed.* Winchester, Mass.: Faber & Faber, 1966.

Maslow, A. *The Farther Reaches of Human Nature.* New York: Viking Press, 1971.

Maslow, A. *Religions, Values, and Peak Experiences.* Columbus, Oh.: Ohio State University Press, 1964.

Rogers, C. *On Becoming a Person*. Boston: Houghton Mifflin, 1961.
Wallerstein, J. and Blakeslee, S. *Second Chances: Men, Women & Children a Decade After Divorce*. New York: Ticknor & Fields, 1989.
Wilber, K. *No Boundary*. Wheaton, Ill.: Theosophical Publishing House, 1981.

Chapter 8

Chang, Jolan. *The Tao of Love and Sex: The Ancient Chinese Way to Ecstasy*. New York: E. P. Dutton, 1977.
Chia, Mantak. *Awaken Healing Energy Through the Tao*. New York: Aurora Press, 1983.
John, Da Free. *Love of the Two-Armed Form*. San Rafael, Ca.: Dawn Horse Press, 1978.
E. J. Gold and C. Gold. *Trantric Sex*. Playa del Rey, Ca: Peak Skill, 1988.
Leonard, G. *The End of Sex: Erotic Love After the Sexual Revolution*. Los Angeles: J. P. Tarcher, 1983.
Muir, Charles and Caroline. *Tantra: The Art of Conscious Loving*. San Francisco, Ca.: Mercury House, 1989.
Ramsdale, D. A. and E. J. Dorfman. *Sexual Energy Ecstasy*. Playa del Rey, Ca.: Peak Skill, 1985.
Singer, J. *Energies of Love*. Garden City, N.Y.: Doubleday, 1983.

Books on Sex Education

Brecher, E. *The Sex Researchers*. Boston: Little, Brown and Co., 1969.
Katchadourian, H. and Lunde, T., M.D. *Fundamentals of Human Sexuality*. New York: Holt, Rinehart and Winston, Inc., 1972.

Chapter 9

Adamson, S. and R. Metzner, "The Nature of the MDMA Experience and Its Role in Healing, Psychotherapy, and Spiritual Practice." In *Revision: The Journal of Consciousness and Change* 10, no. 4.
Grof, S. *LSD Psychotherapy*. Pomona, Ca.: Hunter House, 1980.
Hoffer, A. "LSD: A Review of its Present Status." In *Clinical Pharmacology and Therapeutics*. 183, 1965.
Huxley, A. *Moksha: Writings on Psychedelics and the Visionary Experience*. Edited by Horowitz, M. and Palmer, C. Los Angeles: J. P. Tarcher, 1982.
Mogar, R. W. "Psychedelic Drugs and Human Potentialities." In H. Otto (ed.), *Explorations in Human Potentialities*. Springfield, Ill.: Charles C. Thomas, 1965.
Rogo, D. "Ketamine and the Near Death Experience," *Anabiosis: The Journal of Near-Death Studies* 4, no. 1, 1984.
Sandison, R. and J. Whitelaw. "The Therapeutic Value of LSD in Mental Illness," *Journal of Mental Science*. 100, 1954.
Sandison, R. and J. Whitelaw. "Further Studies in the Therapeutic Value of LSD in Mental Illness," *Journal of Mental Science*. 103, 1957.
Spencer, A. M. "Permissive Group Therapy with LSD." In R. Crockett, R. Sandison, & A. Walk (eds.), *Hallucinogenic Drugs and their Psychotherapeutic Use*. London: H. K. Lewis and Co., 1963.
Schultes, R. and A. Hofmann. *Plants of the Gods: Origins of Hallucinogenic Use*. New York: McGraw Hill, 1979.
Tart, C. "Marijuana Intoxication: Common Experiences," *Nature*. 226, 1970.
Tart, C. *On Being Stoned: A Psychological Study of Marijuana Intoxication*. Palo Alto, Ca.: Science and Behavior Books, 1971.
Weil, A. *The Natural Mind*. Boston: Houghton Mifflin, 1972.

Yensen, R. "From Mysteries to Paradigms: Humanity's Journey from Sacred Plants to Psychedelic Drugs." In *ReVision: The Journal of Consciousness and Change* 10, no. 4. Spring, 1988.

Chapter 10

References on the Process of Transformation
Griscom, C. *Nizhoni: The Higher Self in Education,* in preparation.
Grof, S. and C. Grof. *The Stormy Search for the Self.* Los Angeles: J. P. Tarcher, 1990.
Hendricks, G. and B. Weinhold. *Transpersonal Approaches to Counseling and Psychotherapy.* Denver: Love Publishing Co., 1982.
Leonard, G. *The Silent Pulse.* New York: Bantam Books, 1981.
Masters, R. A. *The Way of the Lover.* West Vancouver, B.C.: Xanthyros Foundation, 1988.
Mindell, A. *Working with the Dreaming Body.* London: Routledge & Kegan Paul, 1985.
Raheem, A. *Soul Return: A Guide to the Whole Person Through Transformational Integration.* Aptos, Ca.: self-published, 1987.
Small, J. *Transformers: The Therapists of the Future.* Marina Del Rey, Ca.: DeVorss, 1982.
Smith, F. *Inner Bridges: A Guide to Energy Movement and Body Structure.* Atlanta, Ga.: Humanics New Age, 1986.

References for the Gaia Hypothesis
Bateson, G. *Mind and Nature: A Necessary Unity.* New York: E. P. Dutton, 1979.
Bohm, D. *Wholeness and the Implicate Order.* London: Routledge & Kegan Paul, 1980.
Lovelock, J. E. *The Ages of Gaia: A Biography of Our Living Earth.* New York: W. W. Norton, 1988.
Lovelock, J. E. and Margulis, L. "Gaia and Geognosy." In M. B. Rambler. *Global Ecology: Towards a Science of the Biosphere.* London: Jones and Bartlett, 1984.
Perry, J. W. *The Heart of History: Individuality in Evolution.* Albany, N.Y.: State University of New York Press, 1987.
Sagan, D. and Margulis, L. *Microcosmos.* New York: Simon and Schuster, 1986.
Sahtouris, E. *Gaia: The Human Journey from Chaos to Cosmos.* New York: Simon and Schuster, 1989.
Toffler, A. *The Third Wave.* New York: William Morrow, 1980.

Chapter 11

Bragdon, E. *A Sourcebook for Helping People in Spiritual Emergency.* Los Altos, Ca.: Lightening Up Press, 1988.
Cousins, G. *Spiritual Nutrition and the Rainbow Diet.* San Rafael, Ca.: Cassandra Press, 1986.
Grof, S. and C. Grof. *Spiritual Emergency: When Personal Transformation Becomes a Crisis.* Los Angeles: J. P. Tarcher, 1989.

Index